THE CHOSEN PEOPLE

THE CHOSEN PEOPLE

A Study of Jewish History from the time
of the Exile until the Revolt of Bar Kocheba

by

JOHN M. ALLEGRO

HODDER AND STOUGHTON LTD
LONDON   SYDNEY   AUCKLAND   TORONTO

Acknowledgements are due to the following: Messrs. William Heinemann
Ltd., for permission to quote from the English translations in their Loeb
editions of Josephus; to Messrs. Edward Arnold for the quotation from
E. Bevan's *The House of Seleucus*, i (1902) p. 207, in ch. IV. Biblical quotations
are mostly from the Revised Standard Version by permission of Thomas
Nelson and Sons Ltd., and from the Authorised Version of the Apocrypha.
The photographs of coins showing the heads of Antony and Cleopatra (plate
15 a, b) are reproduced by kind permission of the British Museum.

Contents

List of Plates

List of Figures

Preface

No race has received so much attention from historians, philosophers and theologians as the Jews. For all that, their ethnic and cultural origins have remained shrouded in mystery, largely because the main source of information, the Bible, is self-contradictory in this regard. The Hebrew and Aramaic writings that are contained within the biblical corpus come from a wide area of space and time, and the unity that has been impressed upon them derives largely from the wishful thinking of the Jewish theologian of a comparatively late date. In fact, as recent research is showing ever more clearly, the myths and traditions of the Bible were very, very old long before they were ever collected or even written down in their present form, and stem in large measure from pre-Semitic strata of Near Eastern culture. The task of sifting fact from fancy, history from pious hero-worship, becomes increasingly difficult as the heterogeneous nature of biblical traditions becomes more evident.

Nevertheless, it is plain that the Babylonian exile of the Jews in the sixth century BC played a decisive part in the formation of what we call Judaism, and that thereafter the distinctive features of the cult, particularly its exclusiveness, become more and more emphasised even if they were not then actually created. The Israelite religion of the post-exilic years was a very different thing from that which had preceded the catastrophe of 587 BC, and it is to this crucial period, culminating in the even greater disasters of the first and second centuries AD, that we should look for a better understanding of the Jewish problems of today.

Some new understanding of the relentless forces at work within Judaism of this period has now been made possible through the discoveries outlined in my recent book, *The Sacred Mushroom and the Cross*. We now know, for instance, that the pious belief of later Judaism and Christianity that Yahweh/Jehovah was from the beginning a "pure" desert god, utterly opposed to the popular fertility cults of contemporary Canaan, was quite false. He can now be philologically

related to the Indo-European Zeus, and their common name inter-
preted from its Sumerian origin to mean "spermatozoa", the sacred
juice of created life. Many of the other divine names of the ancient
Near East were similarly sexually oriented, all bearing witness to the
original fertility concepts of the religions of this homeland of man's
earliest civilisations. Furthermore, the discovery of the ancient cult of
the sacred fungus, whose hallucinatory drug gave priest and prophet the
fancied belief that they could communicate with the divine source of
life, has at last given the key by which ancient Israelite mythology can
be positively related to the oldest strata of Near Eastern culture. Abraham
and Moses are as Sumerian in origin as Gilgamesh.

This lifting of cultural horizons means that we can now view the
later, esoteric developments within Israel, like Essenism, Zealotism and
Christianity, in a wider and very much more satisfactory perspective.
Now, for the first time, we can begin to understand how these self-
destructive religio-political movements stemmed from the most
ancient features of Israelitism, and we can better sympathise with the
Roman and more moderate Jewish authorities who saw their dangers
and tried, too late, to root out the extremist elements before they could
bring disaster upon themselves and all Jewry.

If this tragic saga of the Chosen Race has any lesson for us today, it
must be that religious emotionalism, however stimulated and for
whatever motives, is an extremely dangerous and unpredictable force.
Moral and patriotic idealism that springs from a racialist religion is a
perilous philosophy that can soon burst through the bounds of rational
control. Modern heralds of the New Era, from whatever gods they claim
their authority and wherever they raise their prophetic voices — the
Jerusalem of Knesset, the Meccan kiblah or the platforms of Carnegie
Hall or Wembley Stadium — should appreciate the power of the spoken
word to unleash the mighty forces of religious fanaticism. Modern
facilities for mass-communication and hypnosis make the stimulatory
drugs used by Zealotism, early Christianity and medieval Islam,
unnecessary. Their calls to a Holy War against supposed moral, political
or racial enemies can be now more terrifyingly effective than ever before,
and more fearful in their consequences. Let the reformer and the patriot
seek the infinitely more difficult and painstaking way to the Promised
Land through reason and rationality.

Introduction

Jerusalem fell to the Babylonian army in July 587 BC. The burning heat of summer, famine and its attendant plague had sapped the people's will to resist any longer. As the battering rams breached the north wall, Zedekiah the king and what remained of his army slipped through the southern gate and fled towards the Judaean Wilderness. Nebuchadnezzar had reasserted his control over another rebellious province in his western empire. He had also changed the course of human history.

The capture and destruction of Jerusalem was a watershed in the development of Israel, matched in importance only by the city's catastrophic fall to the Romans some six hundred years later. In those intervening, ruthless years, the exclusive cult of Judaism that we know today was conceived and bred. It was born in blood and nourished in the agony of despair and loneliness. The dismemberment of her State and despoiling of her most sacred shrine bred into the Jewish soul a ruthless self-assertiveness that has spared neither her own people nor those she has proclaimed her enemies. When the Babylonian prince dragged the flower of the Jewish nation to an alien soil in Mesopotamia, he created Judaism and the Jewish problem. He tempered the steel of a racial character with the fire of humiliation, and ground its edge with suffering. From thenceforth Judaism was a sword, whose sheathing during periods of political subjugation merely served to preserve its deadly brilliance for the day of emancipation.

When the exiles were allowed to trickle back to their home-land, following the fall of Babylonia in October 539 BC to the armies of the Persian Cyrus, they found barriers of sullen hostility had replaced the walls thrown down by Nebuchadnezzar. Their lands and houses had been taken over by the peasants the invaders had left undisturbed. To the south Edomites, forced northwards through incursions from Arabia, had moved into King David's proud land of Judah; to the north the Samaritan aristocracy, claiming suzerainty over the remainder of the land, actively resented the return of the Jewish nobility to challenge their power. Drought and crop failures brought the returned exiles to destitution. The work of restoring the shattered Temple, which alone could induce their tribal god Yahweh to return to his people, ground to a halt. The materials for the work promised by the Persians failed to arrive and all the people's energies were needed merely to remain alive. The proud dream of a second restoration from Exile, led by another Moses and Joshua into the Promised Land, and of a new theocracy centred upon a resplendent Temple to which even foreigners would stream in submission to a Jewish god, fell and shattered on the cold stones of reality. Like their patriarchal forbears, the exiles began to think wistfully of the fleshpots they had left behind, and of their brethren in the Jewish quarters of Babylon, growing sleek and fat on the profits of their business houses. They remembered the grand prophecies of the Second Isaiah, and the universal rule of Yahweh he had foreseen, and contrasted it with this barren land, soured by the hatred of their neighbours. On the Temple Mount, the pathetic skeleton of sticks and stones mocked Ezekiel's vision of God's House, filled with the glory of the Lord. What unatoned sin barred the Chosen People from the favour of their god? Had not their prophet proclaimed their penance paid in full, even to double the extent of their iniquity, and did not his hymn of comfort promise the end of all their warfare?

From the turmoil of their disillusionment and heart-searching came fresh accusations of their shortcomings, and pious directives to Israel's restitution to grace. She had compromised her religious purity by accepting foreigners with their syncretistic worship in her midst. Only by purging the community anew of these alien elements could her cultic innocence be restored. No sacrifice was too great to achieve this end. Loving husbands must banish their foreign wives and children from their homes. Jewish women must leave their gentile husbands and forsake their offspring. Only when the nation had purged itself racially would Yahweh fulfil his promises conveyed through the prophets. Then, as the Elect of God, they could turn their undivided attention to re-building the Temple, as the prophet Haggai demanded. His contemporary, Zechariah, offered them through his apocalyptic imagery the vision of a new world that might give them hope and assuage their self-inflicted pain. Persian power, they were promised, would soon be smashed, even as the old Babylonian empire had crumbled before Cyrus. Even now the rumblings of revolt throughout the Persian world heralded the fall of its present ruler Darius. Arise, Jews still in hated exile! Flee while there was yet time, and return to the new Jerusalem to welcome the messianic King. Soon every knee would bend before the Jewish god, and those who resisted his rule would be consumed by famine and plague.

In March 515 BC, a Temple of sorts was in fact completed and dedicated with great rejoicing. But it was a poor thing compared with Solomon's, and the messianic leader so highly proclaimed, Zerubbabel, was no David. The scattered Jews remained within their foreign counting-houses, and feasted from their fleshpots. Darius mastered the rebellions within the empire. It was still he, and not a Jewish king who ruled the world. Yahweh had not yet returned to his Holy Hill.

Seventy years later affairs in Jerusalem were no better. Political pressure upon the city state had increased from the north and south; morale was low and was reflected in cultic and moral laxity. Racial discrimination was breaking down again and intermarriage becoming common. Jewish separatism was being threatened from within and without, and once more the cry went out from Jerusalem to world Jewry for financial and political support to maintain Israel's religious and ethnic integrity.

In December 445 BC, a deputation arrived in Susa at the Persian court of Artaxerxes, and contacted a Jewish official, Nehemiah, brother of the company's leader. Aware of the king's present concern for the stability of Palestine and the safeguarding of his lines of communication to an Egypt in turmoil, Nehemiah prevailed upon his royal master to foster the growth of an independent state centred upon Jerusalem's strategically vital position. It was to be a defended area, meaning that the walls beaten down by the Babylonian invaders would have to be rebuilt. Jerusalem's political subservience to Samaria would be ended, and her loyalty to the Persian king thenceforth guaranteed by his appointing Nehemiah himself as the city's new governor.

Some seven weeks after his arrival in Jerusalem Nehemiah had managed to reconstruct a makeshift city wall. The first physical barriers between the post-exilic Jew and the gentile world had been erected. Nehemiah had begun to translate into tangible reality the separatist policies advocated by the prophets. In those lines of heaped stones and rubble around Jersualem we might discern the foundations of the walls that bounded the ghettos of medieval Europe, the gas-chambers of Auschwitz and the battle-lines of modern Palestine.

The political and strategic planning of Nehemiah was complemented by the priestly activity of Ezra. Together they purged anew the Jewish cult and reformed it around the Mosaic Law. This corpus of Hebrew moral and religious legislation, set in a framework of ancient mythology, was endued with a mystic aura of sanctity. It was the very Word of God, almost God Himself, incarnate. It had a corporate entity and authority greater than the sum of its literary parts. It was not a law, or many laws; it was *the* Law, the Teaching, par excellence. Together with the Temple, as seat of the god and fount of all interpretative inspiration, it formed the focus of worship and the directive power of post-exilic Judaism. In granting Nehemiah authority to rebuild Jerusalem's walls and shrine, the Persian king had unwittingly given his sanction to the erection of a centre of inevitable dissension astride his empire's most vital line of communication. He had helped create a kingdom, not only politically autonomous, but containing within its constitution an avowed intention to rule the world.

The Samaritans under their local governor Sanballat saw the danger. He had close links with the Jerusalem priesthood, and himself a Yahwist, knew too well the political extremes to which Nehemiah's separatism must lead. He alerted governors of the surrounding districts, Tobiah in Transjordan, Geshem in north-west Arabia, and the inhabitants of the old Philistine coastlands to the west. Raids were mounted from all sides to harass the wall-builders, threatening their villages and families and so to keep them from their task of fortification. It became a race against time as Nehemiah strove to complete the work before the warnings sent urgently back to Susa by the local governors could have their effect and the royal decrees be cancelled. Within the city the priesthood and leading families saw the inevitable end no less clearly and tried to frustrate the work. But it was of no avail. The labourers were organized into shifts working under the protection of the arms of those who rested. Men in outlying villages were forced from their fields to assist in the labouring and standing guard. At length, despite all opposition, the walls were finished and in pomp and religious cere-monial were dedicated to the glory of Yahweh: "and the joy of Jerusa-lem was heard afar off". Judaism had been born again, fathered by religious sentimentality from a strange land, on the child-bed of political opportunism and amid birth-pangs which predicted an even greater anguish.

A generation after Nehemiah's second term of office in Jerusalem, ostensibly establishing a loyal outpost of the Persian empire for his master, Egypt rebelled and remained free for some sixty years. Simultaneously, Artaxerxes faced and crushed a revolt on the part of his brother Cyrus the Younger who, with thirteen thousand Greek mercenaries raised in Asia Minor, thrust eastwards into Babylonia. Xenophon in his *Anabasis* records the retreat through the perils of winter of ten thousand survivors after their defeat at Cunaxa. Nevertheless, the writing was on the wall. It was from Europe that the fatal challenge to Persian supremacy in the ancient world was to come. Despite the skilful use by Artaxerxes II of bribes to sow discord among the Greeks and to bring all Hellas to the point of exhaustion, it was the Macedonian Philip II who, half-a-century later in 338 BC, achieved by his victory at Chaeronea the hegemony of the Greek states. Two years later his son Alexander succeeded to the throne. In five short years the Persian empire was no more. A major European power had entered decisively into the Near Eastern lists and under Alexander extended its influence beyond the Indus.

When Alexander died in Babylon, Palestine became a succulent bone pulled this way and that by the Ptolemaic and Seleucid dogs that tore the short-lived empire to pieces. Ptolemy Lagi seized control of Egypt and established his capital at the new city of Alexandria, while his brother-general, Seleucus I, had by 312/11 BC made himself master of Syria, Babylonia and Iran. His capitals were at Antioch in Syria and Seleucia on the Tigris in Babylonia. By the end of the century Ptolemy had manoeuvred himself into control of Palestine and Phoenicia and his dynasty maintained that position for a century. During this time the Jewish population of Egypt increased considerably by the influx of new immigrants, willingly or unwillingly brought south by the fortunes of war or the scent of business opportunities. Alexandria became the prime centre of Jewish political and commercial power in the ancient world. The old cultural languages of the Jews, Hebrew and Aramaic, gave way to Greek, the *lingua franca* of the new world. Even the Bible had to be translated into Greek for the benefit of Jewish communities in Egypt. The foremost Jewish thinkers were busy forcing their traditional religious and mythological concepts into Greek moulds, making them "respectable" to western thought. From now on, the Holy War of conservative Jewry was to be waged not so much against alien marriages within the fold as against the more insidious Hellenization of the Jewish cult.

Following a period of erosion in its control over the northern

B

provinces, the Seleucid empire stirred to new life with the accession in 223 BC of Antiochus the Great. He reasserted Seleucid domination from Asia Minor to the frontiers of India and eventually, after an initial set-back, snatched the prize of Palestine from Ptolemaic grasp in 198 BC by a decisive victory at the source of the Jordan. In Jerusalem the Jews received their new rulers with apparent delight. However favourable their treatment had been under the Ptolemies, the war seems to have hit them hard, the Temple had been damaged and the community disrupted. The Jews took up arms against the Ptolemaic garrison in the city, and were rewarded by the victors with tax reductions and state aid for the upkeep of the cult and the repair of the shrine. Doubtless some acknowledgment of Seleucid suzerainty was required to be shown by the religious leaders in return for this official recognition of their cult, but if it did manifest itself within the Temple worship any dissident voices were hushed in the wave of relief that followed the end of the war. Later such pricks to the proud exclusiveness of their religion were to fester and burst in the Maccabean revolt. For the time being Jerusalem settled down again to political submission and apparent religious autonomy.

However, in the west another growing monster watched the trend of events in Asia with increasing interest. Rome had crushed Carthage at Zama in 202 BC; Hannibal had fled to the Seleucid court and sought an ally for continuing his struggle against the western power. Unwisely Antiochus, fired by a zeal for asserting Seleucid control over all the territories of Hellas, marched into Greece. At once the mighty bear struck out against the intruder. In 192 BC Antiochus was driven from Europe and two years later he was forced to give up all Asia Minor apart from Cilicia, along with his war elephants, his navy, many hostages including his own son, and a crippling indemnity. The great House of Seleucus was plunged into virtual bankruptcy.

What remained of the empire had to foot the bill. Tax demands became ever more extortionate; temples were obliged to yield up their treasures, and, for all their cultic independence, the Jews of Jerusalem were not exempt. Antiochus III was killed in 187 BC whilst robbing an Elamite temple, and his successor, Seleucus IV, attempted through internal Jewish dissension and intrigue to lay hands on private bank deposits in the Temple treasuries. The High Priest, Onias III, was obliged to travel to the court and argue his case before the king. The cracks in the supposed independent structure of the cult were now showing through. The price of political peace was rising, and the strains inevitably imposed by the maintenance of a theocracy within an alien empire were again making themselves felt. Furthermore, the Jews were themselves dangerously divided. The Faith had been more imperilled by the seductive glamour of Hellenism than had ever been achieved by outright physical persecution. New generations of intelligent Jews found the religion and culture of their forefathers less and less relevant to the modern world. They were not semi-nomads in the deserts of Sinai, nor plunderers of sown lands from across the Jordan. The Sabbath was a nuisance, circumcision a disfigurement and disgrace when they performed naked in the Jerusalem gymnasium. They sacrificed to the gods of the games, like any civilised Greek, and they wore Greek dress. The tax-free emoluments of the Temple priesthood became a prize to be sought by smoothing the palms of imperial officials and even of the king himself. If the bribe were not immediately available, arrangements could be made for liquidating sufficient of the Temple funds to pay the cost after take-over. In the atmosphere of religious scepticism then prevailing in the Holy City, the sacred offices of the cult seemed no more than executive positions in a highly profitable company formed to attract funds from the Diaspora. Certainly the capital assets of the Temple, subscribed by pious Jews from all over the world, must have been considerable to judge from the inroads made upon them by their directors and political "protectors".

Antiochus IV, "God Manifest" (Epiphanes), succeeded his assassinated brother Seleucus IV in 175 BC. Six years later, when returning from a successful invasion of Egypt, Antiochus replenished his failing coffers en route by looting the Jerusalem Temple to the extent even of stripping the gold leaf from its façade. The following year he was again in Egypt, this time entering the ancient capital of Memphis and advancing on Alexandria. However, on this occasion the Roman bear took active note of this extension of Seleucid power, and growled menacingly. Antiochus promptly turned tail and went home licking his wounded pride. On the way he was told that his personal representative in Jerusalem was finding it increasingly difficult to "persuade" the Jewish hierarchy to accept his master's instructions. Antiochus decided that a display of force might prove a useful reminder to the Jews where their true interests lay and to whom they owed their political fealty. He accordingly despatched a force of mercenaries to Jerusalem which they promptly looted and partially destroyed. The walls were torn down and a citadel was erected within the city over against the Temple enclosure and equipped with a Seleucid garrison to remind the Jews continually of their subservience and to give constant support to the imperially appointed High Priest and his minions. Thus, in effect, a Greek *polis* was established in the undefended city and the Temple became virtually a city shrine devoted as much to Zeus as Yahweh. Judaism was fast becoming another Syro-Hellenic cult, organized by the State as part of the trappings of Seleucid imperialism. Real integration of the Jew into his pagan environment was at last becoming an established fact and this time with the active collaboration of a sizeable and influential part of the population, priestly as well as lay.

Antiochus determined to press this Hellenization of Jerusalem even further. Perhaps had he waited, exclusive Judaism might have died a natural death and crumbled away as effectively as the broken walls that symbolized her hard-won autonomy. But, impatient of pockets of conservatism that resisted his changes, Antiochus decreed the cancellation of the special rights and privileges of the Jews and in effect forbade the practice of distinctive Judaism. Regular sacrifices were suspended, the observance of the Sabbath and traditional festivals forbidden, circumcision of children made a crime and copies of the Law were ordered to be destroyed. Pagan altars were erected throughout the territory and Jews were forced to participate in the attendant rites and to eat swine's flesh. Later chroniclers saw as the climax to all this sacrilege the introduction in December 167 BC, of the cult of the Olympian Zeus into the Temple, and the erection of some kind of image, probably phallic, to represent the god (the "abomination of desolation" of Daniel) within the holy place.

The severity with which these measures were enforced upon the Jews, in callous disregard of any scruples of individual conscience, crystallized opposition which, in turn, made Antiochus even more brutal in his suppression of the Jewish cult. Groups keeping the Sabbath secretly were sought out and massacred by Greek soldiers; women persisting in circumcising their children brought upon themselves and their offspring an immediate death penalty; similar fates awaited those who refused to eat ritually unclean food. Passive opposition centred around a sect known as the "Pious Ones" (Hasidim), who for a time resisted pressures to take up arms against their persecutors. Inevitably, however, the call for more active measures of retaliation found a response among less pacifically inclined Jews. In a village called

Modein, in the foothills east of Lydda, an old man named Mattathias killed both a king's officer and a Jew making impure sacrifices and the assassin became the rallying centre for armed revolt. Mattathias and his five sons, John, Simon, Judas, Eleazar and Jonathan, took to the hills and began to harass the occupying forces by guerrilla action. Mattathias died in the following year, 166 BC, and leadership passed to his third son, nicknamed "The Hammer", Maccabeus. A new dynasty of rulers had arisen in Israel. The religious and political autonomy that had been previously sought from the dominant powers by diplomacy, bribery and voluntary submission, was for a century to be won and held by force of arms.

Some initial victories by the terrorist forces, largely made possible by Antiochus's increasing involvement in the east, gave the faithful cause to believe that Judas's comparatively small forces were under divine protection. By 164 BC Judas was able to restore Jerusalem's defences and garrison the city with his troops. In December, three years after its profanation on the orders of Antiochus, the Temple was ritually cleansed and the Feast of Dedication (Hanukkah) was cele-brated to mark the event.

The Jewish freedom fighters still had their problems, however. Attached religiously to the Jerusalem community were pious Jews in other provinces of Palestine, particularly in Galilee and regions to the east of the Jordan. Judas and his brothers launched campaigns in these areas against the occupying forces with some measure of success. Although they could not hope to maintain for more than brief periods the control their raids brought them, it made possible the emi-gration to Judaea of those traditionalist Jews who sought the spiritual sanctity of the Holy City. This helped to strengthen Judas's hand at home and to stiffen resistance there to those Hellenistic Jews who distrusted the Maccabean war aims and maintained their allegiance to the Seleucid garrison still resident in the citadel. When Judas returned from his campaigns and laid siege to this centre of dissension in the heart of the city, the cry to Antiochus for help went up not only from the Greek forces but from a considerable part of the Jewish population. The king responded so effectively that Judas was driven to fortify the Temple area itself and retreat there with his men, unable to defend his lately won positions to the south of Jerusalem. Only internal strife within the Seleucid state saved the situation for the Jewish rebels. The Greek army withdrew after promising Judas and his friends freedom to worship in accordance with their traditions. The oppressive restrictions imposed by Antiochus IV were rescinded, and the religious autonomy of the Jewish community was restored. Thus the cause of exclusive Judaism had triumphed even in its moment of weakness. A legitimate High Priest was appointed, one Alcimus, and the Pious Ones, who had been ultimately persuaded to share in the fighting alongside the Maccabees, thankfully laid down their unaccustomed arms and resumed their devotions in peace. It is true that Seleucid troops were still active in the Holy City, and that the Hellenistic Jews were no more sympathetic to Jewish extremism and the Maccabean cause than they had been. But the immediate battle had been won; Judaism had its own undefiled cultic centre and its pious devotees could practise their religion undisturbed within the political structure of an alien empire. Surely this was sufficient.

The Maccabees thought otherwise. The real divisions between them and their more quietist compatriots and co-religionists were now starkly demonstrated. They had tasted political freedom and smelt the hot blood of battle. A father and five sons, backed by a motley crowd of fanatical guerrilla fighters, had routed professional Greek troops. They had lain in wait in rocky defiles, pounced and seen the enemy run for his life, leaving rich booty for the taking. They had glimpsed the vision of a Jewish kingdom holding a gentile world in servitude. Above all, Judas and his brothers had learnt that in the power-game physical force could be outwitted by guile and by craftily playing off one foe against another. Where the balance between mighty forces is most delicate, the lightest touch will often tip the scales and its threat will offer opportunities to the unscrupulous for blackmail. With such tactics as these in their armoury, Judas and his brothers saw no reason for resting content with religious autonomy. Empires were collapsing, new powerful friends were to be won; even mighty Rome was looking for allies, however small, on her empire's eastern frontiers. It was a time for opportunism, not retrenchment.

Judas made overtures to Rome and at the same time hampered the activities of the newly appointed High Priest, for all his legitimate claim to the sacred office. Alcimus appealed for Seleucid help and for a time it seemed that Judas had overplayed his hand. In April 160 BC, during an almost hopeless engagement with the Greeks, Judas was killed and his youngest brother Jonathan took over command. Set-piece battles were avoided thereafter and the guerrillas restricted their activities to

harassing the enemy with minimum losses to themselves, in the meantime seeking more powerful support from elsewhere. In this regard they
were for the time being unsuccessful, and the rebels were again on the
point of losing hope when another series of internal disputes forced the
Seleucids to seek a quick settlement. The result of these parleys was that
Jonathan was able to establish himself without further Greek opposition
at Michmas, a few miles north-east of Jerusalem. From this stronghold
he laid claim to the traditional Israelite office of "judge" of the people.
For the time being he let the priesthood have its way in Jerusalem,
preferring to wait on the sidelines and hold himself free to dabble as
profitably as he could in more secular affairs. The year was 157 BC, and
he had not long to wait.

In 153 BC, a certain Alexander Balas laid claim to the Seleucid throne,
giving himself out to be the son of the infamous Antiochus IV ("God
Manifest"). The legitimate king, Demetrius, desperately seeking allies
against the intruder, begged even the support of Jonathan who, nothing
loath, demanded and received permission to maintain an army. Thus
protected he moved back into Jerusalem, fortified the Temple area, and
maintained a careful watch over the Greek garrison in the citadel. He
needed now the spiritual authority to match his secular power and
obtained it from none other than the pretender Alexander, to whom he
made the same promises of support as he had just offered Demetrius.
Alcimus the High Priest had died some years previously and his sacred
office had remained unfilled in the meantime. Now, at the great autumn
festival of 152 BC, Jonathan himself solemnly donned the sacerdotal
robes. Thus, at the instigation of a foreign pretender, a member of a non-
Aaronite and non-Zadokite family (and thus by lineage outside entitle-
ment to the high priestly office) was made at once supreme head of
religious Jewry and a deputy-king of the Seleucid empire.

For two years Jonathan the priest-king danced the diplomatic tight-
rope between Demetrius and Alexander Balas. Finally he was forced to
choose between his patrons and the inevitable clash drew near. He
chose Balas, rejecting Demetrius's tempting offers which included
tax-exemption and rich donations to the religious community of
Jerusalem. He chose correctly; Demetrius was killed in battle against
Alexander Balas in 150 BC. Jonathan was invited to Ptolemais and there
honoured as "general" and "joint-ruler" in the Seleucid state. In
Jerusalem and elsewhere the opposition among the pious Jews and the
suspicion of the Hellenists was no longer voiced openly. They could now

only wait and watch with anxiety the inexorable pressures that must build up against any policy of moderation and appeasement towards the gentile world. Judaism had been set upon a course to political domination of her neighbours, and disaster.

Jonathan's almost incredible diplomatic agility in changing sides at opportune moments eventually led him to his fate in 143 BC. He was succeeded by Mattathias's second eldest son, Simon, who achieved the long-sought Maccabean goal of ridding Jerusalem of the hated Seleucid garrison in the citadel, and with it the core of dissident Hellenistic Jews. He had it resettled with compatriots faithful to his cause and enclosed the area within an enlarged city wall. Well might he have himself called "governor and leader of the Jews", and proclaim his rule as the beginning of a new era. Certainly under his son John Hyrcanus and his grandsons Aristobulus and Alexander Jannaeus, Jewish leadership continued to be a secular rather than religious function. Even when Seleucid power disintegrated from within, the Jewish state could only be maintained by constant wars with its neighbours, and the disquiet felt from the beginning by the religious sections of the community was intensified. Jannaeus's rule in particular was marked by internal dissension, culminating in open revolt among his compatriots and their invitation to the Seleucid Demetrius III (Eukairos) to help them overthrow their own king. Thus far had come the popular Maccabean revolt against Greek tyranny! Nevertheless, the extent of Jannaeus's kingdom was greater than even that of David and Solomon in all their glory. It must have seemed to many Jews that, despite its price in blood and hatred, the restoration of the Davidic princedom was a sign of God's renewed favour to his Chosen People.

When, in 64 BC, great Pompey strode upon the Palestinian stage, the history of Israel moved into its last and most desperate phase. No matter how effectively the new Jewish rulers played the power-game, and the Herods were quite as unscrupulous as the Maccabees, Roman power was of a very different category from that of the crumbling Seleucid empire. Never again were the Jews to win political autonomy like that achieved by Judas and his brothers. Whatever favours the Idumaean family, and particularly Herod the Great, wheedled from their masters, there could never be any doubt about who was ultimately in charge of Palestine.

In 63 BC, Pompey completely reorganized Syria-Palestine as a Roman province under a governor. The Maccabean kingdom was divided up, Judaea was separated from Samaria which, like the Jerusalem community,

I   Ancient Zion, on the south-east hill of Jerusalem, site of the old Davidic city and probably of the Acra.

2   The site of Docus (the hilltop on the right), seen from the tell of ancient Jericho. Christian tradition identified Docus with the Mount of Temptation.

3   Rabbath Ammon (Philadelphia), modern '*Amman*: the Roman amphitheatre.

4   A view north-eastwards from Mount Gerizim. On the left is Mount Ebal, on the northern
side of the east-west pass through the central hills. Northwards the road runs to Beth-shan
and Galilee. Commanding the east-west pass is the mound of ancient Shechem.

was allowed to practise its own religious cult. The coastal cities and those inland urban communities that joined to form the "Decapolis" (Ten Cities) were given independent status. Galilee, although considered part of the Jewish religious community centred on Jerusalem, was nevertheless separated from it by politically independent districts, as was Perea to the east of the Jordan. The Roman principle was thus followed of permitting, even encouraging divergent religious expression among the subject peoples of Palestine, allowing their cultural grouping to take account of religious loyalties, but ensuring that politically they remained divided. Each district had a degree of autonomy but all owed allegiance to the Roman governor. In this way, the characteristic religious tolerance of the empire was sensibly demonstrated alongside the need to preserve the *pax Romana*.

In 40 BC, the Roman senate appointed Herod king of Judaea and three years later he was able to take possession of his kingdom and the then desolated city of Jerusalem. At first his domain encompassed no more than the area Pompey had left to the religious community of Jerusalem, that is, Judaea with Idumaea to the south, and Galilee and Peraea to the north and east. To these had been added villages in the plain of Jezreel and, more important, the sea port of Jaffa. Later, however, after the death of Antony and Cleopatra and a swift change in allegiance, Herod was able to add the whole of the coastal plain to his kingdom, as well as the city and province of Samaria. By 23 BC, he had practically all the remainder of Palestine, apart from the free cities of the Decapolis.

Herod was undoubtedly a great king. He was a master of diplomatic trickery and a builder on a huge scale in both civil and military undertakings. He lived and loved and massacred in the grand manner. He was the epitome of an oriental despot. But he was no Judas Maccabeus; indeed, he was but half a Jew. His reconstructed Jerusalem, of which the Temple was the crowning glory, was a showpiece to the world, built to the everlasting glory of Herod, not Yahweh. The religious circles of Jerusalem could not feel at ease under his rule, however great the material benefits it brought the city and the Temple clergy. He was a friend of Rome, a foreigner, and as such despised. His death in 4 BC was the signal for an outbreak of rioting, directed as much against Rome as Herod's successors. The inevitable reaction by the authorities was swift and vicious, and brought more anti-Roman hostility in its train. In AD 6, that part of the kingdom lying to the west of the Jordan, in the centre and to the south, was deprived of its independence and

reconstituted as a procuratorial province. It was now an inferior dependency ruled by a governor living in Caesarea. He controlled Jerusalem
through a military garrison stationed in the Antonia fortress, built by
Herod at the north-western corner of the sacred area, overlooking the
Temple court. Thus the pious worshipper was made continually aware
of the presence of Big Brother watching his every move. Even when, later
on another Herod called Agrippa, obtained the kingship over practically the whole territory formerly controlled by his grandfather, and
even tried to extend and refortify Jerusalem, he was never accepted by
the religionists of the city as anything more than a tool of the hated
Roman overlords. Much as he played the part of a devout Jew and a
generous benefactor of the cult whilst in the city, outside Jerusalem he
behaved no differently from any other rich Hellenistic king, glorying in
regal ostentation and lavishly sponsoring the pagan arts. At Agrippa's
death in AD 44, unlamented by his Jewish subjects, the whole of this
territory reverted to a procuratorial province, ruled by governors living
in Caesarea. The stage was now being set for the last bloody conflict.

Behind the political scenes, there was stirring within Judaism an
underground movement more intensely fanatical and dangerous than
anything that religion had yet produced. It was the almost inevitable
outcome of allying an exclusive cult to political ambition. While
Jewish leaders were able to exercise some degree of political independence, howbeit limited to the periods of internal weakness of their
masters, the extremists were kept in check. Their energies could be
used to fight Israel's battles and they were susceptible to a measure of
restraint by the nation's rulers. However, once the Romans had arrived
and taken over the running of the country with a firmness of control that
left no hope of restoring the Davidic and Maccabean kingdoms as an
ideal theocracy, pious hopes turned once more to a divine intervention
in Israel's affairs. The ancient messianic expectations became even
more politically oriented. What mere mortals could not achieve on their
own, God would bring about with his heavenly hosts under the leadership of a war-Messiah, a scion of the royal house of David, a Son of
God. He would be the right arm of a new kingdom; his very breath
would slay the wicked who dared to assert themselves against Yahweh's
intention that his Chosen People would rule the world. But this new
era would only dawn if there could be found among the Faithful a band
of ruthless men willing to sacrifice their lives and those of their less
enthusiastic compatriots to attain that end. These would be the

Chosen Ones, equivalent in these Latter Days to the corps of elite who surrounded King David a millennium before. They called themselves in Hebrew the *Qannā' īm*, which their contemporaries understood to mean, "the Zealous Ones", jealous for their god's unique power amidst the no-gods of the pagan world. There now seems reason to believe that the name actually refers to the ancient drug source from which much of their fanatical energies derived, like the "Assassins" of medieval Islam.

It was around these so-called "Zealots" that the revolt of AD 66 exploded, and they were the malevolent power that directed its end remorselessly to the destruction of the nation. For in the event no angelic legions swooped from on high to blast the Roman armies. The walls of Jerusalem fell before the siege engines, and the August sky of AD 70 darkened with the smoke of the burning Temple. The Zealots who escaped the funeral pyre of Judaism and fought their way back to Herod's fortress by the Dead Sea, died by their own hands three years later. The ruthless years of this tragic chapter in Israel's history finished on the same note of tragic disillusionment as had marked its inception; worse, the barriers that had been erected to safeguard the purity of Judaism have served ever since to provoke the envy, distrust, and even hatred of the gentile world.

CHAPTER I

Origins and Exile

"Your origin and birth are of the land of the Canaanites," the exilic prophet Ezekiel is bade declaim against Jerusalem, "your father was an Amorite and your mother a Hittite" (16^3). He goes on to describe his compatriots in terms of the bastard child of a whore, exposed in the open to die, weltering in her mother's blood, unwanted and despised. Her god rescued her from the dung heap and nourished her, and when she began to show physical signs of puberty covered her nakedness with fine clothes and ornaments. Her beauty attracted lovers, however, and unable to resist their blandishments she became as great a whore as her mother.

This highly uncomplimentary picture of Israel as the product of miscegenation among resident Canaanite tribes is much closer to the truth than the idealized mythology which saw her as fathered by a "wandering Aramaean" who emigrated from Mesopotamia to Egypt, and whose family so multiplied and prospered that it evoked the envy of the native princes (Deut $26^{5\text{ff.}}$). According to this account, the people were forced into slavery and remained in that unhappy state until rescued by a hero Moses. He led them out through the desert of Sinai, where they were taught the secret name of their god and later permitted to enter Canaan. In fact, the names of the patriarchal heroes, as that of the god himself, are non-Semitic, as our recent researches have shown, and go back to the earliest known civilisation of the Near East, indeed of the world. The language to which we can now trace these names is called Sumerian, and seems to have been the fount of both Semitic and Indo-European and was in use long before these two linguistic families went their separate ways. The divine name Yahweh (its purposeful mispronunciation as "Jehovah" was intended to preserve its secrecy from the uninitiated) turns out to have been merely a dialectal form of the Greek god-name Zeus, and both meant "spermatozoa", the source of all life. The very common Semitic word for "god", *El*, in its various forms, has a similar connotation, and cognate names like *Ba'al* and *Hadad*,

Seba'oth (the Hindu *Siva*), and the like, refer to the male organ of generation with which the god was mythologically identified. He was envisaged as a mighty penis in the heavens which, in the thunderous climax of the storm, ejaculated semen upon the furrows of mother Earth, the womb of creation.

The widely expressed view that Yahweh was some kind of "pure" anti-sexual deity, holding himself aloof from the Canaanite *ba'alim* is seen to have been the product of a much later age. The Hebrew prophets may have portrayed Yahweh as the enemy of the local gods, and seen his worship as a purifying flame cutting its way through the heinous sexual practices of Canaanite "high places", but we now know that his origin was no less related to the dependence of an agricultural people on regular rainfall and the fertility of their fields. Equally false was the biblical idealisation of the desert wanderings as a time when Yahweh wooed his bride Israel on the steppes of north Arabia before she became tainted with the gross perversions of agricultural fertility cults. The whole concept of the desert god owed more to the efforts of later theologians to historicise their mythology than to any authentic tribal memories of Israel's early experiences. We are now able to pinpoint the source of the patriarchal myths in a particular form of the fertility religion, centred on the cult of the sacred mushroom. Its devotees conceived the fungus as a manifestation of the phallic god, and believed that eating it brought them into a direct relationship with the deity and enabled them to share in the heavenly secrets. The cap of the mushroom, the *Amanita Muscaria* (see below, Ch. XVI), contains a hallucinatory drug which imparts a sense of euphoria, coupled with violent physical energy, followed by periods of acute depression. This cult was as old as the name Yahweh, and similarly derived from the Sumerians.

The school of thought which produced the historical corpus of the Old Testament we call Deuteronomic (that is, Deuteronomy—Kings, compiled around the seventh century BC), found in the "father Abraham" myth a justification for their concept of a centralized cult. While the tribal divisions of the people persisted, it was hardly possible to elevate one shrine, and thus one community, above the others, religiously and politically. When external pressures forced a unification of the tribes under a monarchy in the eleventh to tenth centuries, centralization of the cult became more feasible, even if it meant taking over a foreign Jebusite shrine at Jerusalem (II Sam 6), to avoid tribal jealousies. The political unification of the tribes did not long survive David's son Solomon (I Ki 11, 12), but two centuries later the forceful arrival of Assyria on the Palestinian scene reduced the nation to a single tribal dependency, Judah, with the capture and resettlement of the northern kingdom in 721 BC. In these circumstances, a State religion, based upon a single shrine at Jerusalem became possible, and the religious reforms of Hezekiah (715–687/6 BC; II Ki 18$^{3-6}$; cp. II Chr 29–31) and Josiah (640–609 BC; II Ki 22^3–23^5; cp. II Chr 34^1–35^{19}), were largely aimed in that direction. The old sanctuaries in the outlying areas were disestablished and Yahweh worship directed towards Jerusalem (II Chr 30; II Ki 23^8). Along with this geographical centralisation of Yahwism went a deliberate attempt to purge out those elements of the cult deemed unworthy of the new unified religion, however rooted in the past they may have been. Hezekiah even removed from the sanctuary the serpent image (II Ki 18^4), traditionally connected with Moses, whose name actually means "emergent snake", with both phallic and fungous significance.

To bind the remnant of the people closer together in face of the perils from Mesopotamia, the historicisation of the old desert mythologies became urgently necessary. If all Israel sprang from the loins of Abraham, then even the heterogeneous collection of people left in Judah could look back in their imagination beyond a loose confederation of twelve tribes to a single progenitor, and pride themselves on a purity of race unmatched in the whole of Palestine. They were a single family, chosen by their god whilst still wandering in the desert, and brought together into the Promised Land. Above all, they were *different* from their Palestinian neighbours. Their god was not Ba'al, and those features of their traditional religion like sacred prostitution, prostration before the erect phallic images of the Asherah, worship of the mother goddess Ashtoreth, and dedication of human semen at the mouth of the vaginal passage to the earth's womb, the Kidron valley outside Jerusalem, had all to be banished, no matter how reluctantly. From now on they had to deny their mixed heritage, and to consolidate their precarious political position on the basis of a fanciful ancestry and an exclusive religion.

Such reorientations of traditional beliefs and practices are not, however, achieved overnight, whether by the stroke of a politician's pen or a prophet's exhortation. Neither Hezekiah's nor Josiah's reformation was long lived. It needed the calamity of the Babylonian

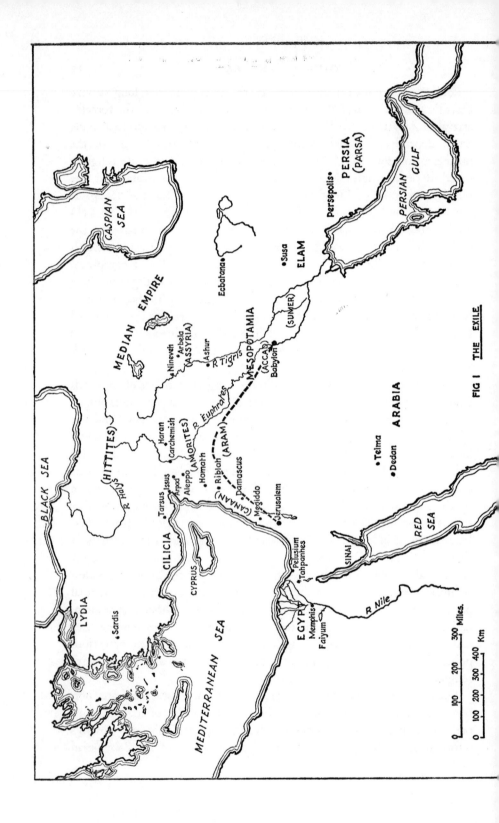

FIG I THE EXILE

exile to establish the new philosophy of racial and religious exclusiveness and bring Judaism proper into being.

Josiah died at Megiddo (Figs. 1, 2) trying to resist an Egypto-Assyrian coalition, and for four years, until 605 BC, Judah was under Egyptian domination. In that year, the Babylonian king Nebuchadnezzar thoroughly trounced the Egyptian forces at Carchemish, and followed it through with another crushing blow at Hamath (Fig. 1). The way to Palestine was open, and in a year or two Judah became once more part of a Mesopotamian empire. Ill-conceived rebellions by Jewish kings, in 601 (II Ki 24[1]) and 588 (v. 20), brought a final dissolution of the state. In July 587 BC, the walls of Jerusalem fell (II Ki 25[2ff.]; Jer 52[5ff.]), the king Zedekiah was caught with his bodyguard trying to escape into the desert, and a month later a demolition party was sent in to raze the city. Some of the city's leading citizens, priestly and lay, were executed before Nebuchadnezzar at Riblah (II Ki 25[18-21]; Jer 52[24-27]), while the remainder of the notables were deported to Babylon (Fig. 1). Thus began the exile which was to change the history of the world. The humiliation of defeat made the Jews more ready to accept the historiciza-tion of their myths, and to glorify the days of their desert wanderings as a Golden Age of religious fidelity. Faith in the past, as portrayed by the romantic historians, was a prerequisite to a hope for the future. As their god had brought them through the furnace of affliction at that time, so in the years of their exile in Babylon he would not fail them, and would bring them back eventually to the Promised Land (Ezek 20[33-38]).

Unfortunately, we have very little first-hand evidence for life in Judah during the fifty years of the Exile. Archaeological excavations have shown that the Babylonian invasion razed most of the important towns in the Judaean hill country and the western slopes (the Shephelah), among them Debir, Lachish and Beth-shemesh (Fig. 2). To the north of Jerusalem, probably counted as part of the province of Samaria, and to the south in the Negeb, the towns remained untouched, but elsewhere the population was decimated by war, plague or deportation. Of the survivors, some thought it best to migrate voluntarily, and one group from Jerusalem, despite Jeremiah's protests, took off for Egypt, dragging their unwilling prophet of doom along with them (Jer 42, 43). Furthermore, unlike the Assyrians, the Babylonians did not replace the scattered populations of conquered districts with others to avoid dangerous political vacuums. So Judah's inhabitants, possibly numbering

C

FIG 2   PALESTINE OF THE EXILE AND MACCABEES

as many as a quarter of a million in the eighth century, were reduced to less than twenty thousand after 587 BC.

After the holocaust and upheaval that followed, some refugees will have drifted back (Jer 40$^{11-12}$), but the dispirited nature of their existence can be gauged from the biblical book of Lamentations. The Temple area was still the centre of worship, however, and pilgrims brought sacrifices there from the north, as the story in Jeremiah 41$^{4ff.}$ indicates. Furthermore, their cult continued to be of the "unreformed", fertility variety, including sacred prostitution and dedication of semen to Molech (Isa 57$^{3-13}$; cp. 65$^{1-5, 11f.}$). Those Judaeans who had made their way to Egypt joined Jewish communities already established there. Refugees would have gone south earlier as the tide of events became plain in Judah, some to settle just within the frontier, like Jeremiah's party at Tahpanhes (Daphnae: 43^7), Fig. 1, 3; others in the cities of Lower Egypt (Jer 44^1; Fig. 3). Later the Egyptian Jews were to form one of the most important and influential centres of world Jewry, rich and powerful enough to play a significant part in imperial politics. Of one Egyptian group we are unusually well informed, thanks to the discovery of a large number of fifth-century Aramaic papyri from their colony at Elephantine, at the First Cataract of the Nile (Fig. 3). The community was already there when the Persians conquered Egypt in 525 BC, and must therefore have been established by one of the Pharaohs of the Twenty-sixth Dynasty, possibly Apries (588–569 BC), or Amasis (569–525 BC). The Jews could thus conceivably have arrived before the fall of Jerusalem in 587. In any case, Yahwism as practised there was certainly not the "pure" cult promoted by the reformers, since they had their own Temple and altar, on which they offered burnt offerings and made animal sacrifices, quite out of accord with the centralising aspirations of the Deuteronomic legislation. Among Yahweh's companions at this sanctuary were deities called Eshem-bethel, Herem-bethel and 'Anath-bethel, possibly merely other manifestations of the one tribal deity, but whose presence in any case displayed highly "irregular" syncretistic tendencies to the Deuteronomist's point of view.

Nebuchadnezzar had taken the aristocracy from Jerusalem for deportation to Babylonia. They represented the cream of the population materially and intellectually and were comparatively few in number. Jeremiah's figures include those led away on the three occasions, in 597, 587 and 582, and in all amount to only four thousand six hundred

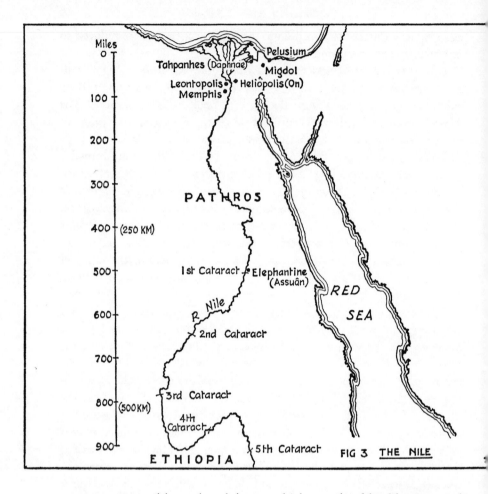

Miles
0
Tahpanhes (Daphnae)
Pelusium
Migdol
Leontopolis
Heliôpolis(On)
Memphis
100
200
300
PATHROS
400 (250 KM)
500
1st Cataract
Elephantine
(Assuân)
RED
R. Nile
SEA
600
2nd Cataract
700
800 (500KM)
3rd Cataract
4th
Cataract
900
5th Cataract
FIG 3   THE NILE
ETHIOPIA

persons, presumably male adults to which we should add wives and children, say three or four times that number (52^{28-30}). To judge from references to these exiles in the writings of Jeremiah and his younger contemporary Ezekiel, they were not harshly treated. They were taken to southern Mesopotamia, not far from Babylon (Fig. 1). Their main centre, according to Ezekiel (1^{1-3}), was in the region of the river Chebar, actually one the canals that crossed and irrigated the alluvial land of the lower Euphrates and Tigris (cp. Ps 137^1). They built houses, farmed, raised families (Jer $29^{5f.}$), and had their own settlements (Ezek 3^{15}; Ezra 2^{59}; 8^{17}). They were allowed to hold meetings, and listen to the exhortations of their prophets and discuss their communal affairs (Ezek 33^{30-33}). In course of time, the Babylonian Jews achieved wealth and high status and were able to bring considerable pressure at court, as we see in the story of Nehemiah's successful intercessions to the Persian king for a relief mission to Palestine (Neh 1, 2).

For all this, the Babylonian Jew could only think of himself as a stranger in a strange land, and brought his children up to believe that their roots lay elsewhere than in Mesopotamia. Distance lent enchantment to faraway Palestine, and the passage of time threw a screen over its local cultic practices. It seemed to the exiles that worship at Jerusalem had exemplified the pure Yahwism preached by the prophets and reformers. This roseate view of the past similarly projected on to the national consciousness a quite unreal picture of their glorious tribal heritage, as far from reality as the picture Ezekiel draws of the Temple (ch. 40–46). Coupled with these dreams of the fancied past went a hatred against those who had banished them from their homes and those who had taken advantage of their absence to rape their lands:

"By the waters of Babylon, there we sat down and wept, when we remembered Zion.

On the willows there we hung up our lyres.

For there our captors required of us songs, and our tormentors, mirth, saying,

'Sing us one of the songs of Zion!'

How shall we sing Yahweh's song in a foreign land?

If I forget you, O Jerusalem, let my right hand wither!

Let my tongue cleave to the roof of my mouth, if I do not remember you,

if I do not set Jerusalem above my highest joy!

Remember, O Yahweh, against the Edomites, the day of Jerusalem, how they said, 'Raze it, raze it! Down to its foundations!'

O daughter of Babylon, you devastator! Happy shall he be who requites you with what you have done to us! Happy shall he be who takes your little ones and dashes them against the rock!"

(Ps 137.)

One interesting result of this combination of religious idealism and a determination to keep themselves separate from alien peoples, was a tendency of the exiled Jews to emphasise certain traditional customs which set them apart from other men. Two in particular, Sabbatarianism and circumcision, were given the sanction of divine ordinances, and promoted as distinctive signs of pure Yahwism. To keep the seventh day holy, and to have one's penis denuded of the foreskin, were the special marks of the Jew. In fact, the origins of both customs are shrouded in the mists of antiquity. The one relates probably to a fertility philosophy that recognized a need for recuperation after the creative act, whether of the lull following harvest, or the peace of mind and body that follows coitus. The same idea is expressed in the biblical injunction to allow land to lie fallow after six years' growth: "in the seventh year there shall be a sabbath of solemn rest for the land" (Lev 25^4).

Circumcision was practised generally in the Syro-Palestinian world, but not apparently in Mesopotamia, nor among the Sea-Peoples from the west, to judge from the scornful epithet applied in the Bible to the Philistines as "the uncircumcised ones". The religious significance of the custom is probably simply that in removing the prepuce, one is preparing the organ for copulation, as on the erection of the penis of an un-circumcised man, the foreskin retracts to reveal the swollen glans. As we may now recognize, the growth of the mushroom was compared by the ancients with sexual stimulation of the penis, and the emergence of its red bulbous cap was envisaged as the emergence of the glans from its enshrouding skin. It is for this reason that we have in the Old Testament a number of curious stories about foreskins as compensatory offerings, and as a "bride-price" (Ex 4$^{24ff.}$; Jos 5$^{2ff.}$; I Sam 18$^{25ff.}$). The general idea behind the "exchange" was that, in removing the protective prepuce, the penis is prepared for its adoption of the "lower lips" of the vulva, one sheathing is sacrificed or exchanged for another.

Keeping the Sabbath and circumcision, therefore, are but two aspects of a fertility cult, and have their origins deep in the consciousness of man. Nevertheless, the observance of these customs became for the exiled Jews an expression of their Faith and a distinguishing mark that set them apart from their foreign environment. Ezekiel refers to the "sabbaths of Yahweh" as a "sign" between the god and his people to be "sanctified" and not "profaned" (20$^{12ff.}$; 22^{8,26}; 23^{38}). Similarly, the post-exilic writer of the so-called "Priestly" stratum of the early stories of Israel connects the Sabbath with the creation of the world (Gen 2^3), and makes circumcision a sign of God's covenant with Abraham (Gen 17$^{10ff.}$). However much these customs may have been recognised among Jews before the Exile, during their enforced separation they took on a far greater significance and served to unify the ex-patriates in a hostile world, and to link them with their real or imagined tribal history. When the "new Judaism" came to be hammered out after the return from captivity, it was around these ancient customs and a historicised mythology that it was fashioned. And the mainspring for this romantic movement came not from the bleak, desolated Jerusalem of reality, but from the emotions of Babylonian Jews feeding their imaginations on unhistorical traditions about their origins, and paying fervent homage to an exclusive religious cult very largely of their own devising.

CHAPTER II

The return

Nebuchadnezzar died in 562 BC. The Babylonian empire had been built by his father and himself, and his death marked the beginning of the end of its short domination of the ancient world. Babylonian supremacy had been made possible by the assistance of the Medes, under their king Cyxares, who helped Nebuchadnezzar to defeat the Assyrians. While the Babylonians were carving their empire out of Assyrian territories in Mesopotamia, Syria, and Palestine, Cyxares was building his own realm, with its capital at Ecbatana (Figs. 1, 4). He subdued the other Indo-Aryan peoples of Iran and pushed westwards into eastern Asia Minor. After a confrontation with Alyattes, king of Lydia, Cyxares was held at the Halys River, Nebuchadnezzar having intervened in 585 BC to help fix the mutual frontier at that point. But with the death of the Babylonian king, a lack of internal stability within the empire gave the Medes an opportunity to take the initiative. The Babylonian throne changed hands three times in seven years, culminating in the reign of Nabonidus (556–539 BC). For some reason, Nabonidus transferred his official residence four years later to the north Arabian oasis of Teima, where he remained for some eight years (552–545 BC), leaving the State's affairs in the hands of his son, Bel-shar-usur (the Belshazzar of the Daniel story). Nabonidus upset the guardians of the Babylonian cult of Marduk by introducing certain religious innovations, and thus aggravated a deteriorating internal political situation by alienating large sections of the priesthood. The city was by now so divided by rival factions that it could only be a matter of time before the enemy at the eastern gates took over control.

The Median king at the time of Nebuchadnezzar's death was Astyages (585–550 BC), the son of Cyxares. He faced a revolt within his dominion from a vassal king of Anshan in southern Iran, called Cyrus. This ruler was a member of the Achaemenian Persian house who had ruled over ancient Elam until its subjugation by the Medes. Nabonidus offered his help to Cyrus in the hope of thereby weakening the Median

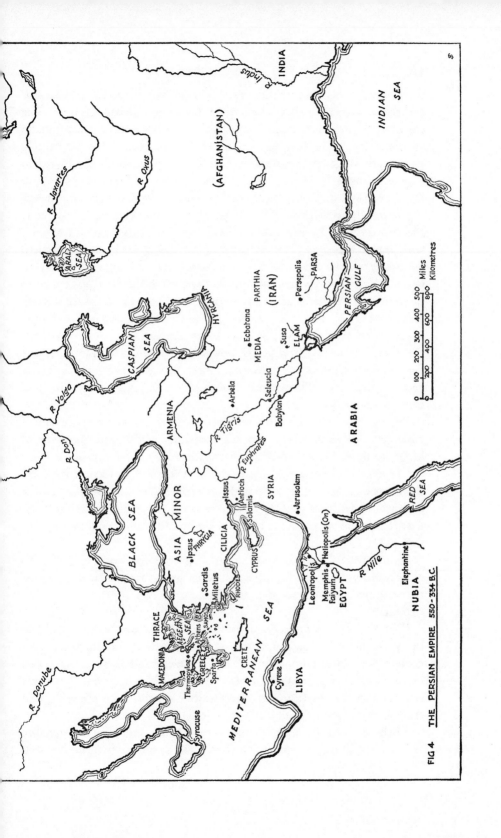

FIG 4   THE PERSIAN EMPIRE   550 - 334 B.C.

threat against his own empire. By 550 BC, Cyrus had taken Ecbatana, dethroned Astyages, and taken over the vast Median empire. The energetic Persian then embarked on a series of devastating campaigns in all directions, and a now thoroughly frightened Nabonidus desperately sought allies against his own protégé in the persons of the Egyptian Pharaoh Amasis (569–525 BC) and Croesus, king of Lydia (ca. 560–546 BC). In one stroke, Cyrus successfully broke up these alliances by sweeping across Upper Mesopotamia, crossed the Halys River in mid-winter, and captured the Lydian capital, Sardis. Nabonidus's defensive alliance with Egypt was a dead letter, since he had lost even his own northern territories. Cyrus could afford to wait for the rich plum of Babylon itself to fall into his lap, and in the meantime pursued his activities eastwards to Afghanistan, and beyond the Oxus as far as the River Jaxartes (Fig. 4). His was now the greatest empire ever known. To the Jewish prophet of the Exile, known to us as Second Isaiah, it seemed that this proud Persian king, the most powerful man of the world, must have derived his authority and prerogative direct from Yahweh, the universal god. He had surely been commissioned by the Lord as his Anointed One, Messiah, or Christ:

"Thus says Yahweh to his Anointed, to Cyrus, whose right hand I have grasped, to subdue nations before him and ungird the loins of kings, to open doors before him that gates may not be closed:

"I will go before you and level the mountains, I will break in pieces the doors of bronze, and cut asunder the bars of iron. I will give you the treasures of darkness, and the hoards in secret places, that you may know that it is I, Yahweh, the God of Israel, who call you by your name . . ." (Isa 45$^{1-3}$).

As the great Cyrus showed himself master of the world as Yahweh's chosen instrument, so the Chosen People would in due time take over the heathen prince's sceptre and succeed to his hegemony over all mankind:

"For the sake of my servant Jacob, and Israel, my chosen, I call you by your name," continues the Jewish prophet. "I surname you, though you do not know me. I am Yahweh, and there is no other, besides me there is no God; I gird you, though you do not know me, that men may know from the rising of the sun, and from the west, that there is none besides me . . ." (vv. 4–6).

"Behold, I will lift up my hand to the nations, and raise my signal to the peoples; and they shall bring your (Israel's) sons in their bosom, and your daughters shall be carried on their shoulders. Kings shall be your foster fathers, and their queens your nursing mothers, With their faces to the ground they shall bow down to you, and lick the dust of your feet . . ." (49 $^{22-23}$).

Babylon's end came swiftly. Upper Mesopotamia had been lost already, as we saw, and the governor of Elam, one Gobryas, had deserted to Cyrus so that this province also was out of Babylonian control. The capital city itself was in a state of panic and had lost all confidence in Nabonidus. The Persian troops massed on the frontier in the spring of 539 BC, and attacked in the summer of that year. The final engagement took place at Opis on the Tigris in October, and it was the defecting governor of Elam, Gobryas, who actually took Babylon, without a fight. Cyrus made his triumphal entry a few weeks later.

According to his own account, Cyrus treated the citizens leniently and respected their religious sensibilities. He claimed that he was led into the captured city by the Babylonian god, Marduk ("Favourer of the womb"), "like a friend and a comrade". Nabonidus had shown the god no reverence by his religious innovations and so alienated his favour. Thus, we are told by Cyrus's own chronicler, "the entire population of Babylon, the whole of Sumer and Akkad, princes and governors, bowed to him and kissed his feet. They were glad that he was king. . . ." So apparently were the local gods and their cultic representatives, since Cyrus made a special point of reinstating their sanctuaries, despoiled by Nabonidus in a last-minute attempt to secure the favours of the various gods by removing their images to Babylon:

". . . the holy cities beyond the Tigris whose sanctuaries had been in ruins over a long period, the gods whose dwelling is in their midst, I returned to their places, and housed them in lasting dwellings. The gods of Sumer and Akkad whom Nabonidus, to the anger of the lord of the gods, had brought into Babylon, at the command of Marduk, the great lord, I settled in peace in their dwellings, resting-places of delight. May all the gods whom I have placed in their sanctuaries address a daily prayer in my favour before Bel and Nabu, that my days may be long . . ." (The Cyrus Cylinder).

Quite apart from his hopes that the combined efforts of the restored Mesopotamian deities might affect his longevity, Cyrus was fully aware that the only way he could continue to rule the world was to keep his subjects happy, and particularly those closest to his home base. His own rise to power by overthrowing his lord and master, whilst a vassal king of Ansham, had taught him to beware of governors entrusted with the rule of local provinces. They could too easily play upon the outraged emotions of cultic or ethnic groups convinced that the foreign ruler had trampled on their religious or national pride and insulted their local deity. Cyrus therefore played safe by demonstrating his obeisance to all the gods, trusting presumably in the broadmindedness of his own Persian deity, Ahura Mazda, not to hold this politically inspired tolerance against his favourite son.

Small wonder, then, that Yahweh's exiled people should welcome the Persian monarch as a saviour sent from God. For the Second Isaiah, Cyrus is almost the equivalent of a second Moses, ordained by Yahweh to lead his people from the desert to the Promised Land:

"A voice cries: 'In the wilderness prepare the way of Yahweh, make straight in the desert a highway for our God' . . ." (40^3).

". . . saying to the prisoners, 'Come forth!' to those who are in darkness, 'Appear!' They shall feed along the ways, on all bare heights shall be their pasture; they shall not hunger or thirst, neither scorching wind or sun shall smite them, for he who has pity on them will lead them, and by springs of water will guide them . . ." (49^{9-10}).

"The wilderness and the dry land shall be glad, the desert shall rejoice and blossom. . . .

And a highway shall be there, and it shall be called the Holy Way; the unclean shall not pass over it, and fools shall not err therein. No lion shall be there, nor shall any ravenous beast come up on it; they shall not be found there, but the redeemed shall walk there.

And the ransomed of Yahweh shall return, and come to Zion with singing, with everlasting joy upon their heads; they shall obtain joy and gladness, and sorrow and sighing shall flee away" (35^{1-10}).

The prophet, like his predecessors, Hosea (2^{14-20}), Isaiah (10^{24-27}), Jeremiah (31^{2-6}), and Ezekiel (20^{33-38}), drew upon the old "Egyptian bondage" mythology to express their present plight, and saw hope of a similar release from slavery in the belief that history repeats itself:

"Thus says Yahweh, who makes a way in the sea, a path in the mighty waters, who brings forth chariot and horse, army and warrior . . . I will make a way in the wilderness and rivers in the desert . . . to give drink to my Chosen People, the people whom I formed for myself that they might declare my praise" (43^{16-21}; cp. $48^{20f.}$).

"Depart, depart, go out thence, touch no unclean thing; go out from the midst of her, purify yourselves, you who bear the vessels of Yahweh.

For you shall not go out in haste, and you shall not go in flight, for Yahweh will go before you, and the God of Israel will be your rear guard" ($52^{11f.}$).

Indeed, Second Isaiah reaches back even further into Near Eastern mythology for his portrayal of the expected return from exile in cosmic terms. This great event was to be the climax of all Creation, a supreme enactment of the Creator God in man's history:

"Awake, awake, put on strength, O arm of Yahweh; awake, as in days of old, the generations of long ago. Was it not thou that didst cut Rahab in pieces, that didst pierce the dragon? Was it not thou that didst dry up the sea, the waters of the great deep; that didst make the depths of the sea a way for the redeemed to pass over? And the ransomed of Yahweh shall return and, come with singing to Zion . . ." (51^{9-11}; cp. Job 26^{12}; Ps 89^{10}). Rahab was the equivalent of the Mesopotamian Tiamat whom the creator god Marduk divided in two to make the earth and the heavens. The conception derives from the old mushroom cosmology that saw the vulva or womb of a great primeval fungus split apart, leaving the hemispherical "cup" below, while the stem or supporting "pillar" (the "ladder" of the Jacob story, the trunk of mighty Hercules and Atlas of classical mythology) pushed up and supported the canopy of heaven, the mushroom cap. Since the fungus was also seen as a serpent emerging from the ground, charmed to erection like a human penis sexually excited, the primeval serpent nomenclature became attached to the "divided vulva" legend of the earth's creation. The prophet combines the old Rahab "serpent-womb" cosmology with the "Red Sea crossing" legend of Exodus (ch. 14, 15).

In pursuance of his declared aim of resettling subject peoples and restoring their cultic shrines and practices, Cyrus decreed the return of the Jewish exiles in the first year of his reign in Babylon (538 BC). There are two reports of this enactment in the Old Testament: the first, in Hebrew (Ezra 1^{2-4}), and the second, usually deemed more authentic, in Aramaic (Ezra 6^{3-5}). It is in the form of an oral decision by the king, recorded and filed in the state archives, and provides that the Jewish Temple be rebuilt in Jerusalem at State expense, lays down certain dimensions and details of its construction, and requires the return of the gold and silver vessels brought by Nebuchadnezzar to Babylon. The Hebrew version proclaims not only that Cyrus has ordained the rebuilding of the Temple, but that Jews in Babylon wishing to do so may return to Palestine, and their fellows who wish to remain where they are should assist the returning exiles with "silver and gold, goods and beasts, besides freewill offerings for the house of God which is in Jerusalem".

The post-exilic Jewish writer to whom critics usually ascribe the title, The Chronicler, and to whose hand is credited the books of Ezra-Nehemiah as well as I and II Chronicles, names the "prince of Judah" who was put in charge of works decreed by Cyrus as Sheshbazzar (Ezra 1^8; cp. I Chr 3^{18}). How many Jews accompanied this dignitary we do not know; the list in Ezra ch. 2, repeated in Nehemiah ch. 7, belongs to a later time. Doubtless the richer members of the community were content, at least at this stage, to send the brave travellers on their way with pious exhortations and suitably costly donations to the Temple furniture (Ezra 1^6). To judge from documents of a century later from Nippur (437 BC and later), the Jews were well established in their business houses, as they were at least sixty years earlier in Egypt. Josephus, the first-century Jewish historian, adds to his account of the affair: "many remained in Babylon, being unwilling to leave their possessions" (*Ant* I xi 3 § 8). We are equally uncertain of Sheshbazzar's exact legal position. One of the Aramaic source documents quoted in Ezra (5^{14}) says Cyrus had appointed him "governor", whatever that word means in this context, but since his nephew and successor, Zerubbabel, with whose career the Chronicler seems at times to confuse Sheshbazzar's, was called "governor of Judah" (Hag $1^{1, 14}$, etc.; cp. Ezra 6^7), the appointment does seem to have had a political, semi-autonomous status.

Sheshbazzar apparently began work immediately on restoring the Temple (Ezra 5^{16}), but little else is known of the fate or achievements of these pioneers, not least because of the confusion in our sources between Sheshbazzar and Zerubbabel, just mentioned (cp. Ezra 3^{6-11}; Zech 4^9). It seems certain that the enterprise made little progress, and the vision of the glorious homecoming, prelude to the new era of peace and prosperity for all mankind, faded before the harsh reality of desolation and suspicion among the local residents. Zechariah, to whom with Haggai and so-called Third Isaiah (ch. 56–66) we owe a prophetic view of the events of the return, calls it "a day of small things" (4^{10}). If Yahweh were indeed behind the project, as the Babylonian visionaries had assured their listeners, he showed no evidence of his favours in terms of weather and crops. Haggai (520 BC) saw the drought and failures that dogged the repatriates' efforts as divine punishment for not putting first things first and finishing the god's house:

"Consider how you have fared. Go up to the hills and bring wood and build the house, that I may take pleasure in it and that I may appear in my glory, says Yahweh. You have looked for much and, lo, it came to little; and when you brought it home I blew it away. Why? says Yahweh of hosts. Because of my house that lies in ruins, while you busy yourselves each with his own house. Therefore the heavens above you have withheld the dew, and the earth has withheld its produce. And I have called for a drought upon the land and the hills, upon the grain, the new wine, the oil, upon what the ground brings forth, upon men and cattle, and upon all their labours" (1^{7-11}).

Proof that this was so was shown by the improvement in agrarian affairs when eventually the foundation of the Temple was laid anew:

"Pray now, consider what will come to pass from this day onward. Before a stone was placed upon a stone in the Temple of Yahweh, how did you fare? When one came to a heap of twenty measures, there were but ten. When one came to a winevat to draw fifty measures, there were but twenty. I smote you and all the products of your toil with blight and mildew and hail; yet you did not return to me, says Yahweh. Consider from this day onward, from the twenty-fourth day of the ninth month. Since the day that the foundation of Yahweh's Temple was laid, consider: Is the seed yet in the barn? Do the vine, the fig tree, the pomegranate, and the olive tree still yield nothing? From this day on I will bless you" (2^{15-19}).

The hostility of the elements was only part of the trouble besetting the pioneers. However enthusiastically their comrades in Babylon had sent them on their way, their reception in Judah was predictably less warm. The Samaritans in particular regarded the country as theirs, and those Jews who had never left not unnaturally resented the influx of strangers claiming the lands as their own because their fathers or grandfathers had been banished some fifty years before. It cannot have helped the situation when the newcomers echoed the words of their prophet Ezekiel, maintaining that the residents had forfeited any rights they may have possessed by their indulgence in immorality and cultic practices deemed by the "new Yahwism" to be pagan:

"Son of man, the inhabitants of these waste places in the land of Israel keep saying, 'Abraham was only one man, yet he got possession of the land; but we are many; the land is surely given to us to possess.' Therefore say to them, thus says the Lord Yahweh, 'You eat flesh with the blood, and lift up your eyes to your idols, and shed blood: shall you possess the land? You resort to the sword, you commit abominations and each of you defiles his neighbour's wife; shall you then possess the land?' Say this to them, 'Thus says the Lord Yahweh: As I live, surely those who are in the waste places shall fall by the sword; and him that is in the open field I will give to the beasts to be devoured, and those who are in strongholds and in caves shall die by pestilence. . . . Then they will know that I am Yahweh, when I have made the land a desolation and a waste because of all their abominations which they have committed'" (33^{24-29}; cp. Hag 2^{10-14}).

In any event the glorious project petered out. Probably the Persian subsidies for the work never materialised, and what with insufficient material resources, bad harvests and sullen hostility all about them, the adventurers seem to have given up the struggle. Eighteen years later Haggai speaks disparagingly of their efforts:

"Who is left among you that saw this house in its former glory? How do you see it now? Is it not in your sight as nothing?" (2^3; cp. Ezra 3^{12}).

Sheshbazzar was succeeded by his nephew Zerubbabel, who had apparently led a further group of returned exiles to Palestine. Just when this was we have no certain knowledge, but it was more likely to have been during the time of Cyrus than later, when Darius became emperor (522 BC). Between those reigns the Persian empire underwent severe disruption, and Darius's first years were concerned very largely with quelling revolts which threatened the stability of the whole of its vast territory.

Cyrus died in 530 BC, during a campaign against nomadic tribes beyond the Jaxartes river, and he was succeeded by his son Cambyses (530–522 BC), who for some years had acted as his deputy in Babylon. In the course of the inevitable scrimmage for the throne that follows on the sudden death of the incumbent, Cambyses thrust aside his brother Bardiya and had him assassinated. He then proceeded, in 525 BC, to add Egypt to the already mighty Persian empire, and it was on his return from a campaign in that area that he learnt, three years later, that an upstart Gaumata, claiming to be the dead Bardiya, had seized the throne. For some unknown reason, Cambyses committed suicide, and a member of his entourage, Darius by name, also of royal lineage, rallied the army behind him and confronted Gaumata in Media. The usurper was executed, Darius installed on the throne, and immediately anarchy was loosed throughout the empire. Every vassal ruler seems to have decided the time was ripe for revolt and for seizing what he could of the

Persian dominions. Rebellions broke out in Media, Elam, Parsa, Armenia, across Iran to the eastern frontier, and the rumblings were felt westward in Asia Minor and in Egypt. Even in Babylon, a self-styled son of Nabonidus, one Nidintubel, gave himself the throne name Nebuchadnezzar III and remained in control for some months before Darius was able to find time to remove and execute him. The next year, the same thing happened with another "Nebuchadnezzar", claiming to be the son of Nabonidus, and he, too, managed to hold on to the throne for some months before being impaled. For two years Darius had his hands full in his efforts to hold the empire together. The shock waves reached the returned exiles in Judah and bestirred them to fresh hopes of political independence.

The books of Haggai and Zechariah reflect the wild imaginings that the apparent loosening of the imperial control awakened in Jewish hearts. Haggai's utterances are dated between August and December 520 BC, and Zechariah began his prophecies in the autumn of that year. Darius had not yet mastered the rebellious situation, and the prophets thought they recognized in the turmoil the hand of Yahweh preparing the way for his direct intervention. Now, at last, the old Davidic kingdom was to be re-established in its long-promised glory. But since the god could only return to his people and land if he had somewhere to live, the Temple must be rebuilt. Thus, spurred on by prophetic exhortations, and under the sacerdotal guidance of one Joshua (Jeshua), a priest of the old Zadokite lineage, born in exile (Hag 1^1; Ezra 3^2, etc.), Zerubbabel organized the work (Ezra $5^{1f.}$; 6^{14}). Haggai could hardly contain himself in his enthusiasm. Their leader Zerubbabel was surely the long-awaited Davidic ruler who was to come and rule the world (2^{23}; cp. Zech 6^{9-15}). The building on which the people laboured under his direction may not look much now, but wait awhile! Shortly Yahweh would shake the nations so vigorously in the cataclysmic upheaval which was even now presaged by rebellions through the empire, that their gold and silver would cascade upon Jerusalem and fill the Temple with such wealth as not even King Solomon's treasuries could match (Hag 2^{6-9}).

Zechariah, speaking for the most part after Darius had regained control, expressed his dreams in more esoteric forms. His visions have to be deciphered, and are the forerunners of apocalyptic ("revealed") writings of intertestamental and Christian literature. He projects his hopes for the future with no less certainty of their ultimate fulfilment

D

but, in view of the hard facts of Darius's renewed hegemony, with a rather vaguer chronology. Nevertheless, he shares Haggai's belief that the current upheaval marked the beginning of Yahweh's divine intervention in man's affairs, and urged Jews still living in Babylon to flee from the wrath to come and take their rightful place in Jerusalem, future capital of the world (2^{6-13}), "overflowing with prosperity" (1^{17}) in which they will share (8^{12}). But they must make sure of their place, for the city will prove so attractive to others that it will spread beyond its present walls and have to rely for its protection on the power of the god dwelling within (1^{17}; 2^{1-5}). Even gentiles will find its abundance irresistible, and cling on to any Jew they meet, begging to be allowed to accompany him to the land of plenty: "ten men from the nations of every tongue shall take hold of the robe of a Jew, saying, 'Let us go with you, for we have heard that God is with you'" (8^{23}).

Meanwhile, it was important to rebuild Yahweh's house. The present residents would find that once the work had begun others would rush to help (6^{15}), and Zerubbabel, who had undertaken the task at the god's behest, would see it through to its end (4^{6-10}). Alongside this royal saviour would stand the anointed priest, Joshua, and in this duality of messianic office ("the two anointed": 4^{14}), Zechariah sets the pattern for later conceptions of the twin messiahs, priestly and lay, ruling the ideal theocracy of the future. Zerubbabel, as the lay messiah, scion of David's house, the "Branch" of Jeremiah's promise (23^5), would be the military and administrative right arm of the kingdom (6^{9-15}), working in close accord with the sacerdotal representative, through whom God's Law would be reinterpreted for mankind (ch. 3).

Viewed in the cold light of reality, these high hopes and specious promises for a re-establishment of Jewish rule in Palestine and over all the earth, must seem pathetic, if not ludicrous. But they were dangerous. That kind of talk in an empire passing through a revolutionary phase of the kind that faced Darius on his accession was not to be tolerated. Furthermore, renewed building activity, even if confined for the time being to the walls of a religious sanctuary, was suspicious, and the Persian governor of the Trans-Euphrates satrapy ("the province beyond the River": Ezra 5^3) began to take notice. He was told the Jews were doing no more than had been permitted them by the great Cyrus himself eighteen years previously. Search was made in the royal archives, and eventually the record of Cyrus's verbal decree was discovered in the Median capital of Ecbatana. Building was allowed to continue during the search, so clearly the Jewish leaders had been able to allay the satrap's anxieties (Ezra 3⁵). Darius confirmed the old decree and even, according to the document reproduced in Ezra, ordered that the costs of rebuilding and of providing animal sacrifices should be made available from State revenues of the Trans-Euphrates province (Ezra 6⁶⁻¹²).

In March 515 BC, the Temple was finished and dedicated with great rejoicing (Ezra 6¹⁵ᶠ·). The cult was organized in accordance with the new, "purified" dispensation now propounded as having been decreed by Moses (Ezra 6¹⁸), and Yahwism was set, however precariously, upon the path laid out for it by Exilic idealism. It fell far short of the political domination envisaged by the dreamers, for the Temple's very existence depended upon the patronage of a heathen king, and whatever autonomy may have been vouchsafed to Sheshbazzar and Zerubbabel, it does not seem to have lasted very long. The "scion of David", the "Christ" of the new kingdom of God, disappeared without trace, possibly because the Persians were not quite so blind to the political motives behind the re-establishment of the Jerusalem shrine and cultus as the records seem to infer. In any case, none of Zerubbabel's family succeeded him, and in the time of Nehemiah, administration was in the hands of the successors of the High Priest Joshua (Neh 12²⁶). Darius still ruled the empire, and the Jews of the Exile were not so overwhelmed with admiration of what had been achieved in Jerusalem or attracted by its prosperity that they yet felt the call to leave the fleshpots of Babylon to secure their places in the brave new world.

CHAPTER III

Building the walls

Before the end of the sixth century BC, Darius I Hystaspes had cast his imperial mantle over the greater part of the known world (Fig. 4). From the Indus valley to the Aegean, from the Jaxartes to Libya, in Thrace and the Balkans to the Danube, Darius's lieutenants administered their provinces, watched over by the military and periodically inspected by roving ambassadors of the king. The eyes of the ever-watchful central authority were everywhere, and yet each satrapy maintained a large degree of autonomy. The benevolent despotism of this system of government encouraged and sponsored large projects. This was the day of magnificent building programmes, as at Persepolis, of the canal that linked the Nile with the Red Sea, of road-making and easy communications throughout the vast empire and other prerequisites of enlarged trade, like standardised coinage and reformed legal procedures. Only in one area of endeavour did Darius fail: his conquering of Greece. A storm destroyed the Persian fleet off Mount Athos; Miltiades and his Athenian troops held the Persian army at Marathon (Fig. 5). It was left to his son Xerxes (486–465 BC) to defeat the Spartans at Thermopylae in 480, capture Athens and set fire to the Acropolis. But his victory was short-lived. At Salamis a third of the Persian fleet was destroyed, and a year later the rest was lost at Samos, whilst the army was cut to pieces at Plataea (Fig. 5). By 466, Xerxes had been thrust out of Europe altogether, and his fleet banned from Aegean waters.

Following his assassination in 465 BC, Xerxes was succeeded by his younger son, Artaxerxes I Longimanus (465/4–424 BC), and it is during his reign that the light of history begins to filter through once more upon the fortunes of the returned exiles in Jerusalem. Apparently the people of Samaria at one time during Artaxerxes's reign became not unreasonably worried when the Jews began fortifying Jerusalem (Ezra 4⁷⁻²³). They complained to the Persian king, saying that "if this city is rebuilt and its walls finished, you will then have no possession in the province Beyond the River" (v. 16). The king's researches discovered that

Jerusalem had always been a hotbed of revolt and we ordered the work to be forcibly stopped (v. 21). Unfortunately we cannot more precisely date this activity, and the writer has chronologically misplaced the incident. For further information about the state of affairs prevailing in Judah during this period we have to look to the memoirs of Nehemiah, whose

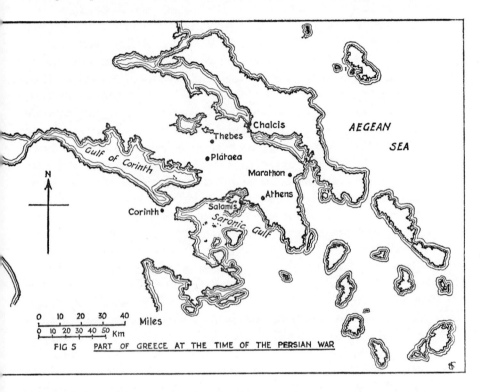

FIG 5   PART OF GREECE AT THE TIME OF THE PERSIAN WAR

activity in Jerusalem began in 445 BC, and to the contemporary prophetic writings of Obadiah (probably early fifth century) and Malachi (about 450 BC).

In the south, the Jews were having continual trouble with the Edomites who had been forced out of their own lands by Arab pressure and had already occupied most of southern Palestine to a point north of Hebron. Malachi's oracle on Edom would indicate that the Arabs had taken over her territory completely by his time (1^{2-5}), and archaeology confirms that Edomite territory remained without settled population for the whole of the Persian period. Obadiah gives vent to unrestrained fury against the descendants of Esau whom he saw as intruders into the

land of Jacob. Characteristically, the prophet looks forward to a vindi-
cation of Jewish territorial rights with fire and the sword, and the
eventual domination of Edom from Mount Zion (v. 21).

There had been a continual drift back of exiles to Jerusalem (cp.
Ezra 4^{12}), and the population list in Ezra ch. 2 and Nehemiah ch. 7,
puts the total residents of the province at about fifty thousand, perhaps
double what it had been before the Return. Some of the previously
depopulated towns, like Tekoa, Beth-zur and Keilah, were now re-
inhabited (Neh ch. 3), and members of the Jewish community were to
be found in Jericho, around Bethel, and even as far as Lydda (Lod;
7^{37}: Fig. 2). Nevertheless, Jerusalem was still without many inhabitants,
"and no houses had been built" (7^4). Administratively the province
seems to have been under Samaritan domination, and the taxes levied
by their officials caused real hardship. Nehemiah boasted later that he
had not lived off the Jews he had come to help, unlike "the former
governors who were before me (and) laid heavy burdens upon the people,
and took from them food and wine, besides forty shekels of silver", and
whose servants "lorded it over the people" (5^{15}).

Measured against the high ideals set by the absent planners, the
religious and moral standards of the Holy City were deplorably low.
Priests were accepting less than the best of the flocks to burn to their
jealous god on the altar (Mal 1$^{6-14}$), their doctrinal teaching was faulty
(2$^{1-9}$), and the tithes were not flowing into God's House (3$^{7-10}$), so that
the Levites were having to work in their own fields to live instead of
performing their cultic duties at the expense of the worshippers
(Neh 13$^{10f.}$). The rich were flourishing and the poor were becoming
poorer, as their mortgages were foreclosed and they and their children
reduced to slavery (Neh 5$^{1-5}$), or they were cheated out of their wages
by unscrupulous employers (Mal 3^5). Worse, the principle of the Jewish
master-race, founded upon the myth of racial purity, was being jeo-
pardised by intermarriage on an increasing scale. Nehemiah complains
of the situation thus:

"In those days also I saw the Jews who had married women of
Ashdod, Ammon, and Moab; and half of their children spoke the
language of Ashdod, and they could not speak the language of Judah,
but the language of each people. And I contended with them and
cursed them and beat some of them and pulled out their hair; and I
made them take an oath in the name of God, saying, 'You shall not give
your daughters to their sons, or take their daughters for your sons or

yourselves. Did not Solomon king of Israel sin on account of such women? . . . foreign women made even him sin. Shall we then listen to you and do all this great evil and act treacherously against our God by marrying foreign women?'" (13$^{23-27}$).

Once again, it was from outside Palestine that the driving force came to correct matters. As the Jews of Babylon had instigated the Return from Exile, and at least partly financed the re-establishment of the cultus in Jerusalem on their terms, so it was in Persia, at the court of Artaxerxes I, that action was taken by the exiles to restore their control over Jerusalem. The personal cup-bearer of the king, one Nehemiah, happened to be a Jew with a brother among the repatriates in the Holy City. In December 445 BC, this brother, Hanani, headed a delegation of Jewish settlers to Susa, and laid a formal complaint about the treatment meted out to them by their Judaean neighbours. He begged his influential brother to seek redress on their behalf from the king (Neh 1$^{1-3}$). Their news greatly distressed Nehemiah who was able, four months later, to seize an opportunity to raise the matter before his royal master. One day, when handing over the cup that cheers, Artaxerxes found the happy occasion marred by his officer's gloomy countenance. "Why is your face sad," he asked, "seeing you are not sick?" The earnest servant lost no time in discoursing at length upon the plight of his fellow-Jews and their Holy City, lying waste and its gates destroyed. He besought his master to let him go and help rebuild the city, and, perhaps in the circumstances not surprisingly, the king urged him to go and discreetly asked how long he might be expected to stay away (2$^{1-8}$).

Nehemiah seems thus to have persuaded the king to reverse his previous decree, made at the instigation of the Samaritan governors, that this very project of rebuilding Jerusalem as a defendable fortress site should be nipped in the bud (Ezra 4$^{17-22}$). When Nehemiah arrived in Palestine, accompanied by units of the imperial army and bearing the king's letters, the local officials were disquieted (Neh 2^{10}), less, perhaps, because he had come "to seek the welfare of the children of Israel", than because his intention was to secure the defences of a potentially hostile enclave within the empire's Palestinian possessions. For then or subsequently Nehemiah was given the power of a provincial governor (5^{4}; 10^{1}), and thus made independent of Samaritan control.

There is some doubt about when Nehemiah actually arrived in Jerusalem and began work. The Bible gives the impression that he

started from Susa straight away (Neh 2^9), but Josephus (*Ant* XI v 7 §
168), following the Greek Septuagint text, the first part of which is
preserved in I Esdras, makes him go first to Babylon and collect volun-
teers to accompany him, not arriving until 440 BC. In any case, he lost
no time in putting his plans into action. Three days after his arrival he
made a secret nocturnal inspection of the city walls, telling no one, not
even the Jewish priests and notables (2^{12-16}). Only when he had assessed
the work to be done did he disclose his full intentions, and the Samaritan
officials were left gasping at the audacity of what appeared to be open
rebellion within the realm, apparently with the emperor's blessing!
(2^{19}).

Chief among Nehemiah's enemies was one, Sanballat, whose
governorship of the Samaria province is confirmed from the Elephantine papyri (cp. Neh $4^{1f.}$). To judge from the names of his sons,
Delaiah and Shelemiah, he was a Yahwist, and he was allied by
marriage with the high-priestly family in Jerusalem, indicating that
opposition to the Mesopotamian inspired plans of Nehemiah was by no
means confined to non-Jews. There were plenty of people in Judah who
realised what was happening and who shared with Sanballat and his
friends apprehension of the likely outcome of building a fortress near
one of the empire's main strategic routes, however impressively
authorised its architect might appear to be with the king's credentials.
Outside Judah, also, the feverish building activity of the Jerusalem
reformers was viewed with disquiet. With Sanballat is mentioned
Tobiah, governor of the province of Ammon in Transjordan (2^{10}, etc.).
His family were also Yahwists, and of considerable renown even as late
as the second century. Apparently they tried to counter Nehemiah's
religious persuasiveness with prophecies designed to strike fear into the
hearts of his followers, and probably bearing more closely on reality
than the promises of prosperity purveyed by the Jewish leader (6^{14}; cp.
2^{20}). That the opposition of Sanballat and Tobiah was not inspired by
motives of religious jealousy is shewn by the fact that they counted
among their supporters a very powerful pagan Arab chieftain from
north-west Arabia, one Geshem (Gashmu) from Qedar (Dedan: Fig. 1),
whose territory we know to have included Edom and southern Judah
(2^{19}; $6^{1,6}$).

The allies made plans for concerted attacks on the wall-builders to
stop the work (4^{7-12}). Nehemiah was now fighting against time. He
had to finish the defensive positions before either Artaxerxes rescinded

his orders or the surrounding governors won enough support among the Jews in and around the city to abort his plans. He armed his workers, "each with one hand laboured on the work and with the other held his weapon" (4^{17}). Furthermore, the shifts were so arranged that those not actually fetching and carrying were protecting the workers, and behind them all stood the leaders, watching (v. 16). By what methods the labourers were kept at the task under such conditions we are not told. Certainly the temptation to give up and return home to protect their families in the outlying areas must have been strong indeed, since they were under constant attack during the absence of their menfolk (vv. 10–12). To counteract this tendency to desertion, Nehemiah had the families of his workpeople brought into the city, and thus made as dependent upon the success of the building operations as the normal residents: "Do not be afraid of them. Remember the Lord, who is great and terrible, and fight for your brethren, your sons, your daughters, your wives and your homes" (v. 14).

The work-parties were scattered along the length of the walls, and so susceptible to attack concentrated on the thinly defended sections. Orders were given that in this event, Nehemiah and his attendant bugler would run to the place of attack and sound off a rallying call to draw all the defenders to the spot. He and his officers were kept so busy that "none of us took off our clothes; each kept his weapon in his hand" (v. 23). He resisted all his enemies' efforts to lure him out of the city for a parley, however much they bullied or cajoled him, and threatened to reveal to the king the true object of his frantic endeavours:

"It is reported among the nations, and Geshem also says it, that you and the Jews intend to rebel; that is why you are building the wall; and you wish to become their king, according to this report. And you have also set up prophets to proclaim concerning you in Jerusalem, 'There is a king in Judah'. And now it will be reported to the king according to these words . . ." ($6^{6f.}$).

Fifty-two days of ceaseless work saw the completion of some kind of continuous rampart around the city (6^{15}). The gates were hung and Nehemiah's brother Hanani received his just reward of governorship of Jerusalem, aided by one Hananiah, keeper of the castle (7^2). Everyone entering and leaving the city was checked, and guards were everywhere (v. 3). We gather that there was no great enthusiasm from the Jews to live within the walls of what was virtually a blockade. To swell their numbers for defensive purposes, Nehemiah ordered a ballot among the Jews of surrounding towns, by which every tenth family was required to move into Jerusalem. Just how reluctantly they went may be judged by the remark that those who volunteered to go were "blessed" by everyone else (11²).

Having thus procured for himself some security from the outside world, Nehemiah now started the more vital task of indoctrinating the people of the "new Jerusalem" with a sense of racial cohesion. From henceforth they were to be a holy people, a chosen race, ordained by their god for a world mission. They must learn to recognise each other as privileged members of a very special society, distinct from all other men. They were brothers in Yahweh and must learn to treat each other with a respect not due to the gentile. For a start he insisted they cancel all outstanding debts, and no longer exact interest from each other:

". . . I and my brethren and my servants are lending them money and grain. Let us leave off this interest. Return to them this very day their fields, their vineyards, their olive orchards, and their houses, and the percentage of money, grain, wine and oil which you have been exacting from them" (5¹⁰ᶠ·).

However, much more than fiscal measures was required to weld this heterogeneous collection of peoples together into an organic whole. There had to be an emotional rallying-point, overriding all other allegiances, ethnic, even familial. It could only be religiously inspired, and at its centre must be a supra-national god, a single deity to whose creative acts was owing all life, on earth or in the heavens, and to whom was thus due the homage of all men. The traumatic effects of the Exile upon the minds of the intellectual elite of Judah had already produced the monotheistic ideal of Second Isaiah (ch. 40–55), who uncompromisingly identified the tribal god Yahweh with the sovereign Lord of all history. In fact, as we may now appreciate, he was doing no more than perceive in the deity the fertility concept that had been implicit in his name, "Sperm of life", from the beginning. Yahweh, like his exact philological counterpart, the Greek Zeus, and his semantic equivalent El, chief god of the Semites, was always the one creator god, the source of all life, and only secondarily appropriated as a tribal deity. The Jewish philosopher, wrenched from his homeland by a foreign conqueror, was forced to project his understanding of Yahweh's dealings with his people against a backcloth of world politics. If Israel's god had any reality at all, he must be able to act over a far wider area than Palestine, and to be able to demand the allegiance of many more peoples than the

Jews and the Canaanites. The prophet saw Yahweh as a cosmic deity, lord of the heavenly hosts and forces of nature, but at the same time still the special god of Israel, a tribal deity whose main interest was the welfare of his Chosen People. Thus it followed that whatever the grand strategy in the Creator's mind, it involved the destiny of the Jews, and all history was directed to their glorification.

Here we have the core of the doctrine of the Chosen Race, whose working out in practical politics was to wreak such havoc among the nations of the world and to bring successive disasters upon the Jews themselves. The idea was formulated among the Babylonian exiles, although its elements were already embedded in tribal mythology and religion. From afar they manipulated events and people in the cradle of Jewish political ambitions, Judah, where their hero-king David had five centuries earlier by cunning and courage won domination of Palestine. Their servant in this endeavour was Nehemiah, and his first task was to implant into the minds of the Palestinian Jews, residents and repatriates, the idea that however lowly their present status and meagre their resources, Yahweh was working out through them his great purpose which would result in their taking their rightful place as head of the nations. The signs of this divine control might be seen all about them. Had they not rebuilt the city walls in record time against overwhelming odds? Even their enemies recognised in this endeavour the influence of some superhuman power and were afraid, "for they perceived that this work had been accomplished with the help of our god" (Neh 6^{16}). The Jews themselves must recognise that their defeat at the hands of the Babylonians, their Exile, and the hardships they had borne on their return, were but necessary tribulations to temper the steel of their endurance for the mighty works to come. Their present situation was the culmination of a tribal history stretching back to "the affliction of our fathers in Egypt" (9^9), and now was the time to make a new covenant with their god (v. 38).

Prime mover on this religious aspect of the reconstitution of the Judaean community was one Ezra, "the Scribe", learned, as we read, "in matters of the commandments of Yahweh and his statutes for Israel" (Ezra 7^{11}). He, too, was a designate of the Babylonian Jewish community, and sent apparently with the king's blessing and letters of authority (7$^{12-26}$). He came to Jerusalem armed also with a copy of the Law and power to enforce its provisions on all Jews in Palestine who claimed allegiance to the cult community of Jerusalem: "whoever will not obey the law of your god and the law of the king, let judgment be strictly executed upon him, whether for death or for banishment or for confiscation of his goods or for imprisonment" (v. 26). Money and offerings for the Temple cult were abundantly supplied by Ezra's Babylonian Jewish patrons, and supplemented from the royal treasuries (vv. 15–20). Cult personnel were exempted from taxes (v. 24).

The chronological relationship between Nehemiah and Ezra is in doubt. While Nehemiah's dates seem quite certain, supported to some extent by the Elephantine papyri's references to Sanballat, his arch-enemy, the traditional view that put Ezra's ministry in Jerusalem before Nehemiah's, in 458 BC, is now largely discredited. The picture given of the more or less settled city in which Ezra worked reflects more the state of affairs after Nehemiah's administrative efforts than that obtaining before he had come. Again, Nehemiah's memoirs in respect of the abuses he found prevalent among the people contain no hint that Ezra had already called upon them to respect the Law he brought with him. For these and a number of other reasons, scholars today usually favour a date for the Scribe's visit as around 428 BC, immediately following Nehemiah's first period of governorship of twelve years ending in 433 BC (Neh 5^{14}). At that time he returned to his king's service at the Persian court, but was shortly back again, making his presence felt amongst the renegades who had immediately taken advantage of his absence to return to their own religious customs (13$^{6ff.}$). It was probably in this second term of office that Ezra arrived, despite the Chronicler's impression that the Scribe preceded his political counterpart by some thirteen years (Ezra ch. 7–10; cp. 7$^{7t.}$ with Neh 1^1; 2^1). In any case, there is no doubt that Ezra's mission was a necessary complement to Nehemiah's, for in the body of inspired teaching, the Torah or Law, that he brought with him, he gave the community a focus of faith and practice that was to serve it through periods of political disruption and frustration down to the present time. From the day that Ezra climbed up on to a wooden platform in the city square before the Water Gate and intoned the "book of the Law of Moses" in Hebrew and Aramaic "from early morning until midday" until the people wept (Neh, 8$^{1-9}$), Judaism became a religion of The Book. This "Law", probably the Pentateuch, or first five books of the Old Testament, was not merely a piece of legislative literature. It was a manifestation of God's will, to be venerated and adored as though it were Yahweh made manifest on earth. It was a living expression of the divine will for Israel for all time, capable of infinite application and interpretation.

It is difficult for a non-Jew to appreciate the nature and significance of the Torah for Judaism. We may wonder at the gross superstition that attended its every word at a later time, when it was decreed so sacred that not a "jot nor tittle" might be changed, even though errors in the text were plain and easily rectified. Our present text of the Bible has been given vowels sometimes quite at variance with the consonants to which they are attached (Semitic writing normally is written without vowels), and the reader is directed to follow the revision for the sake of sense, even though he is forbidden to change the written word in copying! For the pious Jew the Law is the utterance of God, and as such is sacrosanct, and any change made in even the smallest detail is blasphemy. Absurd as the gentile might consider the extremes to which this respect of the written word was taken, they are merely the irrational projections of the basic thesis of a divine revelation through the mind and speech of specially inspired men like Moses. In the Pentateuch, Ezra gave the New Israel a much-needed focus of faith and conduct, and something that was distinctively Jewish. It was designed to exclude the outsider no less effectively than Nehemiah's wall. Its Law demanded an obedience that was more a religious attitude than mere observation of certain moral and cultic precepts. It was the mark of a Jew no less exclusively than the practice of circumcision and Sabbatarianism. Other men had laws; only the Jew had the Torah. Other cultures had their heroic mythology; only the Jew made his tribal legends historical episodes in the one God's unfolding plan for all mankind. It was a Jewish god who had created the world, who had walked in the Garden of Eden, who had revealed his will to Moses, and who had, in these latter days, created anew his divine community in the Holy City. The history of the Jews as revealed in the Torah was thus in a sense coextensive with the story of mankind, and in Adam's supremacy over the beasts of the field (Gen 1^{26}) could be seen figured from the Creation the eventual dominion by the Jew of the whole world.

It is in this light that we have to understand the fierce intolerance and ruthlessness of Nehemiah's measures to protect the supposed racial purity of the restored community in Palestine. Wives of foreign extraction were wrenched apart from their husbands, children of mixed marriages made outcasts, and the priesthood was cleansed of "everything foreign" (Neh 13$^{23-30}$). These terrible walls that Nehemiah and

Ezra built around Judaism in the fifth century before our era have lasted until the present day. Unwittingly the master-planners of Babylon and their administrative and religious executors laid the foundation of an anti-Semitism which was thenceforth to blot the pages of human history.

CHAPTER IV

The Greek enchantment

The Chronicler ends his narrative with Ezra, around 427 BC. Thereafter, until the books of Maccabees take up the story of the Jews in 175 BC, we have virtually no first-hand knowledge of their fortunes. From biblical and extra-biblical Jewish writings we may assess something of the religious developments of this period, but they impart very little direct historical information. Of the world at large during this time much is known, however. Artaxerxes I died in 424 BC, and was succeeded after the assassination of the rightful heir Xerxes II, by his son Darius II Nothus (423–404 BC). By the time the Peloponnesian War had ended with the capitulation of Athens in 404 BC, Persia had been able to manoeuvre herself into an even stronger position in Asia Minor. Under Darius's successor, Artaxerxes II Mnemon (404-358 BC), however, colonial troubles, particularly in Egypt, threatened to disrupt the empire completely. That country seized her freedom in 401, and remained autonomous for some sixty years through the Twenty-eighth, Twenty-ninth and Thirtieth Dynasties. At the same time, the king's own brother Cyrus (the Younger) raised an army in revolt in Asia Minor, including thirteen thousand Greek mercenaries, and reached Babylonia before being killed and his army routed. The Spartans noted the march of Xenophon's Ten Thousand survivors through Persian territory, and dared to take advantage of the absence of the Athenian protective "umbrella" over the Greek cities of Asia Minor, to campaign there in a crusade of (lucrative) liberation. The Persians in retaliation set dissension among the Greeks by recruiting more Greek mercenaries and using their gold to subsidise Greek states to disrupt the Spartan peace elsewhere. In 387 BC, the Spartans were obliged to cede all the Asiatic mainland to Persia and to concentrate their energies on maintaining order in Greece. Now it seemed that the Persians were able to exercise a dominating influence on the Greeks of Europe, as Darius I and Xerxes had tried without success to do by frontal assault. But more trouble faced Artaxerxes.

With the example of Egypt's successful revolt to encourage them, and an increasingly heavy taxation burden to goad their people into support, the satraps of the western empire rose against the central authority. They were nominally controlled by the Persian monarch, and owed him allegiance and feudal dues, but many of them were hereditary kings over their own peoples. They formed a coalition and issued their own coinage, and formed an alliance with Pharaoh Tachos of Egypt who, around 360 BC, moved north into Syria to their assistance. The allies crossed into Mesopotamia, and for a time it seemed as though the Persian empire was to lose the whole of its western dependencies. At that crucial moment, Pharaoh Tachos faced an uprising back home in Egypt, and was forced to surrender, leaving his allies unprotected. One by one they acknowledged defeat, and the revolt of the satraps was over. When Artaxerxes died in 358 BC, the Persian empire was nominally still intact, apart from Egypt's defection. But the readiness with which the western satraps had risen and banded together showed the extent of the empire's basic instability. Furthermore, in the Greek world, Philip II of Macedon had come to royal power (359 BC), and the picture of hopeless disunity and inter-state feuds was beginning to change.

Philip was an able administrator, diplomat and general. The Macedonians were a fairly homogeneous people, and needed only a strong hand to organise them and create an effective force. In Philip they found their natural leader, and, having secured his position, he annexed Thessaly (352 BC), Thrace (342 BC), and any adjacent Greek colony that fell to his hand (Fig. 6). The Athenians, dependent upon their control of the straits leading to the Black Sea for their corn supplies, noted with apprehension the rise to power of Macedon, but, even so, could not believe the threat it presented was anything more than a temporary affair. In fact, Philip had so prepared the ground with supporters in the majority of Greek states, that his ability to take over Greece piecemeal was already assured. His potential domination was made absolute when, with the young Alexander, he defeated the Thebans and Athenians at Chaeronea in 338 BC. The rest of Greece ceded their hegemony to Philip at the Congress of Corinth. Two years later Alexander succeeded his father. Few could have guessed that even then the days of the Persian empire were numbered.

Artaxerxes III Ochus saw his prime function as one of pounding the empire back into total subjection. He rose to power ruthlessly, killing all his brothers and sisters as potential rivals to his claims. Once on the

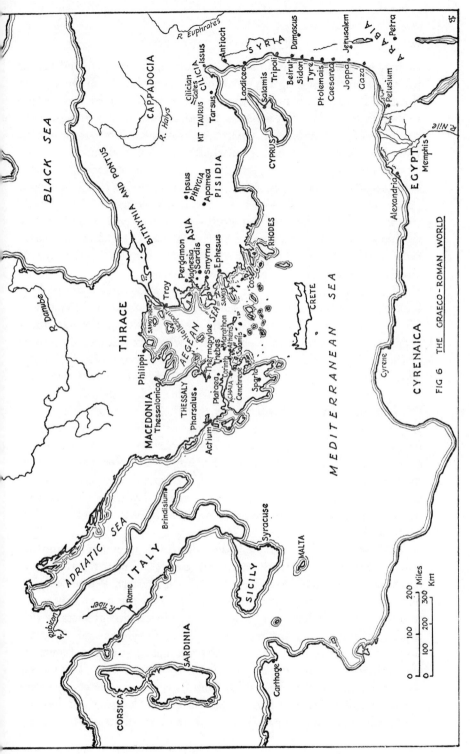

FIG 6   THE GRAECO-ROMAN WORLD

throne, he cracked down on rebellious subjects everywhere and turned his attention to restoring Egypt to the Persian fold. When he achieved this goal in 342 BC, it might have seemed that the empire was back to its old strength. But the weaknesses had already shown through with the revolt of the satraps, and Artaxerxes's violent death by poisoning four years later, and the same fate suffered by his son and successor Arses after a reign of only two years, were further indications of internal corruption in the body politic. The next king, Darius III Codomannus (336–331 BC), had to be sought from as distant a branch of the family tree as the grandchildren of the brother of Artaxerxes II, such had been the bloody inroads made upon the Achaemenian house. Even as Darius came to the throne, the young Alexander succeeded to the rule of Greece and dreams of a mighty eastern empire.

Of the Jews during these stirring times we know practically nothing for certain. As regards the Egyptian Jews, the texts from the colony at Elephantine break off at 399 BC, and we may presume the settlement ended during the reign of Nepherites I, who succeeded to the throne of the Pharaohs in that year and founded the Twenty-ninth Dynasty. This community had always been loyal to Persia and would thus have been politically suspect when Egypt won her independence in 401 BC. Of the Samaritan Yahwists we know that they accepted the Pentateuch as their supremely authoritative religious book, since that continued to be the only part of the Jewish Scriptures they acknowledged as canonical, and they built their own temple on Mount Gerizim, for it was there in the early second century BC (II Macc 6^2). But they never acquiesced in the political ambitions of Judah, and even today their communities in Palestine have more in common with their Arab neighbours than modern Jews.

Judah seems to have retained some degree of autonomy during the fourth century. She struck her own coinage, imitating the Attic drachma then current over the whole of the western Persian empire, but having the name *Yehud* (Judah) stamped on the coins. There are traditions that the Jews were involved in political disturbances at this time, and even that some were deported to Babylonia and Hyrcania (Fig. 4), but, again, little is known for certain of these events. However, of one thing we can be sure: the doctrine of the Chosen Race, a people set apart from the non-Jewish world, must have been undergoing severe strains at this time. The Palestinian world was changing and looking westwards more and more for its culture. For all its walls and its exclusive cult, Jerusalem could not keep entirely apart from the international stream of human and trade relationships that had long been so much part of the Fertile Crescent. There had always been plentiful contacts with the Aegean lands, and in the fifth and fourth centuries BC these increased as Greek traders, mercenaries and other adventurers were constantly coming and going throughout western Asia. The trade routes from the Mediterranean led through the ports of Phoenicia, through Judah and south to Arabia, and Greek artefacts and pottery have left their traces throughout Palestine.

To survive commercially, the Jews could not afford to keep entirely to themselves. The first recognisable step was the abandonment of Hebrew as the common speech in favour of its sister language Aramaic, already established as the *lingua franca* and official tongue of the Persian empire. Epigraphic evidence shows that already by the fourth century this process was well advanced, and it is presumably the tendency to adopt a more common dialect that so concerned Nehemiah: ". . . half their children spoke the language of Ashdod, and they could not speak the language of Judah, but the language of each people" (13^{24}). Hebrew was by no means dead, but it became more and more reserved for religious writings, and its revival during times of political resurgence was more a mark of self-conscious nationalism than the needs of social intercourse. Furthermore, a knowledge of Greek was becoming more and more essential for trade and, latterly, for cultural advancement. On the other hand, from the east came a steady stream of religious and philosophic ideas that left a profound mark upon the Jewish consciousness, as intertestamental literature amply demonstrates.

Alexander crossed the Hellespont in 334 BC, and a year later met and routed the main Persian army at Issus, by the gulf of Alexandretta. Darius fled, to be assassinated by one of his own satraps after an unsuccessful last stand two years later at Gaugamela, near Arbela (Figs. 1, 4). In the meantime Alexander had stormed through Palestine, entered Egypt as its liberator, turned eastwards again and taken Babylon, Susa and Persepolis. Thence he marched to the farthest boundaries of the empire and campaigned beyond the Indus (327/6 BC). When he died in 323 BC, still only 33 years of age, a new era had dawned in world history. The long and gradual infiltration of Greek trade, customs and ideas into the eastern lands had become a flood-tide of planned Hellenization. Alexander's ideal had been to unite East and West under one cultural banner, Hellenism. He arranged mass marriages between his Greek troops and native women, and instituted a policy of settling his veterans and other Greeks in colonies throughout his empire. In their wake followed adventurers, traders, savants, and a continual flow of emigrants from overpopulated Hellas. Greek-speaking and thinking communities were to be found everywhere, not as isolated ethnic groups in an alien world, trying to preserve their culture from barbaric contamination, but as dynamic centres propagating their speech and ideas in the cities and outlying districts where they had taken root. Greek now became the *lingua franca*, and its use gave the traveller access to bazaars and seats of learning throughout the empire. The capital cities, like Antioch and Alexandria (Fig. 6), became Greek centres, spreading their influence far beyond their immediate localities. Alexandria in particular became the focal centre of Hellenic culture, and through the great minds that dwelt and taught there, influenced the thinking of the contemporary and later world for all time.

Of the details of Judah's political submission to Alexander's forces during their progress southwards through Palestine, we know little. Josephus records at some length an account of how Alexander was diverted from taking vengeance upon Jerusalem for an initial rebuttal of his advances by seeing a vision of the Jewish god, dressed in the robes of the High Priest, urging him to take over the Persian empire. Thus when he came storming down upon the city, and was met by the priest and his retinue, attired in their robes and offering him open entry without opposition, he prostrated himself before the company and then went on to offer sacrifice to Yahweh in the Temple (*Ant* XI viii 5 § 329 ff.) All of which probably adds up to a valid tradition that the Jews of the city hastened to show allegiance to the new master, news of whose sweeping victories would have long since reached them. In any case, the real submission of many Jews was not to Greek arms but to the all-pervasive Hellenic culture. This was to become the greatest enemy to Jewish exclusivity that the New Israel had had to face since the Return.

The Jews of the extra-Palestinian communities fell easily under the spell. In Egypt, where there had long been strong Jewish communities, the time of Alexander and his immediate successors saw a vast increase in their numbers, and Alexandria became a centre of world Jewry. It is said that by the first century AD there were a million Jews in the country, and their presence in various localities is attested by contemporary documents. Between the third and first centuries BC, the Scriptures were translated into Greek for the benefit of Jews who no longer spoke Hebrew, and this translation, known as the Septuagint (from a fanciful story about its translation being the work of seventy-two scribes working simultaneously and independently and arriving at exactly similar renderings of the sacred text), became in due course the Bible of the early Church.

Even in Palestine, the Jewish communities could not avoid the influence of Greek colonies founded all over the land, such as those at Acre (Ptolemais), south of the Sea of Galilee (Philoteria), ancient Beth-shan (Scythopolis), Samaria (Sebaste) and old Rabbath Ammon (Philadelphia, modern Amman: Fig. 7). There are marks of Greek Stoic thought even in the later books of the Bible, like Ecclesiastes, and in extra-canonical literature like the writings of Antigonus of Socho (latter part of the the third century BC), to whose disciples later Jewish tradition credited the Sadducaean and Boëthusian heresies which rejected the doctrine of an afterlife and retribution after death.

Somewhat later it became fashionable to try to harmonise Greek and Hebrew thought, in an attempt to commend Judaism intellectually to the Greek world. Thus in the third book of the Sibylline Oracles (c. 160 BC), part of that collection of post-biblical literature called the Pseudepigrapha, the writer has clothed his Jewish thoughts in Greek dress, claiming the authority of the pagan Sibyl to extol the glories of the Jewish people. Again, in the fourth book of Maccabees, to be dated in the two or three generations over the turn of the era, the writer, an orthodox Jew, enlists the Stoic values in his commendation of Judaism to his readers. He adopts the Stoic virtues of judgment, justice, courage and temperance, insisting that these are best attained by men born and brought up under the Law of Moses. The greatest exponent of this attempt to marry Jewish and Greek thought was Philo Judaeus (c. 30 BC–AD 45), a native of Alexandria. In fact he owed far more to Greek philosophy than Jewish, his main sources being Plato, Aristotle and the Stoics. He is recognised for his contribution to ancient thought mainly as a mediator between Hellenistic philosophy and both Christianity and Neoplatonism.

The sudden death of Alexander the Great left his mighty empire in disarray. By 315 BC, four of his generals achieved supremacy, and of these, one Antigonus, evoked the envy of the other three by claiming succession to Alexander. The two of greatest concern to the story of the Jews were Ptolemy Lagi and his immediate subordinate, Seleucus. Together they defeated Antigonus at Gaza, but when Ptolemy returned to Egypt,

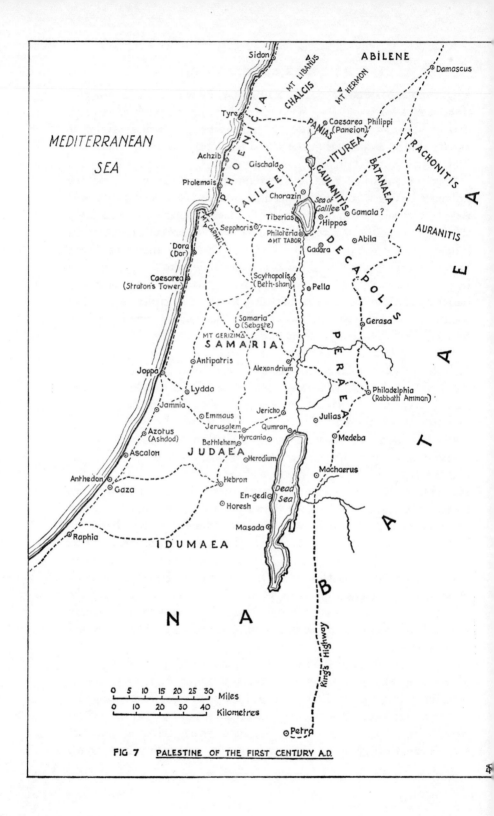

FIG 7   PALESTINE OF THE FIRST CENTURY A.D.

which he had seized after Alexander's death, Seleucus instituted his own dynasty by conquering Babylonia (312/11 BC) and then extending his power westward to Syria and eastward across Iran, with capitals at Antioch in Syria and Seleucia on the Tigris (Fig. 4).

Antigonus was finally eliminated from the empire-sharing through his defeat by the other generals, including Seleucus (but excluding Ptolemy who preferred to wait in the lists) at Ipsus in Phrygia (Fig. 4), in 301 BC. With the death in battle of Antigonus, his Asiatic empire came to an end. Palestine (Coele-Syria) fell to Ptolemy, although his right to that part of the spoils was disputed by his supposed allies since he had not taken part in the decisive battle. He managed to retain a *de facto* control of the area, but it was thereafter a bone of contention between the respective houses of Ptolemy and Seleucus, and the subject of intermittent wars during the third century BC.

Syria-Palestine had always been strategically important; it still is. Its position and significance has been described thus:

"The land which we call Syria is created by the line of mountains which go from the Taurus on the north as far as the Gulf of 'Akaba in the Red Sea. These mountains prevent the Arabian desert, traversed by the Euphrates and Tigris, from extending quite to the eastern shore of the Mediterranean. From its position Syria has always been the bridge between Egypt and Asia. But it was not only traversed by a world-route going north and south, it was crossed east and west by the routes from Babylon and the Further East, which found on its coasts their nearest outlet to the Mediterranean, and in the Cilician Gates their natural door into Asia Minor. It belongs to the Mediterranean lands and at the same time is of those lands the most closely connected with the great seats of Asiatic civilisation" (E. Bevan, *The House of Seleucus* i, 1902, p. 207).

Set in the midst of such a vital bridge between two worlds, eyeing each other with envy and ill-concealed malice, it is small wonder that for the next two or three centuries Judah was caught up in international events. For the first hundred years or so of Ptolemaic domination we have little direct information on the fortunes of the Jews in Palestine. Apparently they were left in peace, the administration of their area being little different from that imposed by the Persians. The only direct evidence in this regard is some papyri discovered in the Faiyum of Egypt (Figs. 1, 4), representing the correspondence of one Zeno, an agent of the finance minister of Ptolemy II Philadelphus (285–246 BC).

Two letters among the collection are from Tobiah of Ammon, a descendant of the Tobiah of Nehemiah's time, a governor of Transjordan. So that part of the country at least was being administered on the Persian lines.

It was not until the accession of the energetic and powerful Seleucid ruler, Antiochus III, the Great, in 223 BC, that the northern kingdom was able to achieve its long-cherished ambition of controlling Palestine-Syria. The first attempt, in 221 BC, broke unsuccessfully against the strong fortresses of the Lebanon, and Antiochus was obliged to withdraw to deal with troubles elsewhere. Two years later he tried again, at first with some measure of success, but a four months' truce enabled the Egyptian army to recover their strength and reorganize. In 218 BC, Antiochus pushed on southwards and seemed within sight of achieving his ambition. But the regrouped Egyptian army defeated him soundly at Raphia (Fig. 7) in June 217 BC, on the very frontiers of Egypt, and he was driven back out of Syria, to lick his wounds, and wait.

In 203 BC, the victor of Raphia died, and his succession by his four-year-old son Ptolemy V Epiphanes (203–181 BC), with the internal struggles for power that his minority evoked, gave Antiochus the chance he had been awaiting. He began operations in the spring of 202 BC, with apparently little success, since he continued them the following year. He appears to have reached Gaza, where he was held by the local population who remained loyal to their Egyptian masters. The delay gave the Egyptian general Scopas time to regroup and drive the Syrians back to the sources of the Jordan, at Panium (Baniyas), the Caesarea Philippi of the New Testament (Fig. 7). There Antiochus routed the Egyptians, who fled to Sidon and were besieged by land and sea, and starved to surrender. In 198 BC, the whole of Syria-Palestine was incorporated into the Seleucid empire.

Josephus tells us that the Jews of Jerusalem received their new lord with joy, freely admitting him to the city and providing "abundant provision for his entire army and his elephants" (*Ant* XII iii 3 § 133). They also gladly joined his soldiers in their attack on the Egyptian citadel which Scopas had left within the city. How much the Jewish welcome was a matter of necessity, and how much relief at the end of a continuing struggle which must have devastated their lands every time the opposing armies passed through, we can but guess. The Temple seems to have been damaged in the fighting, since, according again to Josephus, Antiochus in his gratitude for the help given him by the

Jews, ordered that they be assisted to obtain all the materials needed to restore the fabric. Furthermore, the native population seems to have been decimated by slaughter and enslavement, and Antiochus made provision for encouraging a repopulation of the area by means of a relief from taxes for three years for new residents (§ 143). He also ordered that the provisions of the Jewish cultic laws be strictly observed by everyone in the city, Jew or pagan, that no foreigner might enter the Temple area or bring ritually unclean flesh into the city. Again, how much of this report of Antiochus's overwhelming enthusiasm for his new Jewish subjects is to be believed, is very dubious, and when Josephus goes on to cite a letter the king is supposed to have written to his satrap of Lydia, Zeuxis, praising the Jews as models of political fidelity (§ 147ff.), our credibility is strained to breaking-point. After all, Jerusalem and its pious subjects had only just been prised loose from a century of faithful subservience to the Egyptian royal house!

Scarcely had Antiochus brought Seleucid dominion to its most far-reaching extent than he collided with an even greater force to the west. Rome had lately broken the Carthaginian forces at Zama (202 BC), and their general Hannibal had fled to the Seleucid court for protection and help to continue the fight. Antiochus unwisely allowed himself to be persuaded that his destiny involved suzerainty of all Hellas, in Europe as well as in Asia, and he marched into Greece. Rome reacted immediately, driving Antiochus from Europe (192 BC), and following him into Asia, defeated him at Magnesia, between Sardis and Smyrna (190 BC). In the words of Daniel: "Afterwards he shall turn his face to the coastlands, and shall take many of them; but a commander shall put an end to his insolence; indeed, he shall turn his insolence back upon him. Then he shall turn his face back towards the fortresses of his own land; but he shall stumble and fall, and shall not be found" (11 18f.). Antiochus's final fall was in fact three years after this defeat, which involved a humiliating loss of nearly the whole of Asia Minor, his war-elephants and navy, and a crippling indemnity. He was killed robbing a temple in Elam trying to find money to pay off the Romans.

The chronic shortage of ready cash with which the Seleucid house was thereafter plagued drove provincial administrators and their tax-farmers to put ever-increasing burdens upon their subject peoples. Something of this situation is reflected in the story recounted at length in II Maccabees of how one of the Temple governors sought diplomatic advantage over the Jewish High Priest, with whom he was quarrelling at the time, by unwisely revealing to the Syrian governor of Coele-Syria the existence of large private bank deposits in the Temple treasuries (3^{4-40}). The king, now Seleucus IV (185–175 BC), promptly despatched his treasurer Heliodorus to Jerusalem with orders to expropriate these assets. The High Priest, Onias the Just, did his best to persuade the Syrian official that the money, although admittedly not earmarked for cultic purposes, was nevertheless destined for "the relief of widows and fatherless children", and had been deposited in the Temple bank in virtue of the "holiness of the place, and the majesty and inviolable sanctity of the Temple, honoured over all the world". The Syrian Chancellor of the Exchequer was unmoved, however, and took immediate steps to realise the cash assets of this unexpectedly profitable enterprise within the empire. We are told that he was deterred only at the last moment by a frightening apparition of the Jewish god, mounted on a charger and supported by two handsome and athletic warriors. The defenders of this early House of Rothschild set about the wretched Heliodorus to such good effect that only his abject contrition and Onias's kindly intercession for him with Yahweh saved him from certain death. When, later, Seleucus asked him whom he might send to try again to seize the Temple deposits, Heliodorus weakly suggested anyone the king did not over-much care for (v. 38). Daniel repeats the tradition in the form of a "realised prophecy" thus:

"Then shall arise in his place one who shall send an exactor of tribute through the glory of the kingdom; but within a few days he shall be broken neither in anger nor in battle" (11^{20}).

Seleucus IV was, in fact, "broken" by being assassinated by Heliodorus in 175 BC, and, with the accession of his brother Antiochus IV, Epiphanes, the "contemptible person" of Daniel 11^{21}, the stage was set for the next great climax in Jewish political history.

CHAPTER V

The Maccabees

Now that foreign eyes had gazed covetously upon the Temple's riches, the pious Onias decided he must journey to Antioch to plead his people's case for preserving the inviolability of their sacred institutions. But the quarrel within the Temple hierarchy which had betrayed the presence of the private safe deposits in the first place persisted back in Jerusalem. During the High Priest's absence his own brother Joshua, known better by the Greek version of his name, Jason, made a bid for the high priestly office by offering the newly-installed Antiochus Epiphanes a considerable cash sum for the appointment and deposition of his brother. Furthermore, he asked to be allowed to further the Hellenization of Jerusalem and its youth, by building in the city a gymnasium after the Greek fashion (II Macc 4$^{7-9}$).

This period of Jewish history is unusually well documented, thanks largely to the two books of Maccabees. These writings have come down to us through their incorporation into the Greek Bible of the Church, the Septuagint. The First Book of Maccabees was probably written in Hebrew but has survived only in a Greek translation. It relates the events between 175 BC and 134 BC, probably using contemporary records. It is thus a valuable historical source. At the same time, it is strongly biased in favour of the Maccabean leaders, the heroes of the story, and tends to paint all opposition to their militaristic faction in the darkest colours. The Second Book of Maccabees deals only with the period from 175 BC to 161 BC, and, on its own witness, forms part of an otherwise unknown history written by one Jason of Cyrene (2$^{23\text{ff.}}$). He had apparently written a five-volume work which the writer of II Maccabees tried to abridge into a single book. Since this Jason was evidently a Jew of the Hellenic Diaspora, it is probable that he wrote in Greek, so that II Maccabees will probably have been similarly composed in that language. This work gives us more details of the origins and early stages of the Maccabean revolt, but its historicity is marred by the kind of fanciful tales we have just mentioned regarding the salutary appearance of Yahweh and his handsome warriors before Heliodorus at the Temple treasury. There are, furthermore, discrepancies between the First and Second Books in their descriptions of events, and it is usual in such cases to give more credence to the First Book.

The activities of the anti-Onias faction within Temple circles are portrayed in our sources as irreligious and covetous, eager to Hellenize their city for their own monetary gain. Onias and his friends, on the other hand, are shown as upholders of pure Yahwism, resisting the demands of hostile compatriots and aliens to "modernise" the Jerusalem society for fear of compromising post-exilic racialist policies, now inseparably connected with the cult. Thus to encourage people to speak Greek, adopt Greek customs of dress and recreation, was to betray the Jewish religion. Judaism was not just the worship of Yahweh and the observance of certain cultic laws and customs; it was an exclusive way of life. Its protagonists vehemently asserted that it was as old as Abraham and Moses and the Covenant on Sinai. On their part, the progressives could point to the large number of Greek-speaking Jews of the Diaspora who, from reasons of sentiment or deep religious emotion, regularly visited the shrines of the Holy Land. Their fidelity to their race and Faith could not be questioned, as the cost in money and discomfort of their periodic Holy Land tours witnessed; yet they dressed, spoke and acted like Greeks.

The struggle between the sympathisers of Onias and the Hellenizers of Jason and his friends was crucial for the future history of Judaism. At stake was the success of policies of exclusivism formulated and ruthlessly carried out three centuries earlier by Nehemiah, Ezra, and the Babylonian planners of the New Israel. Had the religious extremists of 175 BC and later lost the battle, and the Jews of Jerusalem become integrated into provincial Hellas, the world, and Jewry in particular, might have been spared much of the anguish of the succeeding centuries. As it was, the popular trend that would almost certainly have submerged the exclusive racialism of the religionists was checked and even reversed by the inept handling of the situation by the Greeks themselves.

A central feature of imperial policy in the administration of their subject peoples by the Persians and their Greek successors, Ptolemaic and Seleucid, had been religious tolerance. Common sense had shown that, throughout history, religious cults attract far more allegiance from ordinary folk, and thus can be a much more effective means of discipline, than any monarchical institution. Kings can change, sometimes with bewildering frequency, but the national gods, no less fickle and through their priests no less demanding on the material resources of their devotees, go on for ever. Kings can sometimes be avoided, or if necessary assassinated, but the god watches everything, himself unseen, and his retribution for acts of disobedience is the more terrible in its unpredictability. One never knew when he might strike with famine or ill-health, so it was best to keep perpetually in his good graces by obeying the cultic rules. By allying themselves ostensibly with the native gods, empire-builders could thus command the fidelity of their subjects, and the cost of the odd sacrifice or two, or the timber, stone and masons to help build or rebuild their temples and altars, was a small price to pay for political stability. The system was admirable and nothing but the most severe pressures, political and financial, could have persuaded the Greek rulers to transgress this first rule in the manual of good government. Antiochus III, as we have seen, confirmed the privileges granted to the religious community of Jerusalem when he wrested Palestine from the Egyptians. But his successors were plagued with financial problems, and the wealth of the temples within their realm proved too great a temptation for their itchy fingers. The humiliating peace of Apamea in 189 BC had plunged the empire into debt to Rome, and internal discord as well as external pressures denied the administration the period of calm and retrenchment that its parlous financial condition demanded. Antiochus III had been required by the treaty to send his son Antiochus to Rome as a hostage. When the king was assassinated, another son, Seleucus, succeeded to the throne and obtained his brother's release by offering his own heir Demetrius in his place. When Seleucus was in turn murdered, Antiochus seized power over the head of the still exiled Demetrius. Thus the state was torn apart from the very inception of Antiochus's reign in 175 BC. Furthermore, the Romans were paying more and more attention to the eastern world, and were backing the Egyptians in the south in their renewed efforts to win back their former Syrian possessions. Antiochus IV found it necessary to make several costly campaigns to stave off these attacks from the south by the ruling Ptolemy VI, Philometor (181–146 BC).

On one such occasion in 169 BC, Antiochus was returning from a victorious campaign in Egypt when he stopped off in Jerusalem and helped himself to the Temple treasures, even stripping gold leaf from its façade (I Macc 1$^{17-24}$; cp. II Macc 5$^{15-21}$). The High Priest at the time was one Menelaus, a renegade who had managed to bribe himself into office in the place of Jason who had reached the sacred calling the same way only three years previously. Jason had been driven to take refuge across the Jordan, while Menelaus set about raising cash for his promised take-over bid by liquidating the "company funds" (II Macc 4²⁷⁻³²).

It has been suggested that Antiochus's excuse for plundering the Temple on his way back from Egypt was that he believed that the city was in a state of revolt against him, or rather, against the Seleucids, for rumour had reached the city that Antiochus himself had been killed in the battle (II Macc 5⁵⁻¹⁰). Hearing the report, Jason had staged a come-back from his sanctuary across the Jordan, and with a thousand followers had marched on Jerusalem, driven Menelaus to take refuge in the citadel, and embarked on an orgy of slaughter among the Jews, presumably those who had supported Menelaus's take-over bid for the high priesthood. When Antiochus arrived, Jason in turn was driven out, and Menelaus was reinstated in his sacred office. In gratitude, he accompanied his deliverer on a conducted tour of the Temple, culminating in the plundering of its treasures just referred to (II Macc 5¹⁵ᶠ·). Whether, in fact, this incident of Jason's attempted return to power is to be related to Antiochus's plunder of the Temple treasures, cannot be certain, but the whole sorry tale clearly demonstrates first the political intrigues within the ruling factions of Jerusalem, and the secular nature of the high priestly office which made it so valuable a prize, and also the concern shown by the Seleucid king over any hint of rebellion within the strategic area of his supply lines to Egypt. Trouble in and around Jerusalem might affect this important route at a crucial moment in his campaigns in the south, when ready communication with the north was vital to success. In such circumstances, the religious susceptibilities of the native population had to take second place to the security of the empire. Antiochus needed a staunch ally in charge of the cultus of Jerusalem, and to ensure the High Priest's loyalty, he installed there a royal commissioner, as he had done elsewhere in the province (II Macc 5²²ᶠ·).

In 168 BC, Antiochus ventured again into Egypt and triumphantly entered the ancient capital city of Memphis. Thence he began his march on Alexandria, and at that point the Romans decided Syrian aggrandizement had gone far enough. Through the legate Popilius Laenas, they ordered Antiochus out of Egypt. Daniel describes the encounter thus:

"At the time appointed he shall return and come into the south; but it shall not be this time as it was before. For the ships of Kittim (properly 'Cyprus' but used here, as in the Dead Sea Scrolls, cryptically for 'Rome') shall come against him, and he shall be afraid and withdraw, and shall turn back and be enraged and take action against the holy covenant" (11^{29}).

Antiochus was too well acquainted with Roman power to try to resist this peremptory command; he had, after all, spent a number of years as a hostage in Rome. So he returned the way he had come, realising that the day might soon come when he would have to face a Roman-backed Egyptian army seeking revenge and a recovery of their Palestinian possessions. He determined to settle the Jewish problem once and for all. Jerusalem would have to be thoroughly Hellenized, even if it meant severing relations finally with the religious conservatives in the city. He could take no chances with a cult that was so stubbornly independent in character, and one, furthermore, which embodied doctrines capable of fanatically racialist interpretation. Antiochus therefore ordered Apollonius, commander of his Mysian mercenaries, with a large force of men to establish firm control of the city (I Macc 1^{29-35}; II Macc 5^{23-26}). Horrific tales are recounted in our sources of the butchery of innocent people which resulted from this surprise attack. The truth is probably that Apollonius met resistance from the "conservatives" and was obliged to treat Jerusalem as an enemy city, amply justifying his master's fears that in the event of a conflict of loyalties, Jewish fidelity to the Greek cause could not be relied upon. The walls were pulled down, and a permanent garrison installed in a citadel, built probably to the south of the Temple area, on the site of the old Davidic city on the south-east hill (Fig. 8). For twenty-five years this "Acra" as it was called, peopled not only by Seleucid troops but other pagans and Hellenized Jews, became virtually the new Greek Jerusalem, a *polis*, with the Temple serving as the city shrine like that of any other Greek centre. The "godless" people who inhabited the Acra, led apparently by Menelaus and his friends, were clearly intent on a complete integration with their Greek neighbours. The exclusive nature of the Yahwistic cult was to be broken and the tribal god identified with the Greek Zeus.

As we saw, this association between the gods was, in fact, perfectly historical and legitimate. Zeus was, indeed, Yahweh in origin; both names meant the same, "seed of life", or spermatozoa, and both had their common origin in the underlying fertility religion of the ancient Near East. Just how far this fact may still have been recognised in

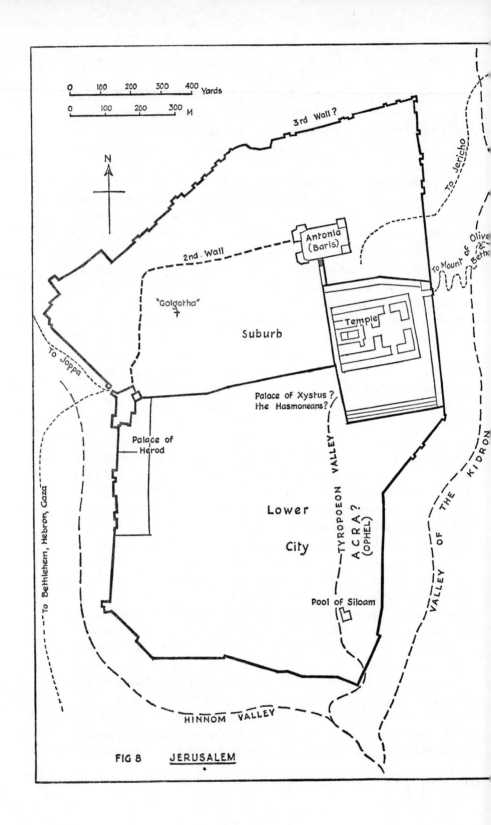

FIG 8   JERUSALEM

popular tradition, even as late as the second century BC, we cannot know. Our records were composed by writers utterly hostile to this synthesis. For such people, religious and political Judaism depended for its continuance on the pivotal assumption that Yahweh was the special tribal god of the Israelites, a "jealous" deity brooking no rival. The Greek Zeus was the prime god of paganism and represented to the Jerusalem authorities not only the political enemy of the Jews, but the threat of absorption into an alien culture.

Resistance stiffened, and Antiochus became more and more obdurate in his demands for religious integration. Once more we have to read our highly prejudiced sources with caution in trying to decide how far the king used violence in suppressing Jewish cult practice. The books of Maccabees speak of women who had circumcised their babies being put to death along with their infants (I Macc $1^{60f.}$; II Macc 6^{10}), and of Jews being killed for refusing to eat ritually unclean food (I Macc $1^{62f.}$). This kind of massacre would have been so contrary to the empire's customary leniency towards foreign cults, however strange and uncouth, and so pointless if the aim was to make the religionists renounce their Faith, that it is simply unbelievable, unless the religious acts had been demonstrations of overt rebellion and deliberate provocations to political unrest. Of such we may almost certainly attribute the official retributive action against those Jews who, it is said, withdrew to the desert with their families and cattle, "in secret places" (I Macc 2^{29-38}), and "in caves" (II Macc 6^{11}). This last passage speaks of "keeping the Sabbath day secretly", indicating a more positive cultic ritual than merely refraining from work. The story in I Maccabees elaborates on the piety of the refugees who, on being discovered, let themselves and their loved ones be cut down by the soldiery rather than desecrate the day of rest by taking up arms to defend themselves. Later, however, realising that their numbers would soon be hopelessly decimated if they continued their policy of passive resistance, the faithful resolved to fight, Sabbath or no Sabbath (I Macc $2^{40f.}$). Before long, these would-be pacifists were joined by others who had "fled for persecution", and by the sect of Jews called the "Pious Ones" or Hasidim. Together they set upon a campaign of terrorizing the Jews of the area who were willing to bow the knee before the Greek authority, and saw nothing amiss in integrating their religion and culture with that of their pagan neighbours:

"So they joined their forces, and smote sinful men in their anger, and

F

wicked men in their wrath; but the rest fled to the heathen for succour"
(I Macc 2⁴⁴).

As is to be expected, we hear all too little of the point of view of those
"wicked men" among the Jewish inhabitants of Judah who tried to
resist the demands of their extremist compatriots. We are told simply
that "many also of the Israelites consented to his (Antiochus's) religion,
and sacrificed unto idols, and profaned the Sabbath" (I Macc 1⁴³), and
that "many of the people" joined the overseers appointed by the king
"commanding the cities of Judah to sacrifice, city by city", forsaking
the Law and committing evils in the land (vv. 51f.). It must have been
all too clear to these "wicked men" that the fanatical racialists among
their compatriots would bring the wrath of the empire down upon the
whole people. They appreciated that Antiochus could not afford to have
religio-political subversion in Palestine at such a time. They were
grimly aware that the Greek methods of suppressing rebellion would be
quite as ruthless, and even less discriminatory than the afflictions laid
upon their fellow-Jews by the "Pious Ones" and their fanatical
brethren. The same kind of situation obtained two-and-a-half centuries
later when the so-called Zealots of the First Revolt of AD 66 massacred
those Jews who dared dissociate themselves from the suicidal rebellion
against the Romans. On this occasion, however, moderate opinion
received more favourable treatment in history, thanks largely to the
writer Josephus whose sympathies lay with the moderates and who
recognised with them the dangers posed for the Jewish people by a revolt
against the power of Rome.

The climax in the Greek campaign to amalgamate the Jewish and
pagan god came, according to our sources, with the introduction of the
so-called "Abomination of Desolation" into the Temple, in December
167 BC (Dan 9²⁷; 11³¹; 12¹¹; 1 Macc 1⁵⁴). The strange Semitic phrase
is customarily explained as a pun on the cultic title "Ba'al of Heaven"
designating the ancient Semitic storm god Hadad, with whom Zeus
(Jupiter) Olympius had been already identified (cp. II Macc 6²). Much
the same syncretism had already been carried out with local approval
in the Samaritan Yahwistic Temple on Mount Gerizim, where the god
was identified with Zeus Zenius, "Defender of Strangers" (II Macc 6²).
Again, historically this identification of the storm deity with Yahweh
and Zeus was perfectly correct. The Jewish god's accompanying title,
Sebaoth, we may now recognise as having originally meant "Penis of the
Storm", reflecting the ancient conception of the phallic deity as a

mighty organ in the heavens ejaculating the precious Yahweh/Zeus spermatozoa in his tempestuous orgasm. The idea is accurately conveyed in the Semitic divine name Hadad, derived from a Sumerian term for "Mighty Father".

Whatever the form (probably phallic) in which Zeus Olympius was represented "upon the altar" (I Macc 1[54]), it was certainly placed there with the active support of Menelaus and the priestly hierarchy of the Temple, and was doubtless as popular among the laity as were the incense altars "at the doors of the houses, and in the streets" (I Macc 1[55]). Furthermore, it is difficult to believe that these cultic "abominations" were instituted overnight; Hellenism had long before made deep inroads into Jewish ideas and practices, and in any case many aspects of Greek religion would have found their echoes in the old Israelite fertility worship which never lay far beneath the surface of the Jewish consciousness. Thus, the worship of Bacchus in which the Jews joined, carrying the ivy-covered thyrsus (II Macc 6[7]), was again only another aspect of the ancient fertility cult, on which our recent studies of the religion of the Sacred Mushroom have cast much new light.

Active resistance to Antiochus's measures gathered around one family, variously known as the Maccabees (from the nickname given to a member of the clan called Judas Maccabeus—"The Hammer"), and the Hasmoneans (from an ancestor called Hashmon, Graecized into Asamonaios—Josephus, *Ant* XII vi 1 § 265). The story goes that in the village of Modein, in the foothills east of Lydda (Fig. 2), there lived a pious Jew named Mattathias, of priestly lineage, and proud father of five sons, John, Simon, Judas, Eleazar and Jonathan (I Macc ch. 2). One day a king's officer arrived in the town and demanded that Mattathias be the first to offer sacrifice at a pagan altar, as his royal master had decreed. The old man refused, but another of the community stepped forward not unwillingly to make the required offering. Mattathias was so incensed at this betrayal of the Faith, that he fell upon the unfortunate collaborator and killed him at the altar. He then slew the king's commissioner, and pulled down the shrine (vv. 24f.). He and his sons fled to the desert and were there joined in the "secret places" by other rebels, as already noted. Their passive resistance turned swiftly to armed revolt, no longer confined to defending their lives, but maintained by guerrilla offensives against Seleucid forces and Jewish settlements whom they deemed dangerously pro-gentile.

Mattathias died peacefully a few months later and was buried in the family vault at Modein (I Macc 2⁷⁰). Such a return home would seem strange if in fact he and his sons were by then such outlaws that their steps were being dogged at every turn by a hostile administration. Actually, Antiochus was busy enough elsewhere and left about this time for a campaign against the Parthians (I Macc 3³¹), though hardly, as is implied, in order to raise money to quell the Maccabees, whose fame we are told was now "world wide" (vv. 25f.). Again, we have to read our sources with a good deal of scepticism over the whole Maccabean affair. It was indeed important, not to say disastrous for Judaism, but the "mighty victories" recorded of the famous Judas and his brothers would have seemed mere pin-pricks to the Seleucid governors, concerned with more serious marks of deterioration in the international situation, and we may doubt whether the Jewish exploits would have "caused great dread to fall upon the nations round about them" (v. 25).

Antiochus delegated responsibility for rounding up the rebels to a subordinate, variously identified in our sources as Lysias, the king's regent in Antioch (I Macc 3³², ³⁸ff.), and, rather more probably, Philip, the governor of Jerusalem (II Macc 8⁸). Again, pious exaggeration has involved the king's right-hand man in what must have been a very local affair, as it has enlarged the numbers of troops taking part out of all reality.

The mantle of the dead Mattathias fell upon Judas, after whose nickname, "The Hammer", the whole family and their wars have been designated in history. To him tradition has credited the dubious honour of turning a passive resistance movement against forced idolatry into a full-scale rebellion for political ends. In 165 BC, Judas achieved some success against the Seleucid forces at Emmaus, on the western side of the Judaean uplands, by attacking the enemy camp whilst the soldiers were out looking for him (I Macc 4³ff.). In the following year he secured an important strategic centre at Beth-zur, south of Jerusalem (v. 29: Fig. 2). It is some indication of the lack of real opposition to the insurgents, and of the more urgent calls on the empire's defenders elsewhere, that after these two victories Judas was able to enter Jerusalem in triumph, seal off the Seleucid forces in the Acra, and take over the Temple area (I Macc 4³⁶ff.).

Rehabilitation of the exclusive Jewish cult was now possible. Zeus was banished from the sanctuary; Yahweh reigned once more supreme, and alone. The desecrated altar was pulled down and its stones put on one side "until there should come a prophet to show what should be done with them" (v. 46). Judas's followers then built a new altar with unhewn stones, as the Law commanded, replaced the sacred vessels with new ones, and generally renewed the whole cultic apparatus of Yahwism (vv. 47–51). In December of that year, 164 BC, just three years after the "Abomination of Desolation" had been placed within the shrine, the Temple was rededicated to the exclusively Jewish god, rejoicing that "the reproach of the heathen had been put away" (v. 58). This celebration of the Hanukkah ("Dedication") festival has been observed faithfully by Jews ever since. Judas, with rather more practical application of his respite from Greek pressure, restored the city's defences, installed a garrison of his own troops, and fortified Beth-zur to guard its southern approaches (vv. 6of.). In three short years, a band of outlaws had managed to terrorize the neighbourhood, throw trained Seleucid troops off balance, and put themselves in charge of a key site in the defence system of the empire. Obviously matters could not rest there.

CHAPTER VI

The rise and fall of the "The Hammer"

In the following year Antiochus IV died. For some reason he placed his eight-year-old son, Antiochus Eupator, into the guardianship of his general Philip, rather than in the care of his appointed regent Lysias. In actual fact the boy-king was already in Lysias's custody, and the regent was not so easily persuaded to give up his power to Philip, but continued to control the realm despite his dying master's instructions. Of course Philip was bound to take action to lay hold on his coveted inheritance, and this unsettled state of affairs gave the Maccabees another chance to achieve the impossible.

From the districts east of the Jordan and in the north, word came to Jerusalem that the local residents were persecuting pro-Maccabean Jews (I Macc $5^{9ff.}$). Doubtless the Hellenists of these places were as well aware of the dangers of baiting their Greek masters as those of the Jerusalem Acra, and realised that the presence of real or potential rebels in their midst would only bring suspicion of collaboration upon themselves. Judas and his brothers, on the other hand, appreciated the weakness of their own position in Jerusalem and its environs against the considerable force of Jews and pagans who actively resisted their political aims. They needed more of their own kind, and accordingly campaigned in the territories of Gilead and Galilee to liberate their oppressed brethren and bring them back with them to the Holy City. The brother Simon went north, while Judas and Jonathan crossed the Jordan to the east and returned leading a second "Exodus" of liberated Jews into the Promised Land of Judah over the carnage and ruins of the villages that stood in their way:

"And Judas gathered together those that came behind, and exhorted the people all the way through, till they came into the land of Judaea. So they went up to Mount Zion with joy and gladness, where they offered burnt offerings, because not one of them was slain until they had returned in peace" (vv. 53f.).

With the added numerical support the Maccabeans now enjoyed in their home base, they were able to undertake more campaigns, to the south in Idumaea, biblical Edom, and south-west in the old Philistia coastlands (vv. 65–68), although here lacking the excuse of liberating their beleaguered co-religionists. It seemed to the faithful that Yahweh was at last intervening on the side of Israel against the hated oppressors, and that the chosen vessel of his grace, Judas, had been given an almost supernatural power to overcome the enemies of the Lord. That this favour resided in the Maccabee alone, was illustrated when a certain Joseph and a fellow-officer Azarias thought to emulate their leader and "get themselves a name" (I Macc 5^{57}), and undertook an expedition on their own account. It turned out disastrously, with the loss of "two thousand men of Israel", "because they were not obedient unto Judas and his brethren, but thought to do some valiant act" (v. 61). Similarly, "certain priests, desirous to show their valour, were slain in battle, for that they went out to fight unadvisedly" (v. 67). Thus we see growing up the concept of the charismatic hero around whom the New Israel might be built, an idea which was fostered to such telling effect for the next century of Hasmonean rule. When, later, the Jews came once more under the domination of a foreign imperialism, that same heroic pattern of leadership was to bring the nation to similar dreams of world conquest and inevitable disaster.

However far his guerrilla forces ranged afield, and however much havoc they managed to wreak among their neighbours, Judas could not rest content until he had removed the thorn from the side of his military base, the Acra garrison with its mixed population of Seleucid soldiers and pagan and Jewish civilians. He accordingly laid siege to the area and mounted catapults to break down the defence walls (I Macc 6^{20}). Some of the inhabitants, however, managed to escape and, along with Hellenist Jews, travelled to see the king (or, rather the regent Lysias) to demand protection against the rebels who, if they were not stopped, "will do greater things than these, neither shalt thou be able to rule them" (v. 27).

Lysias realised now that something urgent and definitive would have to be done to settle the trouble in this outpost of the empire once and for all. It seemed for the moment that his rival Philip was otherwise occupied in the east, so he led his army against Jerusalem from the south, passing through Idumaea, invested Beth-zur, and brought Judas's troops to pitched battle at Beth-zechariah, modern *Beth-iskaryeh*, about six miles south-west of Bethlehem (Fig. 3). The First Book of

Maccabees gives a spirited account of this encounter, characterized by extensive employment of the war-elephant, the ancient equivalent of the modern tank (6$^{33ff.}$).

Each beast was allocated to a thousand infantrymen and five hundred cavalry, and was under the supervision of an Indian *mahout*. On the elephant's back was fastened a wooden construction which served as a platform and shelter for archers firing into the enemy from their positions of advantage. Exactly how the practice of shewing the elephants "the blood of grapes and mulberries" was reckoned to "provoke them to fight" (v. 34), is obscure. In any case, the sight of an advancing horde of men, horses and these trumpeting beasts, "when the sun shone upon the shields of gold and brass" and the mountains "glistening therewith like lamps of fire", and "the noise of their multitude, and the marching of the company, and the rattling of the harness", must indeed have been terrifying. Nevertheless, we are told that one of the Maccabean brothers, Eleazar, spying one elephant larger than all the rest, and clad with the regal panoply, supposed that it carried the leader of the host, and cut his way through its bodyguard until he could slip under its belly. Then he thrust upwards with all his might, penetrated the beast's entrails and was squashed to death as it collapsed on top of him, thus achieving his aim of earning himself "a perpetual name" (vv. 43–46). As it turned out, this is all his courageous, if somewhat improbable exploit did achieve, since the array of Seleucid might was too much for the rebels and they fled to the Temple mount in Jerusalem for refuge.

There Judas prepared for a siege (*Ant* XII ix 5 § 375), but was from the beginning hampered by a shortage of food in the city. Even this disadvantage was laid at the door of piety by our historians, explaining the deficiency as due its being a Sabbatical year, during which, as Josephus explains, "the law obliges us to let the land lie uncultivated" (§ 378; cp. I Macc 6^{53}). Furthermore, since Judas and his brothers had brought in more followers from the outlying territories, there were more mouths to feed, and "they had eaten up the residue of the store" (v. 53). The hardships proved too much for many of the insurgents and they went home, leaving only a few in the sanctuary (v. 54).

It seemed that the Maccabean Revolt had run its course. The high hopes of a Jewish state crumbled into dust, faced with the reality of the still vastly superior power of the Seleucid empire. The charismatic hero Judas appeared for what he was, an adventurer with ideas above his station. And that would certainly have been the end of the affair had

Philip not returned at that moment from the east, still smarting from being cheated out of his inheritance by the regent Lysias. He appeared with an army in Antioch determined to assert his rights to the regency. Lysias had no option but to leave his campaign against the Maccabees at the very moment of certain triumph, and return immediately to confront his rival. The details of the hastily-made pact with Judas are not known. In effect, he left the Jewish leader in command of the Temple area, although he demolished the surrounding walls, and apparently agreed to rescind the laws of Antiochus IV requiring the Jews to give up their exclusive religious customs:

"Now, therefore, let us be friends with these men, and make peace with them and with all their nation; and covenant with them that they shall live after their laws, as they did before; for they are therefore displeased, and have done all these things because we abolished their laws" (vv. 58f.).

Again, it must have seemed to Judas's followers that the hand of Yahweh was to be discerned in these events, for whatever retribution Lysias might have been expected to exact from the insurgents, the death of their leaders, the Maccabees, would have seemed inevitable. But, of course, Lysias must have thought Judas now quite powerless, and the execution of a popular hero would have merely left another wound to fester after his departure. He could not afford more trouble in the provinces as he turned to settle his account with Philip. No doubt, also, the regent saw the futility and danger of denying a subject people their right to worship their god as they wished, and was content to revert to the old Persian and Greek principle of religious tolerance. Unfortunately for him, he had not appreciated that Judaism now involved more than the worship of a tribal god in such comparatively harmless ways as killing and burning certain animals, singing psalms, doing no work on a Saturday, and mutilating the tip of one's penis. Judaism was now inseparably linked with political extremism and fanatical racialism.

On the face of it, Judas and his friends had achieved their goal. They had their sanctuary to themselves and could perform their religious rites in peace. It was the situation that had obtained a year or two previously when the Temple had been cleansed and rededicated, with the added advantage of having this religious freedom now confirmed by treaty with the imperial authority. Furthermore, the High Priest Menelaus who had been prepared to collaborate so freely with the Seleucid integrationists was taken away and later executed, and a certain Alcimus of true priestly heritage appointed in his place (I Macc $7^{9,14}$). But Judas was far from satisfied. Palestine, and Jerusalem in particular, was still very much under foreign control. Within the city, the hated Acra reminded him that he was there under sufferance of the Seleucid rulers, and that outside his little band of admirers he had no real power. The Greek troops were still in the land and would react violently to any further assumption of his chosen role of guerrilla chieftain, scourge of the collaborators.

Once more fate, or Yahweh, played into Judas's ambitious hands. It will be remembered that Antiochus IV Epiphanes had seized the Seleucid throne over the head of the son of Seleucus IV, Demetrius, who had been confined as a hostage in Rome. When Antiochus IV died, he was succeeded by his young son Antiochus V Eupator. Demetrius watched this accession from his exile with envy, and tried in vain to obtain official authority for his release from Roman captivity. The Senate would have none of it, but he managed to escape, arriving in Syria in the autumn of 162 BC to the welcome of people and army. He had his cousin Antiochus Eupator put to death, and himself proclaimed king. Rome, of course, withheld recognition, giving it instead to yet another claimant of the throne, one Timarchus, a satrap of Babylonia and Media. According to I Maccabees, Judas decided to take this opportunity to make contact with Rome, "to make a league of amity and confederacy with them" (8^{17}). What truth there is in the story is difficult to say; the idea that mighty Rome would treat with a virtually powerless leader of some fanatical religionists deep in the Seleucid realm, promising material and military aid in their struggle in return for Jewish help "if there come first any war upon the Romans or any of their confederates throughout all their dominion" (vv. 24f.) is too absurd to be seriously contemplated. But a century later when Rome entered in earnest into the Palestinian arena, Jewish relationships with the bear of the Tiber were to be crucial for her own and world history. That so wily and ambitious a leader as Judas Maccabeus should have seen the inevitable swing west-wards of world power at this early stage, and done something about making overtures in that direction is in itself incredible.

Alcimus, the High Priest, was unacceptable to Judas, not surprisingly. His appointment, whatever his priestly credentials, seems to have been instigated by the Seleucid authorities, which would be sufficient to damn him in the eyes of the Maccabean party. Alcimus appealed for help to Demetrius (I Macc 7^{5-7}), who gave him an officer, one Bacchides, and an armed force, to assist him take up his appointment (vv. 8f.). Of those who went out to greet the High Priest were the Hasidim, the "Pious Ones", who, it will be remembered, had earlier lent their support to the Maccabees against the erosion of their religious freedom by Antiochus IV in 167 BC. Now they seem to have changed sides, seeing in Alcimus "one that is a priest of the seed of Aaron . . . he will do us no wrong" (v. 14). They must soon have realised that the ultimate aim of Judas and his party was not simply the re-establishment of religious freedom for the Jews but of a political state. No one could accuse these Hasidim of being Hellenists, pleading for integration with the alien in their midst, yet they were happy to acknowledge as their High Priest an appointee of the Seleucid ruler, since he fulfilled the hereditary requirements of that office. They were thus in direct opposition to the Maccabees, just as their spiritual successors the Pharisees were later to resist the fanaticism of the Zealots of the First Revolt (AD 66–70). There could be no clearer indication of the essentially political nature of the struggle being waged by Judas and his friends, and the lack of support they enjoyed among pious Jews who longed only for peace to worship their god without interference. And no clearer example of the ability of the Maccabean historian to pervert the plain facts in favour of his heroes may be found than in his description of Judas's vicious reaction to the welcome accorded Alcimus:

"But Alcimus contended for the high priesthood. And unto him resorted all such as troubled the people, who, after they had gotten the land of Judah into their power, did much hurt in Israel. Now when Judas saw all the mischief that Alcimus and his company had done among the Israelites, even above the heathen, he went out into all the coasts of Judaea round about, and took vengeance on them that had revolted from him, so that they durst no more go forth into the country" (vv. 21–24).

The "Hammer" was loose once more, pulverising the region into submission. Bacchides having returned to Antioch, Alcimus's renewed pleas for help brought him an officer called Nicanor with a considerable force (vv. 26ff.). After a preliminary skirmish at Kaphar-salama, possibly modern *Khirbet selma*, some six miles north-west of Jerusalem, a major battle was fought on the 13th Adar, that is March 161 BC, near Adasa, modern *Khirbet 'addāseh*, nearly five miles north of the Holy City (Fig. 2). The Seleucid general was killed and Judas pursued his fleeing troops right down to the coastal plain (vv. 43–45). The perpetual

remembrance of that day of victory by the Jews, recorded in I Maccabees
7[48f.], was perhaps unwarranted. A year later, in April 160 BC, Bacchides
reappeared on the scene with a larger force, the sight of which struck
terror into the heart of Judas's troops, many of whom fled, leaving their
hero with a mere "eight hundred men" (9[6]). Resisting all attempts to
urge him to follow their example, Judas stood firm against the hopeless
odds, and was killed in the ensuing battle (v. 18).

Judas was buried in the family tomb at Modein, and for the time
being at least it seemed that the country might find peace. Bacchides,
with the help of Alcimus the High Priest, did his best to settle the
land, installing garrisons in strategic places, and appointing governors
of his choosing in key cities. He tried to root out the troublemakers, but
succeeded too often in simply driving them into their customary bolt-
holes in the Judaean deserts, where they continued harassing the country
round about with hit-and-run raids. For their leader in place of the dead
Judas they chose his brother Jonathan (vv. 29ff.), who thereupon became
Bacchides's prime quarry (v. 32). The kind of short, sharp engagement
as that recorded in I Maccabees 9[43-49] by the banks of the Jordan, when,
despite the claims of the historian that Bacchides lost a thousand men,
Jonathan escaped only by swimming across the river to the east bank,
merely demonstrates that the rebels had little power at this stage beyond
making themselves a thorough nuisance to everybody.

Jonathan needed, above all else, allies, since he had long ago lost the
sympathy and cooperation of moderate Jewish opinion. He turned to the
Nabateans on the east of the Dead Sea and the natural enemies of the
Seleucid governors of Palestine. He sent his brother John as an emissary,
asking that the insurgents might leave their movable goods with them
while they carried out their raids within their homeland. On the way
with these possessions the party was waylaid and robbed by Arabs from
Medeba in Transjordan, and John killed (vv. 36ff.). Jonathan took
vengeance by ambushing a wedding party from the same tribe, bringing
the bride and her large retinue from Nabatea to meet the bridegroom
with his friends. The spoil thus won probably more than compensated
for the lost baggage carried by the lamented John, and the Maccabeans
ensured that the slaughter of the revellers "turned the marriage into
mourning, and the noise of melody into lamentation" (v. 41). Whatever
satisfaction the affair may have given to John's avengers, it did little to
cement good relations with possible allies east of the Jordan, and we
thereafter hear no more of proffered alliances with Nabatea.

Once again, it must have been internal dissension within the Seleucid ruling house that gave the Maccabees another chance. One can hardly believe, with the historian, that Bacchides became so disheartened by his failure to break the resistance at a Maccabean stronghold, Bethbasi, probably modern *Beit bassa*, south-south-east of Bethlehem on the edge of the Judaean wilderness (vv. 62ff.; Fig. 2), that he decided to go home (v. 69). Even more incredible is the idea that this disillusionment alone prompted the Syrian commander to make a treaty with the rebel leader, acceding to all his demands, and promising "that he would never do him harm all the days of his life" (v. 71). Anyway, whatever the cause of Bacchides's urgent withdrawal, Jonathan seems to have been left to "govern the people" at Michmas, north of Jerusalem (v. 73; Fig. 2), like some judge of ancient Israel. Direction of the Jerusalem cultus remained with Jonathan's enemies of the Sadducaean priesthood, who at this time lacked a High Priest. Alcimus had died two years previously, according to the historian because he had dared to pull down the wall dividing the sacred inner enclosure of the Temple from the Court of the Gentiles (vv. 55f.). Josephus says "a sudden stroke from God seized him, by which he was brought speechless to the ground, and after suffering torment for many days, he died" (*Ant* XII x 6 § 413). The Jerusalem authorities could hardly fail to feel ill at ease with the unsatisfactory state of affairs left by Bacchides. They had been left leaderless, admittedly still with the Seleucid-manned Acra in their midst, but with a ruthless gang of rebels installed some seven miles away at Michmas, "governing" the countryside, and, in the words of I Maccabees, "destroying the ungodly men out of Israel" (9^{73}). They could have been left in no doubt of the probable outcome of this unhappy situation, as Jonathan and his followers coerced by blackmail and violence ever-increasing support from outlying districts for their cause. They must also have been aware that every month they were left without support from their Seleucid rulers, the political situation within the empire would deteriorate and make it less likely that the authorities would be physically capable of sparing men and arms to pacify the Palestinian scene. When after a gap of five years, our records take up the story once more, disputes about the imperial throne had presented Jonathan with more chances to exercise his considerable political shrewdness and thereby to climb several more rungs on the ladder to absolute power.

CHAPTER VII

John Hyrcanus

We saw earlier that, when Demetrius seized the Seleucid throne, he antagonized the Romans, who gave their support to another claimant. He also had to face the opposition of two vassal-kings of Rome, those of Cappadocia and Pergamon (Fig. 6), all allied in their desire to see a weakling in Antioch. The king of Pergamon, Attalus II, ingeniously produced another claimant to the Syrian throne in the person of a youth called Balas. Apparently the young man bore a remarkable resemblance to the dead Antiochus IV Epiphanes, so Attalus proclaimed him as a son of the late king and rightful heir to the crown, giving him the name of Alexander, and installing him some time between 158 BC and 153 BC in Cilicia, close to the Syrian frontier. Attalus then persuaded Antiochus's erstwhile finance minister, Heracleides, to present the young impostor at Rome and bribe support for his claims from the senators. The Romans were happy to give further cause for embarrassment to Demetrius, and with their blessing Alexander Balas in 153 BC obtained a foothold in Ptolemais (I Macc 10[1]).

Demetrius was now in some difficulties. Balas had not only the support of Rome and the kings of Cappadocia and Pergamon, but could also count on help from Ptolemy Philometor, ruler of Egypt on his southern flank. In such circumstances, even the assistance of a rebel chieftain in Judaea was welcome, and I Maccabees tells us that Demetrius sent "loving words" to Jonathan, saying to himself, "Let us first make peace with him, before he join with Alexander against us: else he will remember all the evils that we have done against him, and against his brethren and his people . . ." (vv. 4f.). He supported his "loving words" with authority to raise an army to fight his master's battles and to take over control of Jerusalem, free hostages from the citadel, and refortify the city (vv. 6–11). Outlying fortresses were cleared of Syrian troops, although Beth-zur remained occupied by the Hellenist Jews who had taken refuge there (v. 14). The Acra itself was still manned by Syrians (v. 7; cp. 11[20]; *Ant* XIII ii 1 § 42), although now contained within the larger city fortifications (v. 11).

We now have the extraordinary spectacle of rival claimants for the throne of a still mighty empire falling over themselves to flatter a notorious troublemaker in the very territory they wished to rule. Alexander Balas, hearing of the attentions heaped upon Jonathan by Demetrius, resolved to add honour to his rival's gifts of authority and arms: he appointed him High Priest of the Jews and sent him a robe of royal purple and golden crown, and called him by the honorific title "Friend of the King" (vv. 15–21). Thus far the account left to us by the Maccabean historian is perhaps just credible, but when he goes on to detail the next bid in the "win-over-the-Jews" stakes, the story becomes almost ludicrous. Demetrius, we are told, capped Alexander's offer by declaring a "tax holiday" for all Jews and Jerusalem in particular, freedom for all Jewish captives everywhere, complete immunity for Jews from any molestation during their sacred festivals, allocation of thirty thousand appointments in the king's armies at normal rates of pay, even at the highest ranks, and a guarantee that wherever they served, only men of Jewish race should be their superiors, always careful for their special customs and religious susceptibilities. To Judaea was to be added territories to the north of Jerusalem, and the whole of the city of Ptolemais and its environs was to be given as a free offering to the Jerusalem Temple to pay expenses incurred by the cult. Furthermore, the sanctuary was to receive an annual sum of fifteen thousand shekels of silver from the king's own account, which was also to defray all costs of repairing the Temple, and fortification of the city and elsewhere in Judaea (vv. 24–45). We need not doubt that this extravaganza is a manifesto of some Maccabean election campaign, and would have provoked as much amazed disbelief from Demetrius as it did apparently among Jonathan's followers:

"Now when Jonathan and the people heard these words, they gave no credit to them, nor received them, because they remembered the great evil he had done in Israel. . . . But with Alexander they were well pleased . . ." (vv. 46f.).

Well might Jonathan be pleased. At the great autumn festival of 152 BC, he was installed in the most sacred office of Jewry, at the instigation of a foreign ruler, himself an impostor and not yet confirmed in his usurped regality. Jonathan of the house of the Hasmoneans, of no priestly lineage, a war lord whose hands were stained with the blood of his priestly adversaries, was now High Priest, the anointed of God. We may imagine the reactions of the Hasidim who fifteen years previously had given the Maccabean cause their moral and active support. In those intervening years they had seen the peace and religious tolerance they longed for frustrated by the lust for temporal power of this man and his family, now elevated to spiritual supremacy in Israel. Doubtless many foresaw even then the anguish this brood of Hasmonean priest-kings would bring upon their own people. Had they been able to look beyond the century of warfare Jonathan's inauguration as High Priest portended for Israel, the prospect would have afforded them scarcely more comfort. The Maccabean dynasty, so ill-begotten by the Greeks, was to be followed by a royal line of Idumaean Herods, conceived by Roman patronage.

Jonathan had chosen sides wisely. Demetrius was killed in battle with Alexander two years later. Jonathan was invited to Ptolemais as an honoured guest at the wedding of his master to Ptolemy Philometor's daughter, Cleopatra Thea (vv. 59ff.). A last effort by Jonathan's adversaries to warn the king against his new-found Jewish ally failed, and Jonathan returned with high honour and gifts in triumph to Jerusalem (vv. 61–66). For five years or so all went well. Jonathan was able to establish his position in Judaea, and Alexander enjoyed his voluptuous life as king of the Seleucid empire and son-in-law to an Egyptian Pharaoh. It could not last, of course. Demetrius had left a son, Demetrius II, on any legal reckoning the rightful heir to the throne. In 147 BC, he appeared in Syria with an army to claim his inheritance, and all Alexander's supporters joined the new opposition, save Jonathan. To him fell the task of opposing the turncoat Apollonius, governor of Coele-Syria, and an account of his successes is given in I Maccabees 10^{74-89}. Jonathan first drove the garrison from Joppa, then defeated the governor's army in the plain near Azotus, biblical Ashdod (Fig. 2), despoiled the city and its environs, and set fire to the temple of Dagon over the heads of all those who had taken refuge there (vv. 84f.). Laden with spoils he returned to Jerusalem, and basked in the favour of his patron Alexander, who added the city of Ekron to his already considerable loot (v. 89).

Now Alexander's father-in-law, Ptolemy, perceived from his Egyptian lair the change in the wind of favour. The young pretender's day was drawing to its end, and if Demetrius were successfully to win back his dead father's kingdom, Ptolemy must assert his claim to Coele-Syria

before it was too late. He therefore marched north with a mighty army
(I Macc 11[1ff.]), was met by Jonathan at Joppa with great pomp and the
right hand of friendship (v. 6), and devised "wicked counsels against
Alexander" (v. 8). These included removing his daughter from the
likely loser's establishment and handing her over to the rising aspirant
to the throne, Demetrius (vv. 9f.). At Ptolemy's first appearance in
Syria, Alexander fled to Cilicia, but returned two years later to fight
for his kingdom. However, the combined forces of Ptolemy and
Demetrius met and defeated him by the river Oenoparas, on the plains
of Antioch. Ptolemy was himself wounded, and died three days after
receiving Alexander's head from an Arabian sheikh with whom he had
sought sanctuary (v. 17). Demetrius II was now firmly installed in his
father's place.

Jonathan was not slow to take advantage of the upheaval following
on his friend Alexander's discomfiture. He now turned in earnest to rid
his capital city of the hated Acra, symbol of the alien patronage to which
he owed his high estate. He laid siege to the garrison and at once the
Hellenistic Jews sent a warning message to the new emperor to take
heed of the rebellious governor in Judaea. Jonathan was promptly
summoned to Ptolemais to explain his action. He went, but leaving
instructions to continue the siege. It says much for his diplomacy, the
value of the "divers presents" that he took with him, and the instability
of the Seleucid throne, that Demetrius apparently not only forgave him
for his rebellious acts, but heaped upon him tax concessions, confirmed
him in his high priesthood and ratified the addition of the three top-
archies of Samaria to Judaea, as well as writing a most favourable letter
concerning the honour to be accorded the Jews, "who are our friends,
and keep covenants with us" (vv. 26–37).

Nothing was apparently said about an evacuation of the Acra by
Seleucid troops, so perhaps Demetrius was not so certain of Jonathan's
fidelity as his letter might indicate. His caution was fully justified by
events. An adventurer named Diotus, who took the name of Tryphon,
promoted the cause of Alexander Balas's son, Antiochus, as claimant to
the Seleucid throne, and managed to occupy Antioch (vv. 39ff.).
Demetrius's troops deserted in large numbers, and in desperation he
appealed to Jonathan for help. The Jewish High Priest agreed on condition that the Greeks should leave the Acra and various other fortresses
in the area (v. 41). The king was hardly in a position to refuse, and
Jonathan accordingly sent three thousand men to Antioch. They created

G

such havoc and so despoiled the city that the inhabitants cried for mercy and relief from the Jewish invaders. The situation was thus for the moment saved for Demetrius, and turned out most profitably for Jonathan (v. 51). Nevertheless, it was evident to the Jewish leader that the days left to Demetrius as a source of power and benefit to his ambitions were numbered. He accordingly offered his allegiance to the opposing faction led by Tryphon. His brother Simon was made captain over territory from the so-called "Ladder of Tyre" to the Egyptian frontier: that is, the whole of Coele-Syria with the exception of Phoenicia (v. 59). Jonathan was once more confirmed in his high priesthood by an alien prince and made a king's deputy (vv. 57f.).

Demetrius had now enemies on all sides, and was obliged to attempt to restore the situation in Palestine by bringing his erstwhile faithful ally Jonathan to heel. He sent an army south into Galilee and eventually came to battle in the plain of Hazor (Fig. 2). At first Jonathan's troops were worsted, but after a short prayer and some public lamentation, the heathen were sent packing with heavy losses (vv. 63–74). In a further campaign, Jonathan met Demetrius "in the country of Hamath", north of the Lebanon region (Fig. 1), but succeeded in frightening the Greeks into fleeing out of range during the night before the battle (12^{24-30}). To the south, brother Simon was exercising his role of military governorship, taking over and garrisoning the coastal plain (vv. 33f., 38).

Jonathan was well aware that his clever game of allying himself with successive pretenders to the Seleucid throne, maintaining his loyalty to one just so long as it paid him, and transferring his allegiance just as soon as he sniffed a change in the wind of fortune, could not go on indefinitely. He had already come a long way from the days of his guerrilla chieftaincy in the Judaean deserts. He and his brother virtually had Palestine in their control, but his ability to hold their position lay, he knew, not with successive Greek kings and their backers, but with the mighty power to the west. He accordingly sent messengers to Rome and to Sparta, offering friendship and alliances. He even referred to the strange tradition that the Jews and Spartans derived from common stock, as children of Abraham (v. 21).

Jonathan's doubts of the future of "horse-trading" with the Greeks were soon justified. Tryphon saw the Jewish leader and his brother Simon gaining control of Palestine, and knew that before long they would be in a position to challenge his planned attempt to seize the throne from his protégé (vv. 39f.). Tryphon accordingly moved south to Beth-shan (Scythopolis: Fig. 2), and Jonathan, nothing loath to force a showdown, came to meet him. The two armies faced one another, wavered on the brink of battle, and then thought otherwise. Tryphon invited Jonathan over with gestures of friendship, flattering him with the commanded obsequies of his officers, and suggested he might accompany him with only his personal bodyguard to Ptolemais. There, he promised, he would hand over the city and its defenders and take leave of his Jewish ally. Strangely, Jonathan fell for the ruse, dismissed the main body of his forces and went with Tryphon to Ptolemais. No sooner were the gates of the city shut behind them, than the Greek troops fell upon Jonathan's personal retinue, slaughtering them to a man. Jonathan was kept a prisoner, and Tryphon sent out his army again to round up those of the Jewish forces that were still in the vicinity. Leaderless, the Jews avoided a pitched battle, or (less probably with our historian) the Greeks took fright when the Jews rallied to face them. In any case, a determined attempt by Tryphon to end the menace on his southern flank could not be long delayed. For his part, Simon took over the reins of government and lost no time strengthening his defences in Jerusalem (13^{10}).

Tryphon met Simon's army at Adida, between Joppa and Jerusalem (Fig. 2). The Greek commander had brought Jonathan with him as a hostage, and again the armies paused, glowering at one another. Tryphon sent a message saying that he had merely taken Jonathan in order to ensure that certain moneys owing to the royal treasury should be paid. If Simon would send the cash, a hundred talents of silver, along with two further hostages in the persons of two of Jonathan's sons as a guarantee of future obedience, the Jewish leader would be released (vv. 15f.).

Our writer tells us that Simon was not for a moment deceived by the offer, knowing full well Tryphon's intention. He nevertheless sent across the money and the two children so that the people would not thereafter hold his brother's inevitable death against him, complaining that he might have been yet alive if Simon had acceded to the Greek's demands (vv. 17–19). Sure enough, Tryphon prevaricated, and marched his army south, to approach Jerusalem through Idumaea. Simon blocked his way at every turn, and eventually Tryphon returned home by way of Transjordan. Now that Simon was so clearly in command of the Jewish forces, the value of Jonathan as a hostage had fallen, and Tryphon had him killed on the way, at an unidentified place called Bascama (v. 23).

Israel mourned the loss of her leader, and his brother Simon brought home his body to Modein to lie with his fathers in the family mausoleum, amid great lamentation (vv. 27–30). But the Hasmonean hand never wavered from its iron grip on Jewry. The New Israel was by now firmly set on the road to political domination: it would take more than the death of one of the Maccabean clan to divert its course.

Of the two rival kings in Syria, Simon's favour came firmly down on the side of Demetrius II, against Tryphon and his young protégé Antiochus VI (in fact, in 142/1 BC, Tryphon deposed the boy-king and later, in 138 BC, killed him (vv. 31f.)). Simon continued to secure his defences throughout Judaea and, ignoring Tryphon, addressed himself to Demetrius, who responded favourably, granting the Jews full immunity from taxes (vv. 36–40). This was taken by the people as an authoritative acknowledgment of their political independence, and the year (142 BC) was celebrated as the time when "the yoke of the heathen was taken away from Israel" (v. 41). Simon now had himself proclaimed as "the High Priest, the governor and leader of the Jews", and legal documents were thenceforth dated as of the first and subsequent years of a new era (v. 42). No more certain proof of his domination of Jerusalem could be demonstrated than by his reduction to starvation of the Acra garrison, in the middle of 141 BC, and his replacement of the defenders by men of his own (vv. 49–52). So important was this victory considered that thereafter it was celebrated annually, "because there was destroyed a great enemy out of Israel" (v. 51). Furthermore, Simon extended the frontiers of his province, taking Gazara (Gezer) on the coastal plain, south-east of Joppa, and making it a garrison for the area under the command of his son, John (vv. 43–48, 53). He even achieved for his realm an access point to the Mediterranean by taking Joppa itself (14^5).

For the time being, at least, it seemed that the longed-for Day of the Lord had at last dawned in Israel. The time of Simon's hegemony was looked upon as one of peace and prosperity: "the land was quiet all the days of Simon; for he sought the good of his nation in such wise, as that evermore his authority and honour pleased them well" (v. 4; cp. vv. 8ff.). To mark this high point in Jewish fortunes, the grateful populace resolved to write up the mighty deeds of their leader and inscribe them on brass tablets, to be fixed to pillars in some conspicuous place within the sanctuary (vv. 25–48), with copies to be laid up in the treasury archives for the Hasmonean family (v. 49).

Simon had still to face trouble from the Seleucid rulers, but his position was now relatively secure. Demetrius II was taken prisoner whilst campaigning in the east against the Parthians in 139 BC. This left Tryphon temporarily in sole command in Syria, but soon Demetrius's brother Antiochus VII Sidetes installed himself as king in Antioch and tried to oust Tryphon, appealing to Simon for assistance (15^{1-9}). Simon responded favourably with men and supplies (v. 26), but having in the meantime prevailed over Tryphon, Antiochus spurned Simon's help and demanded that the Jews hand over Joppa, Gezer, the Jerusalem Acra and other fortresses (vv. 28–31). He sent an officer to Jerusalem to accept Simon's surrender, and was there treated to an argument which was to become familiar, and ominous:

"We have neither taken other men's land, nor holden that which appertaineth to others, but the inheritance of our fathers, which our enemies had wrongfully in possession a certain time. Wherefore we, having opportunity, hold the inheritance of our fathers" (vv. 33f.).

Palestine was the Jews' possession by divine right; however long others may have held it, the Chosen People by that same heavenly authority had every justification for taking and keeping it. Not surprisingly, this argument made little impression on the Syrian king. While he himself went off to pursue Tryphon, he ordered his general Cendebeus to wrest Palestine from the Jews. The commander set up his headquarters at Jamnia, and began making inroads into Judaean territory (vv. 40f.). Simon, now an old man, sent his two eldest sons, Judas and John, with infantry and cavalry, to face Cendebeus near the family home of Modein. The Greek troops were utterly routed, and many slain in the vicinity of Azotus (16^{2-10}). From that date (137 BC) until Simon died, Antiochus VII left Judaea alone. It is ironic that, having achieved so much, when this battle-scarred Jewish leader's end came, it was by the hand of one of his own family.

Simon's son-in-law, Ptolemy, a captain of troops stationed in the Jericho district, plotted to seize power and "thought to get the country for himself" (v. 13). He waited an opportunity when next his father-in-law should be visiting his area on a regular tour of inspection. In February 134 BC, Simon duly appeared in the Jordan valley, along with his two sons, Mattathias and Judas. Ptolemy welcomed them and suggested they might like to take some refreshment in the small fortress of Docus, a few miles west-north-west of Jericho (modern 'En-dūk: Fig. 2, Pl. 2). There a banquet had been arranged in their honour, and Ptolemy's assassins concealed around the dining-hall. "When", as the historian says, "Simon and his sons had drunk largely", the armed men sprang upon the guests and slaughtered them (v. 16). Very probably we should see the hand of Antiochus VII behind this treachery, since Ptolemy immediately sent word to the king that the deed had been done, and if he would but send troops, Ptolemy would seize the kingdom on his behalf. At the same time he sent assassins to kill Simon's son John in Gazara (v. 19), and made promises of bribes to Jewish troop commanders around the country if they would support his cause. John, however, was warned in time and was ready for the traitors when they arrived (v. 22).

The Maccabean account ends strangely and abruptly at this point, with but a brief reference for further information to "the chronicles of his (John's) priesthood, from the time he was made High Priest after his father" (v. 24). From this we might gather that John was generally accepted in Simon's place as spiritual leader and secular prince of the people. The Hasmonean clan had sunk its roots too deep into the New Israel to be so easily brushed aside by the treachery of one man, even though clearly Ptolemy must have enjoyed at least the tacit support of those elements of Jewry who hoped still for peace and integration with the rest of the world. For further information on the outcome of the grisly affair at Docus, we have to turn to Josephus, who carries on the story of his compatriots down to the catastrophe of AD 70. For this early period, Josephus's information is somewhat scanty, but it becomes more detailed later on, as he is able to avail himself of more contemporary traditions of current events. Of his two major works, *The Jewish War* and *Jewish Antiquities*, the latter, written subsequently, offers greater detail for the time before the intervention of the Romans.

It is Josephus who tells us that Simon's wife as well as his two sons was involved in the Docus tragedy. Apparently when John marched against Ptolemy in that fortress he was restrained from pressing his siege to the end since his father's murderer still had his mother and two brothers alive in his hands as hostages, contradicting the story in I Maccabees 16[16] which says that the two sons were killed along with Simon. Josephus says that John's mother and brothers were brought up onto the wall of Docus, tortured in the sight of the besiegers, and threatened with being hurled headlong to the ground if the attackers did not desist. The old woman begged her son John not to slacken his efforts, since "it would be pleasant for her to die in torment if Ptolemy, who was doing these things to them, paid the penalty for his crimes against them" (*Ant* XIII viii 1 § 232). The unfortunate John, here called by his surname, Hyrcanus, was torn between his duty to capture and destroy his villainous brother-in-law, and his natural love for his aged parent, whom he saw being "beaten and torn apart" (§ 233). In the end Ptolemy was saved by the inception of the Sabbatical year during which all warfare ceased in Israel, so he killed his hostages anyway and made off across the Jordan to Philadelphia, biblical Rabbath Ammon, modern '*Ammān* (Fig. 7, Pl. 3).

John Hyrcanus I, to give him his full style, now faced more trouble from Antiochus VII Sidetes, whose general Cendebeus he and his brother Judas had routed near the family home of Modein in 137 BC. In the very first year of John's reign, 134 BC, Antiochus invaded Palestine and ravaged the country, driving Hyrcanus back into Jerusalem and besieging him there. Tradition seems to accord a whole year to this investment of the city, during which the inhabitants were reduced to starvation. Hyrcanus tried to relieve the situation by driving out the non-combatants, leaving them to wander outside the walls in no-man's-land in dire suffering. Antiochus's troops hemmed them in from without, whilst the walls and gates of the city were barred to their return. Josephus says that the survivors were saved by the celebration of the Feast of Tabernacles, and the defenders took pity on them and allowed the starving wretches back into the city (§241). This is perhaps credible, but the story he goes on to relate, that Antiochus acceded to a request from Hyrcanus for a seven-day respite whilst the Jews celebrated the festival, takes rather more believing, particularly when our historian adds that the Greek ruler voluntarily contributed "bulls with gilded horns and cups of gold and silver filled with all kinds of spices" to the sacrifices (§242). This remarkable piece of piety on the part of the Syrian king, it is said, so impressed Hyrcanus that he suggested they call the whole thing off, to which Antiochus assented. We must suppose that, in fact, pressure at home demanded his immediate return to Antioch, and shortage of troops and money prevented his effectively garrisoning the country. Hyrcanus seems to have bought relief with money and hostages, and by paying tribute to Joppa and other cities lying on the borders of Judaea. He had to give up his arms and to submit to seeing Jerusalem's walls torn down again (§ 245ff.). Nevertheless, as Antiochus must have appreciated with chagrin as he hurried home, if the campaign had been designed to bring to an end once and for all

Jewish independence and the menace to the Syrian southern flank, it had been a failure. John Hyrcanus was still ruler of his people, and Antiochus was himself too insecure on his throne to maintain a constant military presence in Palestine.

A few years later Antiochus was even obliged to seek in John Hyrcanus an active ally in his wars in the east against the Parthians. As we saw, Antiochus's brother Demetrius II had, in 139 BC, been taken prisoner by the Parthian king, leaving Tryphon a free hand. Now the present king released Demetrius for the purpose of opposing Antiochus. After initial successes, in 128 BC the Syrian ruler was killed in battle and his army routed (§ 256). Demetrius thus became king in Antiochus's place, but was immediately faced with more family feuds about the succession. Neither he nor his successors were thereafter in a position to challenge the Hasmonean hegemony of Palestine. The bitter conflict between the Seleucids and the Jewish nationalists that had been precipitated by the repressive measures of Antiochus IV Epiphanes in 167 BC, came to an end with the later Antiochus's death in 128 BC. Hyrcanus read the signs correctly and swung into action.

CHAPTER VIII

Alexander Jannaeus and the Pharisees

Knowing that for the time being Syria would have been drained of Greek troops by the Parthian wars, John Hyrcanus ranged eastwards across the Jordan, besieging Medebah for six months, and north to the land of the Samaritans. He occupied ancient Shechem and Mount Gerizim (Pl. 4), where he razed the Samaritan temple to the ground. To the south, he stormed through the land of Judaea's traditional enemy Edom, allowing its people to remain in their homeland only so long as they became part of the Jewish religious community and thus subservient to the authority of Jerusalem's hierarchy. To that end they were required to be circumcised and to swear fealty to the Law of the Jewish god, and so submit to the imposition of an alien culture no less harshly enforced than that which had brought the Jews themselves to revolt against Antiochus Epiphanes. Hyrcanus and his friends had quickly forgotten the golden rule of imperialism, forsaken only at their cost by Persians and Greeks beforetime, that religious intolerance breeds rebellion even more surely than over-taxation. From the "Jews" thus created in Idumaea were to come the Herod brood of vipers and their brand of venomous intrigues.

Josephus throws an interesting sidelight on the means by which Hyrcanus was able to mount his campaigns at this time, when he records that he was the "first Jewish king" to have an army of mercenaries, and to pay them he was obliged to rob the royal tombs of Jerusalem (*Ant XIII* viii 4 § 249). In fact, King David was also said to have maintained an army of foreigners (II Sam 8[18], etc.), perhaps accounting in part for the highly improbable story that in his treasure-hunting Hyrcanus opened "the tomb of David, who surpassed all other kings in wealth". The note that Hyrcanus had to find mercenaries to fight his battles for him does, however, ring true, and it was a practice followed by later Hasmonean kings. Later Jewish historians may enlarge piously on the high regard in which Judas and his brothers and their offspring were held by the common people, but the necessity for hiring foreign soldiers hints at a rather different situation. There are other indications of serious rifts in Jewish attitudes towards their priest-king, and, as we have seen, these had their origins from the very inception of the Maccabean adventure.

In the conception of the New Israel, dreamt of by the Jews of the Exile, propounded by their prophets, and hammered out in Judaea by administrators from Babylon Jewry, there existed a fundamental conflict between the religious ideal of a world State governed by Jews and freely accepted by all men, and the practical reality that people are tenaciously conservative over their religions and take unkindly to having their gods chosen for them. When this removal of their freedom of worship is coupled with a particularly uncompromising racialist domination and tight political control, resistance to the alien regime stiffens even further, and will yield to nought but the severest military pressures. From the outset, then, the glorious New Israel was only likely to be achieved by force of arms, and maintained by brute force. The Maccabeans were at least realists, and played the military and political game as shrewdly and ruthlessly as any other tyrants of the ancient world. When it came to converting the gentile to the Faith, to fulfil the spiritual promise of the Kingdom of God, they simply offered the choice between the circumcision scalpel and slavery. Doubtless the practice offered as striking (and religiously meaningless) results in terms of numbers of new adherents to Judaism as centuries later were achieved by devotees of the Prophet welcoming into the Islamic fold those who preferred the Faith to the sword.

There must have been many religious Jews, however, who believed that forceful coercion of this kind had no part in the New Covenant promised by the prophets. God's rule would be primarily in men's hearts, and their submission to Jewish hegemony would be the natural response to Yahweh's claim upon their souls, bodies and property. Of such idealists were the Hasidim, already noticed. They lent their support to the Maccabees in the early days, but withdrew when they realised the political motivation of the movement. Their successors were the Pharisees, supposedly meaning "the separated ones", whom Josephus credits with great influence among the common people (§ 288ff.). Against them stood the Sadducees, or "sons of Zadok", representing the aristocratic priestly hierarchy, rationalist in their emphasis upon freewill and disbelief in a life after death (*Ant* XIII iv 9 § 173). Josephus elsewhere says that the Pharisees "are affectionate to each other and cultivate harmonious relationships with the community", whilst, on the other hand, "the Sadducees, even among themselves, are boorish in their behaviour, and in their intercourse with their peers are as rude as to foreigners" (*War* II viii 14 §164ff.).

The relationship between these two religious parties and John Hyrcanus is portrayed in a curious story recounted by Josephus in *Ant* XIII x 5 §288ff. It is largely unhistorical but nevertheless offers some insight into the traditional antagonism between Pharisee and Sadducee and the peculiar juggling act necessarily performed by the Hasmonean rulers to maintain good relations with one or the other and thus with some part of their Jewish subjects. It appears that John Hyrcanus began with the goodwill of the Pharisees but this turned to violent hostility because of an incident at a dinner-party arranged by the king for his Pharisaic supporters. All was going merrily and everyone was in fine good humour when Hyrcanus happened to expound on the necessity for righteousness, even in a king, and how he had always tried to be good and obedient to the will of God and his Pharisaic subjects, and so on. Warming to his subject, which was clearly going down well with the company, he urged them, nay begged them, that if they should think at any time that he, John Hyrcanus, was not measuring up to his own high standards, they should tell him forthrightly. They expostulated vehemently that none could be better or more virtuous than their own dear leader, and the general good humour was thus sustained, adding piety and reverence to the blessings of the king's ample hospitality.

Unhappily, one churlish fellow, by name Eleazar, "who", we are told, "had an evil nature and took pleasure in dissension", shattered the air of bonhomie by remarking that if the king really wanted to be righteous, he should give up the high priesthood and be content with governing the people (§ 291). Icily, Hyrcanus asked his sole critic why he should give up the sacred office. To which Eleazar replied, "Because we have heard from our elders that your mother was a captive in the reign of Antiochus Epiphanes."

The customs of war being what they were, a woman who had been taken as part of the spoils of victory was naturally expected to have been her captor's concubine. As such she could not thereafter be the legitimate wife of a High Priest who must, by the Law, marry a virgin (Lev 21[14]), and her offspring would be barred from filling that high office, being of impure stock. Hyrcanus seethed with fury and Eleazar's companions were filled with embarrassed indignation. Never backward in stirring up trouble with their old enemies, the Sadducees suggested through one of their number who heard of the accusation (false, according to Josephus), that it was the Pharisees who had put Eleazar up to making his slanderous statement, being themselves unwilling to face the king's wrath. And if Hyrcanus wanted sure proof of this, let him but ask the Pharisees what punishment should be dealt out to the miscreant. Such an insult hurled at a king would merit death; if they suggested less than this it would prove that they were in league with the wretch.

The Pharisees thus charged with pronouncing punishment suggested "stripes and chains"—they were naturally lenient in the matter of punishments, says Josephus. Hyrcanus was thus convinced of their complicity in the slander, and promptly transferred his spiritual loyalty to the Sadducees, declaring null and void the regulations which the Pharisees had traditionally laid upon the Jews.

It will be appreciated that the Law of Moses, proclaimed after the Exile as the final arbiter in matters of religion and conduct, was always painfully inadequate as a code of behaviour covering all manner of daily living. There are aspects of social intercourse for which biblical legislation makes no provision, and many of its injunctions could have no relevance to modern urban life like that of Jerusalem in the second century BC. Thus there grew up a body of casuistic legislation based, often very tenuously, on the Torah, for the compiling and administration of which the Pharisees were largely responsible. If their judgments seem hair-splitting to the point of absurdity, the fault lay not in these moral leaders of their people so much as in the system of an ethical code based rigidly upon ancient writings, often only dimly understood, and frequently quite ill-suited to the legal purposes to which religious dogmaticism had pressed them. The New Testament branding of these pious men as "hypocrites" is quite undeserved and indeed, having regard to the mythical character of the whole Gospel story, never expected to be taken seriously by informed readers. Similarly unreal would have been any such disavowal on the part of the High Priest of Pharisaic rulings; it would have resulted in virtual anarchy, when every man would be his own judge, and the biblical legislation given as many varied interpretations as there were litigants citing its provisions to justify their conduct.

Josephus says that the Sadducees renounced all Pharisaic rulings

(§ 297f.), but enjoyed the confidence of the wealthy alone and had no following among the general populace who gave their support to the Pharisees. It was, of course, the rich man who could afford to make his own laws to suit himself; the poor man looked for justification to the less partial interpretation of biblical injunctions to be expected from his Pharisaic "shepherd".

Hyrcanus died in 104 BC, intending that his widow should take up the reins of government. However, Aristobulus, his eldest son, seized power and declared himself king, the first of the Hasmoneans, according to Josephus, to put the crown upon his head. There is some dispute over this, however; some scholars think that the assumption of monarchy had already been made by his father, while others have suggested that the adventures of Aristobulus may have become confused with the later and more considerable ruler, Alexander Jannaeus. It matters little in regard to power, since John was certainly king of the Jews in fact if not in name. Neither he nor Aristobulus call themselves "king" on their coins, which are inscribed simply "John/Judas (Aristobulus's Jewish name, according to Josephus, *Ant* XX x 3 §240), High Priest, and the community of the Jews", or "head of the community of the Jews". Their diffidence in this regard may have been due to deference to popular religious tradition that only one belonging to the house and lineage of David should sit upon the throne of Israel. In particular, pious expectation looked forward to the coming of a kingly "anointed", Messiah or Christ, who would be a "Son of David", a conception which later became more and more tinged with the mystical and supernatural.

Aristobulus ruled only one year, and contrived in that time to imprison three of his brothers, kill another whom he unjustly suspected of treason, starve his mother to death in prison, and to campaign in the north against the Ituraeans, in the Lebanon region, and forcibly convert them to Judaism. He was of a kindly nature, says Josephus, and was wholly given to modesty, and he quotes other authorities to the effect that this good man "was very serviceable to the Jews, for he acquired additional territory for them, and brought over to them a portion of the Ituraean nation, whom he joined to them by the bond of circumcision" (*Ant.* XIII xi 3 §319).

This short-lived model of Hasmonean "kindliness" left no son, but his widow, Salome Alexandra, released his three brothers from prison, married one of them, Alexander Jannaeus (from *Yannai*, an abbreviation of *Yohanan*, John) and proclaimed him king. They made a finely-matched

pair; when Jannaeus died nearly thirty years later, his subjects could find
no epithet vituperous enough to express their feelings of this pillar of
the Maccabean house. Even then his widow Salome retained enough
power in her hands to take on where her husband had left off. We may
suspect, therefore, that she had been the dominant force behind the
throne from the beginning.

Jannaeus was true to the Hasmonean fighting tradition. He set out
from the start on a policy of territorial aggrandizement, bringing himself
into conflict with Greek rulers fighting for the Seleucid throne in the
north, with Egypt in the south and on the west with a royal pretender
in Cyprus bargaining his way back to the mainland. In Syria,
Antiochus VIII Grypos was struggling with Antiochus IX Kyzikenos
for the kingdom, so Jannaeus took the opportunity to make a bid for
Ptolemais (Acre), and laid siege to the city. It would have been a rich
prize since it offered an outlet to the Mediterranean and a control
position for the hinterland of Galilee. The inhabitants, recognising the
futility of seeking help from the Syrian king, appealed to a certain
Ptolemy VIII (Lathyrus), whose mother, Cleopatra III, had deprived
him of the Egyptian throne, and from whose motherly embrace he had
fled to Cyprus, a dependency of Ptolemais. The hard-pressed citizens
encouraged Ptolemy over to the mainland with the prospect of a general
insurrection in Gaza and Sidon and elsewhere, whose people would be
willing to join forces with him and help him back to power.

The Egyptian prince responded readily; indeed, rather too enthusiastically, thought the people of Ptolemais, who changed their mind even
while he was on his way, thinking apparently it might be better to face
the Jews than have this Egyptian take over the country (§ 330). Furthermore, they reasoned belatedly, his mother was almost certain to take a
hand in the matter to prevent her son establishing himself in Palestine,
and would vent her wrath on his new allies. If this happened Ptolemy
could dash back to the security of Cyprus, while the Ptolemaeans
would be left to face the mother's martial music.

Something of the same logic occurred to Alexander Jannaeus. Faced
with the prospect of fighting Ptolemy's considerable forces if he were to
continue his attack on Ptolemais, Jannaeus himself suggested to Cleopatra secretly that she might like to come north and rid the country of
her offspring's unwelcome attentions. At the same time, he made a pact
with Ptolemy, promising him a fat bribe if he would help him defeat the
ruler of Ptolemais and bring his territory under Jewish domination

(§ 335). All would have been well had not Ptolemy learnt of Alexander's mission to his mother Cleopatra. He promptly broke off these profitable negotiations and began instead to launch a campaign in Palestine on his own behalf, beginning with a siege and eventual capture of the luckless Ptolemais on whose behalf he had come over in the first place. Ptolemy's forces met with a good measure of success and Alexander's troops were mauled at Asophon (biblical Zaphon: Fig. 2) on the Jordan (§ 338ff.).

Cleopatra now decided to take a hand and check her son before he threatened her own position in Egypt. She set out in 102 BC, therefore, with all her forces, under the command of two Jews, Helkias and Ananias (with characteristic feminine prudence she first sent the greater part of her private fortune and her two grandsons to the sanctuary of Asclepius in Cos (Fig. 6), an ancient equivalent of a numbered bank account in Zurich). Her son Alexander (Ptolemy IX) was ordered to sail towards Phoenicia with a great fleet, while she herself came by the land route to Ptolemais with the entire Egyptian army, and laid siege to the city when the inhabitants refused her entry. Her rebellious son thereupon hastened towards Egypt hoping to take it over while his mother had the army engaged elsewhere. Cleopatra, however, had forces to spare and detached an army to drive him out of the country, forcing him to winter in Gaza. She herself pressed on with the siege and finally captured Ptolemais.

The Jewish king Alexander Jannaeus now had to make terms with Cleopatra to ensure, since he had doublecrossed her son, that he had at least one ally. She, on the other hand, began to cast envious eyes around her and to wonder if Egypt might not once again make herself mistress of Coele-Syria, or at least, the Jewish-controlled part of the area. At this point Josephus records a significant exchange between the queen and her Jewish general Ananias (the other, Helkias, had earlier been killed whilst in pursuit of Ptolemy). The commander pointed out how morally reprehensible it would be to deprive such a faithful ally as Alexander of his realm; besides—one can see the steely glint in his eye—"I would have you know that an injustice done to this man will make all us Jews your enemies" (§ 354). A new world force had arrived on the scene: the ability of Jewish money and power in the Diaspora to influence political decisions behind the scenes. The queen appreciated very well the hard truth of the general's warning. Egypt had by now many Jews in positions of wealth and authority, and doubtless Ananias and Helkias were not the only high-ranking Jews in the armed forces. The Palestinian kingdom of Jannaeus thus had protectors in high places wielding power as, or more effective than, brute military strength. Cleopatra took the hint, and made an alliance with Alexander. Her son scuttled back to Cyprus. The Jewish king was once more master in his own land, and prepared to take up his policy of territorial expansion where he had left off.

Jannaeus marched into Transjordan and took Gadara, capturing it after a siege of ten months. Amathus fell next, "the greatest stronghold of those occupied beyond the Jordan" (Fig. 2), and a storehouse of a local chieftain's most valued treasures. He later retrieved his possessions by an attack on Alexander's baggage train, but this did not deter the Jewish leader from pressing on to further conquests. He marched back towards the Palestinian coast near Gaza, storming Raphia, near the Egyptian border, and Anthedon just north of Gaza. Apparently the Jews believed that Ptolemy was still in that city, and when its inhabitants surprised the Jewish camp at night, Alexander thought it was Ptolemy's army and his men scattered. The next morning, on discovering that the attackers were merely Gazaeans, and probably that they were ill-equipped compared with his own men, Alexander regrouped his forces and attacked. The men of Gaza courageously held their ground, vainly hoping for relief from the Nabatean king Aretas in fulfilment of an earlier promise. It never came, and to dwindling supplies and heavy casualties was added rank treachery when the Gazaean general was killed by his own brother. This worthy took over the army and opened the gates to Jannaeus and his troops, presumably on a promise of non-reprisal and peaceful entry. The latter condition was fulfilled by the Jewish troops, but as soon as they were inside the walls, Alexander turned them loose on the inhabitants, "and let his men avenge themselves on them" (§ 362). The Jews had to fight for every inch, however, despite the lack of arms and resources available to the townsfolk. "Some of them, being isolated, set fire to their houses that nothing might remain in them to be taken as spoil by the enemy. Others killed their wives and children with their own hands, as being the only means of saving them from slavery to their enemies" (§ 363). Five hundred elders who had sought refuge in the temple of Apollo—they had been in council session when the attack came—were slaughtered, and the city pulled down in ruins over them. The Jews returned in triumph to their Holy City.

Amid growing signs of disquiet at home, Jannaeus pursued his wars of conquest east of the Jordan, again attacking Amathus, and subduing the inhabitants of Moab and Gilead. He could not help invoking the active hostility of the Nabateans once he invaded these Arab lands. Their king Obedas claimed suzerainty over the whole of Transjordan, as far north as Damascus, since through this region ran the famous "King's Highway" that led northwards from the incense coast of South Arabia to the markets of Asia Minor and Mesopotamia (Fig. 7). Jannaeus and his troops were successfully ambushed by Arabs and the king barely escaped with his life. He managed to make his way back to Jerusalem, only to find that news of his discomfiture had preceded him and had given his Jewish opponents courage to declare a revolt against the Hasmonean rule.

Unfortunately, we lack details of this uprising from a wholly sympathetic source, just as we are all too ignorant of the precise nature and extent of local Jewish opposition to the Maccabean movement from the outset. Its undoubted intensity is illustrated by the repeated attempts by moderate Jewry to overthrow Hasmonean rule despite the bitter cost in broken lives and fortunes. Such rebellions usually failed through lack of independent military resources or over-dependence upon the help of aliens interested only in dominating Palestine for their own ends. Too often such antagonism to the Maccabean priest-kings has been labelled in our sources, and indeed in modern commentaries, as emanating from impious men seeking to undermine the traditional Jewish faith for worldly success or for the softer life promised by contemporary Hellenism. No such judgment can, however, be levelled at the Pharisaic opponents of John Hyrcanus, nor at those Jews now setting themselves against Jannaeus. They wanted an end of this bloody warfare being waged on their behalf by the High Priest and his paid cut-throats from Pisidia and Cilicia (§ 374). Wherever Jannaeus now found his support within Jewry it was not with the religionists who, we are told, on one occasion pelted their spiritual leader with citrons as he prepared to make sacrifice at the high altar. It was at a celebration of the Feast of Tabernacles, when custom required that the worshippers carry palm branches and this fruit (§ 372; cp. III x 4 §245). Furthermore, they again accused this Hasmonean of having no legal right to the high priesthood, with the added reason now that he had married his sister-in-law, Salome, and thus transgressed the law that his wife must be a virgin.

It is the more unfortunate that we lack first-hand information on the names and loyalties of the men principally involved in this clash with Jannaeus, in that there seems to be some reference to the revolt in a fragmentary document from the Dead Sea caves. In a commentary on the book of Nahum, the Essene writer mentions "Demetrius, king of Greece, who sought to enter Jerusalem by the counsel of the Seekers-after-Smooth-Things" (col. i, 1.2; Pl. 5). The incident to which this cryptic remark seems to refer was that recorded by Josephus, when at the end of six years of rebellion by the Jews against their own king, they called in desperation for help from Demetrius III, Eukairos, who was ruling in Damascus. He was the last Seleucid to interfere directly in Jewish affairs. The Greek king marched south to Shechem and met Jannaeus with his combined force of mercenaries and such Jews as supported his cause. Demetrius's forces also included Jewish mercenaries, and in the general conflict of loyalties morale seems to have collapsed on both sides. When battle was finally joined, Alexander was defeated and fled to the mountains, and was there joined by more Jews, according to Josephus, "out of pity" for his present plight. The Essene Nahum commentary would indicate that there had in fact been a split in the ranks of the anti-Hasmonean rebels, some feeling that things had gone far enough with the overthrow of their hated priest-king and that they should now find some new leader who would be a true member of the Zadokite priesthood, of pure lineage and undefiled by illegal marriages or blood of battle. On the other hand, it would seem that there were others who wished to allow Demetrius entry into Jerusalem, perhaps as a first move to reintegration of the community into the civilised world. Of the Greek king's own feelings in the matter we know no more than Josephus's statement that he withdrew from the arena "in alarm". Much as he would probably have wished to accede to the wishes of the Hellenists, he had troubles back home where he was engaged in a struggle with his brother Philip, whom he now proceeded to besiege in Beroea (Aleppo: Fig. 1; Ant XIII xiv 3 § 384).

Now left on their own, the violently anti-Hasmoneans among the Jews tried to make an all-out effort to defeat Jannaeus, but were hopelessly outnumbered and suffered accordingly. The king besieged them in their place of refuge (variously given by Josephus as Bethome and Bemeselis—War I iv 6 § 96), dragged them forth and took them to Jerusalem. There, while he feasted with his concubines "in a conspicuous place"—probably on the city ramparts—he had eight hundred of the wretches crucified for the entertainment of the assembled company. To add to the delight of the onlookers the wives and children of the poor wretches were killed before their dying eyes. Again, there seems to be some reference to this horrible event in the Nahum commentary when the writer speaks of the so-called "Lion of Wrath", possibly Jannaeus, "hanging men up alive" (1.7), and quotes the passage in Deuteronomy 21 22f. where anyone left hanging overnight "on a tree" is reckoned "accursed of God", as remarked by the writer of Galatians (3 13) of Jesus. The rebels who escaped the vengeance "fled by night and remained in exile so long as Alexander lived" (Ant XIII xiv 2 § 383). Since, for other reasons, it seems likely that many of the Essenes of the Dead Sea establishment (Pl. 6) took up their desert sojourn about this time, we might connect them with those committed anti-Hasmoneans who willingly lent their arms to fight Jannaeus but refused to countenance the invitation to Demetrius to enter the Holy City. Unfortunately, from our point of view, they lacked a contemporary "Josephus" to give their side of the tragic tale. Their records so far recovered from the desert caves are too fragmentary, and are in any case couched in too cryptic language for us to glean very much about their part in the affair.

From that time (c. 88 BC) we are told, Jannaeus reigned "in complete tranquillity" being "rid of the trouble they had caused him". While this may possibly have been true on the surface of the Jewish political scene, it certainly was not the case with Alexander's enemies abroad. Antiochus XII, Dionysus, one of the claimants to the remnants of the Syrian kingdom, made two campaigns against the Nabateans to stem their northward advance to Damascus. On the second occasion, the Greek king came through Palestine by the coast route, and Alexander Jannaeus, fearing for the safety of his realm, tried to bar the way with what appears to have been a singularly ineffective ditch and rampart extending some seventeen miles from Chabarsaba, north-east of Joppa, to the sea coast. The Greeks simply pushed their way through it to meet the Arabian king, Aretas III. Antiochus was killed and his army routed, leaving the Arabs in control of the area south, east and north-east of Judaea, up to and including Damascus. Aretas now turned his attentions to the Jews and defeated Jannaeus at Adida, between Joppa and Jerusalem. The war seems to have been fought more with a view to warning off the Jews from interfering with the Arabs' rights in Transjordan than to occupying Judaea, since, after Jannaeus had made certain unspecified concessions to Aretas, the Arab king withdrew (§ 392).

Nevertheless, Jannaeus campaigned again across the Jordan, and for three years, from 83 to 80 BC, he was continually in the field. His continual successes, we are told, brought him the approbation of the Jews (§ 394). Be that as it may, the extent of his kingdom at this time, as given by Josephus (§ 395), far exceeded anything achieved by John Hyrcanus, reaching from the border of Egypt to Carmel along the sea coast, from Idumaea northwards to Seleucia by Lake Merom, and on the east from there down to the Dead Sea. In view of Nabatean strength in this area we may have strong doubts about how effective was Jewish control east of the Jordan and the Dead Sea. In fact, Jannaeus's "conquests" can never have been very permanent; as soon as he was away fighting elsewhere, the conquered territories rebelled. However ruthless and effective the Jewish king's mercenary forces, he lacked the strength and unity of purpose among his own people in Judaea to administer such an empire successfully.

Of course, it is easy enough to condemn the man as a megalomaniac, lashing out on every side at enemies, supposed or real; or to describe him as no more than a power-hungry madman, sacrificing the well-being of his people for an insatiable lust for military conquest. He was undoubtedly all this and more, but he was nevertheless a product of the racialist cult that brought the Hasmoneans to power in the first place. His subjugation of the peoples round about had as its object their incorporation into the Jewish commonwealth, the dream of priest and prophet long before and rooted into the Jewish religion since the Exile. Jannaeus was no more than the sword of Yahweh and perhaps more practical in his interpretation of the role of priest-king in the New Israel than those quietists who awaited the coming of the angelic hordes from on high to usher in the Kingdom of God. Unfortunately Jannaeus's kind of forceful evangelism inevitably inflicts suffering on innocent people. Josephus reports that of the cities subdued in Yahweh's name by Jannaeus, Pella was demolished "because the inhabitants would not agree to adopt the national customs of the Jews" (§ 397), meaning, presumably, circumcision and the Sabbath.

Jannaeus died of alcoholism, according to Josephus, at the age of 49, in the year 76 BC (§ 398). To the last, he was fighting Israel's battles, on this occasion besieging Ragaba in Transjordan (probably modern *Rajib*, 8 miles east of the Jordan and 14 miles west of Jerash, ancient Gerasa: Fig. 2, Pl. 7). His wife, Salome Alexandra, was apparently with him at the time, and was much exercised at the reception she and

her children were likely to receive at the hands of their fellow-countrymen when once it was realised that the king was dead—"you know
how hostile the nation feels towards you"! (§ 399). The dying king
urged upon her the necessity for making peace with the Pharisees, "for if
they praised her in return for this sign of regard, they would dispose the
nation favourably towards her". Thus he instructed the queen: "When
you come to Jerusalem, send for their leaders, and, showing them my
dead body, permit them, with every sign of sincerity, to treat me as they
please, whether they wish to dishonour my corpse by leaving it un-
buried because of the many injuries they have suffered at my hands, or in
their anger wish to offer my dead body any other form of indignity.
Promise them also that you will not take any action, while you are on the
throne, without their consent. If you speak to them in this manner,
I shall receive from them a more splendid burial than I should from
you; for once they have the power to do so, they will not choose to
treat my corpse badly, and at the same time you will reign securely"
(§ 403f.).

This highly improbable dying speech of a reputed dipsomaniac at
least stresses the reality of the antagonism between the ruling house
on the one hand, and the Pharisees on the other, with the moderate
opinion they represented in the country. A young and virile monarch
with a strong army of mercenaries could enforce his will over the
populace, but when he showed weakness or was overcome in battle or by
death, the dynasty was in grave danger of being overthrown, hence
Salome's real concern.

The ruse apparently worked. The Pharisees "stilled their anger
against Alexander" and became his widow's "well-wishers and friends".
They even went to the people and made long speeches in praise of the
dead king, and so moved the people to mourning and lamentation for
their loss that they accorded the corpse "a more splendid burial than
had been given any of the kings before him" (§ 406). Much more to the
point, they took over power in the kingdom, ostensibly leaving Salome
Alexandra the diadem only. She commanded that all the Pharisaic laws
that Hyrcanus had abrogated were to be re-established, and allowed the
Pharisees a free hand to release political prisoners of their own persuasion
and to recall their exiled brethren.

In fact, what the astute queen had done was to make a bargain with
the Pharisees. In return for their having complete power to run the
internal affairs of the State, legal and religious, and thus to keep the

ordinary people happy, they permitted Salome Alexandra to carry on
with the wars of conquest and subjugation where her husband had left
off. She promptly recruited a large force of mercenaries, doubled the
size of her own army, and "struck terror into the local rulers round
about" (§ 409). The Hasmonean "hammer" had passed into faithful
hands.

CHAPTER IX

Enter Rome

Queen Alexandra must have been a truly remarkable woman. Of her Josephus says, "she was a woman who showed none of the weakness of her sex" (*Ant* XIII xvi 6 § 430). She believed in absolute power and scorned those who wore the trappings of kingship and yet shrank from exercising fully its rights of despotism: "for she valued the present more than the future, and making everything else secondary to absolute rule, she had, on account of this, no consideration for either decency or justice" (§ 431). The relationship between the queen and her two sons would make an interesting study of its own. The eldest, Hyrcanus, she despised for his weakness; the younger, Aristobulus, she feared. In him she must have seen her late husband, and knew well that he alone in the kingdom could and would challenge her power.

As a woman, she could not hold the high priesthood, and appointed Hyrcanus to the position, "because", as Josephus says, "of his lack of energy" (*Ant* XIII xvi 2 § 408). Thus, with the Pharisees in her pocket, led by a weakling son as High Priest, she could count on the support of the religious and civil administration, while she controlled the all-important military arm. Aristobulus, however, would not long remain subservient to his mother, and even less to his brother.

The first clash came when the Pharisees demanded vengeance on those who had remained loyal to Alexander Jannaeus during the revolt, and had taken part in the mass crucifixion of eight hundred rebels. Not unnaturally, the queen hesitated in thus rewarding those who, from the Hasmonean point of view, had behaved honourably to their king. They were still well represented in Judaea, even though hated by the mass of common folk and their Pharisaic leaders. Impatient to exercise their newly-won power, the Pharisees would wait no longer for the queen's consent. They began a purge of their enemies, slaughtering them, one after another, in cold blood (§ 410).

The "royalists" clamoured at the queen's palace for protection. Aristobulus saw his chance and joined them. But while they framed their pleas for help with the most loyal of sentiments—their safety was necessary to the royal house, and the queen's welfare was their primary concern—Aristobulus laid the blame for their precarious position on the queen's attitude to the Pharisees. She had betrayed her own supporters who, nevertheless, must bear some responsibility for the situation in that they had allowed "a woman to reign, who madly lusted for power even though her own sons were in the prime of life" (§ 417). The "royalists" hinted that if they were denied protection from the throne, they might have to seek elsewhere: "it would be disgraceful for both them and her . . . if, being abandoned by her, they should be given shelter by her late husband's enemies; for Aretas the Arab and the other princes would consider it of the utmost value to enlist such men as mercenaries, whose very name, they might say, had caused these princes to shudder before even it was breathed aloud" (§ 414).

However, these loyal friends of the royal house appreciated the delicacy of the queen's position with regard to the Pharisees. It may be, they acknowledged, that she was obliged to bow to their wishes for the time being, to placate the people and keep them happy. Nevertheless, Alexandra must also be aware just how fickle could be the mood of the populace and their leaders. To safeguard her own position for the future, as well as giving her friends some security at the present, would it not be a good idea, they suggested, to station each of them in her garrisons scattered round the country, "for, if some evil genius were thus wroth with the house of Alexander, they at least would show themselves loyal, even though living in humble circumstances" (§ 415).

The queen took the point, and sent them to guard all her fortresses, with the exception of three major establishments on each side and to the north of the Dead Sea, Hyrcania (modern *Khirbet el-Mird*) at the foot of the Judaean hills overlooking the Dead Sea (Pl. 8), Machaerus, east of the Sea, and Alexandrium, north of Jericho overlooking the Jordan valley (Fig. 2; Pl. 10). In these she kept her most precious possessions, and doubtless trusted her ambitious son about as much as her other loyal supporters. To keep Aristobulus busy, she sent him off with an army to Damascus to fight Ptolemy, son of Mennaeus, king of Chalcis in the Lebanon region (Fig. 7). He returned, however, "without having achieved anything noteworthy" (§ 418), not least, we may suspect, because he had his mind occupied with matters nearer home.

Alexandra had been sixty-four when her husband died, and for nine years she wielded power, planned and executed military actions, as well as

5   The author at work in Jerusalem, piecing together fragments of an Essene commentary on Nahum, discovered in 1952.

6 The Essene establishment at Qumran, viewed from across the Wadi Qumran, looking
   north-east to the head of the Dead Sea and the hills of Moab.

7 The forum of Jerash, ancient Gerasa, a city of the Decapolis.

8 *Khirbet-el-Mird*, ancient Hyrcania.

coping with factions among her people and a recalcitrant son. At length, even her iron constitution yielded before the strain and she became seriously ill. Aristobulus knew the time had come for decisive action. He slipped away from the palace, leaving behind his wife and three children who alone knew of his intentions. He made first for one of the royalist strongholds where he knew he could find support for his cause and a base of operations. The next day his mother learnt of his departure, and for a time refused to credit the obvious, that her son had raised the flag of revolt. But when messengers began to arrive reporting that first one stronghold then another, and another, had fallen to his standard, she had to acknowledge that her "loyal" supporters had rallied round their new and virile leader. The fortresses in which she had installed them were now centres of armed revolt.

In fifteen days, Aristobulus had twenty-two strongholds in his hands, and, with the resources they contained, he recruited an army of mercenaries, eager for the spoil of revolution (§ 427). Hyrcanus and his Pharisaic supporters watched the storm gathering about them with growing dismay. They knew that with the queen on her death-bed and an army at his command, Aristobulus could at any time take over the government. They trembled for their lives, and saw in their nightmares those eight hundred crosses beneath the city wall, and the avenging spirits of those executioners whom they had cut down for their obedience to the Hasmonean king. They crowded into the chamber of the dying, seventy-three-year-old queen, begging her to take action while still she had breath to issue royal commands.

We may imagine the scene, and the look of utter contempt this dragon of the house of Maccabee must have cast upon her trembling offspring, and the flock of frightened sheep clustering round her bed.

"Do what you like," she rasped with her dying breath, "You've got money in the treasuries and an army in the barracks. Use them; fight your own battles. I'm sick of the lot of you!" Doubtless her indomitable spirit flew to the side of her rebel son as he prepared for battle on the other side of the Jordan. In life two such dominant personalities could hardly remain at peace for long. The weak Hyrcanus might cringe before his mother and accept an unwanted hieratic office because he dare not refuse. Aristobulus craved for the power his mother wielded and refused to surrender, knowing his ruthlessness and impetuosity. She died knowing he would snatch the sceptre from her failing hands; and perhaps for that she died happy.

The army Hyrcanus mustered to meet his brother on the plains of Jericho crumbled before the trained mercenaries Aristobulus had bought with his mother's money. Many of the Jewish soldiers, indeed, deserted to Aristobulus knowing the poor quality of their leadership and the determination of the opposing prince to seize Alexandra's throne. Hyrcanus fled and shut himself in the citadel overlooking the Temple area in Jerusalem, trusting that his brother would respect the sanctity of his office, and would fear for the safety of his own wife and children still imprisoned there as hostages. On either count, it is doubtful whether Aristobulus would have spared Hyrcanus had he a mind to do otherwise, but in the event they reached an agreement that suited both admirably. Hyrcanus retired on a pension to his brother's house, abdicating his claim of primogeniture to the throne, while Aristobulus took up his residence in the palace. The brothers publicly announced their reconciliation, and thus, Aristobulus hoped, calmed the fears of Hyrcanus's supporters.

There now emerges from the shadows a new, sinister figure, whose family was henceforth to play a dominant role in Jewish politics. Under Alexander Jannaeus and his wife, a certain Antipater (Antipas, for short) had been appointed governor in the ancient Edomite territory of Idumaea, whose people had been among those forcibly converted to Judaism by John Hyrcanus. Now Antipater's son, of the same name, began to take a hand in events in Jerusalem. He was rich and had widespread connections with the Arabs, with whom the Idumaeans were ethnically related, and with the people of Gaza and Ascalon. It appears that he saw a chance in the antagonism existing between the ruling parties in Judaea to prepare the way for his own take-over. Aristobulus, although he now had the upper hand, and was certainly the stronger character of the brothers, had against him the weight of the popular party led by the Pharisees. Antipater was astute enough to see that he could not hold power indefinitely against the will of the commons and the clergy. Furthermore, Aristobulus was the match of Antipater in cunning and would prove an uneasy ally in conspiracy.

Antipater thus turned to the weak Hyrcanus, and used his money and influence to stir up trouble against the stronger brother, urging anybody in authority who would listen, to appreciate the illegality of Aristobulus's position, being the younger son (*Ant* XIV i 3 § 11). To Hyrcanus himself, Antipater added the telling argument that Aristobulus was being daily urged by his closest friends to liquidate his brother since, while he lived, his indisputably legal claim to the throne threatened Aristobulus's security. He played on Hyrcanus's nerves to such an extent in this way, that in the end he agreed to follow his Idumaean friend's suggestion and flee the country. Antipater had told him that he could safely throw himself upon the mercy of that most irreconcilable enemy of the Hasmoneans, the Nabatean king Aretas III. If Hyrcanus would but follow Antipater's instructions the Arabs could be induced to act as his ally in the struggle with his brother. Scared as Hyrcanus was, he wanted more assurances that Aretas would give him sanctuary and not hand him straight back to his brother. He therefore asked Antipater to seek sworn promises of safe conduct from the Nabatean king, and these, not surprisingly, were forthcoming immediately. Since the whole scheme had clearly been worked out to the last detail by Antipater and Aretas previously, there was every reason why the Nabateans should welcome Hyrcanus as a defector and a rallying-point for their own sympathetic, or at least unopposed, assumption of power in Jerusalem.

One night, Antipater ushered his protégé out of the capital, and rode hard eastwards across the Jordan and then south to the rose-red city of Petra, hewn from the sandstone rocks south of the Dead Sea (Fig. 7, Pl. 9[a, b]). Once through the long, narrow gorge that was, and is, the city's most convenient access from the world outside, Hyrcanus was safe from his brother, but more than ever under the domination of his new-found "friends". He promised to return to Aretas all the territory and cities his father Alexander had wrested from the Arabs during his campaigns in Transjordan. Antipater offered cash to mount his force against Aristobulus and bring Hyrcanus safely back into Jerusalem as king (§17f.).

Aristobulus met the Arab force somewhere outside the city, was defeated and forced to take refuge within the walls of the Temple sanctuary. His army deserted him, and he was left with only the support of the priestly aristocracy and their money. In the event, this latter blessing proved the most beneficial, but for the moment Aristobulus's position seemed hopeless. The townsfolk had taken the side of Hyrcanus, despite his alien support from the Nabateans now flocking into the city under their king Aretas. All the old anti-Hasmonean hatred seemed about to overwhelm Aristobulus and the priests besieged on the Temple mount. Then from the north came the rumble of a mighty power whose attitudes in the Near East were henceforth to be paramount in the determination of world events.

Pompey, the Roman general, had been pursuing a vigorous campaign in Asia. He had conquered the Pontic kingdom of Mithridates, accepted the surrender of the Armenian king Tigranes, and now prepared to impose Roman suzerainty over the whole of western Asia. The days of the old Seleucid empire were already numbered, its leadership in a state of advanced decay. To take over control, Pompey sent his legate M. Aemilius Scaurus to Syria in 65 BC. In Damascus he heard of the events in Judaea and went immediately to see what pickings he might make for himself out of the confusion, and how Roman power could most effectively be established at the least cost to the empire. He was met by representatives of both sides, each bearing costly gifts and promising a pro-Roman attitude for the future should their present applications for support be successful (*Ant* XIV ii 3 § 29ff.). From now on, this fawning upon the Roman overlord was to be the pattern of Jewish diplomacy. Events in Judaea would be determined by the self-interested decisions of a mightier or more ruthless master than had ever before held sway over that unhappy land. To manipulate by bribery or flattery the will of that giant must therefore be the prime consideration of any aspirant to power. However much—or little—religious motives had actuated the political machinations of the Hasmoneans, from now on the glorious conception of a new Israel ruling the world on behalf of its god had to take second place before the harsh realities of Rome's domination of western Asia.

As long as the empires which successively ruled Palestine showed periodic signs of weakness, or Jewish influence behind the scenes at the imperial courts could obtain special favours for their Judaean brethren, opportunities could be expected to recur for determined local leaders to attain some measure of religious and political autonomy. If, at such times, these leaders took the opportunity to wage war on their immediate neighbours and extend their territory, and to convert some of them to Judaism at the point of the sword, the pious fancy that Yahweh was working out his purpose to bring all nations under his rule, could be kept alive. Now that mighty Rome had entered the arena, Jewish leaders would need all their bribery and wheedling to maintain their offices within the imperial administration, let alone dream of world conquest by a Jewish theocracy. Such hopes must remain the province of prophets and visionaries and ultimately, and most disastrously, the

inspiration of madmen whose drug-induced euphoria blinded them to
military realities.

Scaurus chose Aristobulus's present, mainly, according to Josephus,
because it seemed easier to dismiss Hyrcanus and his ill-trained Arab
supporters and fugitives with a threat of being declared an enemy of
Rome, than to try to force the fortifications of the Temple mount
(§ 31f.). Accordingly Aretas withdrew his Nabateans and re-crossed the
Jordan. Scaurus returned to Damascus, counting his takings, and
Aristobulus waited just long enough for his back to be turned before he
marched forth from his sacred refuge and rushed hotfoot after Aretas.
They met at an unidentified place called Papyron, apparently not far
from Philadelphia (modern 'Ammān) to which Aretas had betaken
himself in his confusion (*War* I vi 3 § 129). The Arabs were defeated, and
among the slain was Antipater's brother. Antipater himself and
Hyrcanus, having lost their Arab ally for the time being, now began to
plan the next move. Antipater appreciated that the influence of money
and shrewd cunning was likely to pay more dividends in the coming
struggle for power than brute force. He had not failed to note that a
mere word from Scaurus was enough to send Aretas scurrying from the
scene. Future words of this sort must be bought with gold and flattery,
and Antipater had a rich store of both to offer.

The following year Pompey himself appeared in Syria and spent the
winter of 64/3 BC in winter quarters. With the spring, he moved to
Damascus and prepared to receive deputations and their gifts. Among
them, needless to say, were messengers and offerings from Aristobulus
and Hyrcanus, the latter's representative being Antipater himself.
There also appeared a delegation from the people asking that the kingship should be abolished and the ancient rule of the High Priest be
re-established, since the two contestants for the crown "were seeking to
change their form of government in order that they might become a
nation of slaves" (*Ant* XIV iii 2 § 41). The claims of Hyrcanus were
advanced on the basis of his primogeniture and his peaceable nature,
whereas his brother was noted for his warlike disposition, as the
rebellions against him by his own subjects witnessed. To support
Hyrcanus, no less than a thousand "of the most reputable Jews"
chosen for the purpose by Antipater were presented to Pompey (§ 43).

Aristobulus, on the other hand, claimed that his brother had been
deposed for his ineffectiveness and weakness of character that "invited
contempt". If Aristobulus had not stepped in and taken over the reins of

government, others, less well disposed towards the Jews, might have ousted Hyrcanus. It appears from the slightly conflicting accounts offered by Josephus in *War* and *Antiquities*, that Aristobulus made a gross error of judgment in the presentation of his case. While Antipater fawned and flattered on behalf of his client, and brought along pious men who said they only wanted peace for their country and religious freedom, Aristobulus behaved truculently before the Roman general. One can almost see the shade of his mother Alexandra standing beside him:

". . . relying on the fact that Scaurus was open to bribery, Aristobulus appeared, arrayed in the most regal style imaginable. But feeling it beneath his dignity to play the courtier, and scorning to further his ends by a servility that humiliated his magnificence, he, on reaching the city of Dium (a city of the Decapolis), took himself off" (*War* I vi 4 § 132).

Antiquities has it that he called to his defence "some young swaggerers, who offensively displayed their purple robes, long hair, metal ornaments and other finery, which they wore as if they were marching in a festive procession instead of pleading their cause . . . without waiting for any of the things to be done of which Pompey had spoken to him, he came to the city of Dium (?), and from there set out for Judaea" (XIV iii 2 § 45–3 § 47).

Pompey took exception to Aristobulus and his protagonists, but at first dismissed the claimants courteously, with the promise that as soon as he had settled matters with the Nabateans, he would come personally to Judaea to resolve the quarrel between the brothers. However, Aristobulus's precipitant departure from Damascus seemed to imply that he was rushing off to prepare resistance against the Roman entry into Judaea. Pompey immediately changed his plans and, taking the army he had prepared to smash Arab resistance, chased after Aristobulus. The Hasmonean hot-head had played the diplomatic game as ineptly as his Idumaean opponent had displayed his native cunning. Antipater had sized up the international situation long before he presented himself before Pompey. He knew he was not dealing with some fraudulent pretender to a Seleucid throne who might be swept away tomorrow with the tide of battle. Rome had come to western Asia to stay, and for the time being Pompey was Rome. This was not the time to flaunt royal robes and rich play-boy aristocrats from Jerusalem in a pathetic gesture of self-sufficiency. The Roman officers would smile at this tinsel parade as disparagingly as Antipater must have watched Aristobulus's tactics.

Aristobulus made for the fortress of Alexandrium in the Jordan valley. It was virtually impregnable, surmounting a mountainous ridge jutting into the plain (Pl. 10). There at least he was safe, and with the respite that his eyrie gave him, came the cold chill of realisation that he had made a fatal error. His followers urged him to make his peace with the Romans, and when Pompey's messengers arrived demanding Aristobulus surrender the garrison, he did so without resistance. Nevertheless, he would not have been Salome's son if he had not made a last attempt to hold Jerusalem against the alien. He therefore rode up to the city and started to prepare its defences against the invader. Pompey moved on to Jericho, and at dawn the next day, he climbed the steep and barren path to Jerusalem (Pl. 11). At his approach, Aristobulus's nerve broke again and he went out to meet the advance party before the attack developed. He promised Pompey money from the Temple treasuries and an open city, surrendered with his own person to the Roman's will. Pompey despatched Gabinius to accept the tribute and occupy Jerusalem, but on his approach the more stubborn "royalists" refused him entry. Pompey was furious, clapped Aristobulus in chains, and prepared plans to storm the city.

Once more the old division of opinion among the Jews became evident. Most wanted peace and knew well that resistance to the invader would only bring more bloodshed and destruction. Among such were probably the party of the Pharisees and supporters of Hyrcanus. On the other side, the fanatical "royalists" of Aristobulus's ruling faction rushed to the Temple mount and cut the bridge by which it was connected with the western hill, preparing for a siege. They were thus in a strong position defensively, since natural ravines encompassed the mount on the east (the Kidron: Pl. 12) and the west (the so-called Tyropoean or "Cheese-makers'" Valley), and walls and ditches shielded the other two sides. In the north-west, there stood the Hasmonean fortress of Baris (later called Antonia by Herod), but it was nevertheless on the north that Pompey made his main attack, since the ground there rises naturally as high as the Temple mount (Fig. 8).

It was three months before the Romans were able to break through on to the Temple mount from the north (*War* I vii 4 §149). The honour of being the first to enter the sacred precinct fell to one Faustus Cornelius, closely followed by two centurions and their companies.

They formed a circle round the Temple court and systematically butchered everyone therein. The priests, we are told, went on with their sacrifices and other religious rites to the end, being cut down even as they poured the libations and burned the incense, "putting the worship of the deity above their own preservation" (§150). Any that did escape the holocaust within the Temple area "perished by their countrymen of the opposite faction".

The numbers of Roman dead were small, but of the Jews a figure of twelve thousand is given (§151). But to later pious historians the worst part of the affair was that the Roman Pompey dared to enter the inviolable sanctuary of the Holy of Holies, the innermost shrine of the Temple. Even the High Priest was allowed entry only once a year into the dwelling of the god himself. Pompey, however, must have found little to interest him, and we are told that he walked out of the Temple without touching any of its gold utensils or sacred treasures. Rather did he command that the day-to-day routine should recommence immediately after ritual cleansing, and thus, says Josephus, "like the able general he was, he conciliated the people". He also pleased the Pharisees by reinstating Hyrcanus as High Priest, "in return for his enthusiastic support of the siege, particularly in detaching from Aristobulus large numbers of the rural population who were anxious to join his standard" (§153).

Aristobulus and his family, including two daughters and two sons, were taken as prisoners to Rome, although one son, Alexander, escaped on the way. In the triumphal procession of 61 BC, the Hasmonean prince was displayed to the Roman people along with other prisoners. Jerusalem was made tributary to the Romans, and Judaea was added to the Roman province of Syria. All the coastal cities were taken out of Jewish control, as well as Samaria in the north and all the gentile cities of Transjordan. The whole province Pompey put under the administration of Scaurus who, with two legions, was now expected to control the area from Egypt to the Euphrates (§ 154ff.; Ant XIV iv 4 § 74ff.).

Looking in more detail for the moment at the territorial and political position now obtaining in Palestine after the Roman reorganisation of 63 BC, we have the following picture. The Hasmonean conquests had for the most part now been lost to Judaea. The coastal cities were independent urban communities under the provincial administration, as were certain Hellenistic cities in Transjordan, like Scythopolis and Pella, which combined to form the "Ten Cities" (Decapolis: Fig. 7).

9 PETRA

(a) The entrance of the gorge leading into the city.

(b) The end of the gorge, and the first of the great rock-hewn tombs to greet the visitor on his entry into the city.

10　Looking towards Alexandrium from a position above the old Jericho–Jerusalem road.

They regarded this "liberation" by the Romans as the start of a new chapter in their history, and counted years from that time on as of the "Pompeian" era. The city of Samaria was similarly counted as an independent urban community, but the surrounding area was placed under the province of Syria. The religious cult on Mount Gerizim, whose temple had been destroyed by the Hasmoneans, was recommenced.

The Romans, like the Persians and Greeks before them, regarded religious tolerance as a mainstay of their imperial policy, for much the same practical reasons of "live and let live". As far as the Jews were concerned, the Roman administration allowed a natural political cohesion between Jerusalem and those parts of Palestine whose inhabitants looked to the Temple as the focus of their cult. Thus the High Priest had a suzerainty, under the provincial governor, over the old territory of Judah, with the addition of Peraea and Galilee. Peraea consisted of a strip of the southern and central land east of the Jordan, bordered on the south by the Nabatean State, still independent, and on the north by the territories of the Decapolis. Galilee owed religious allegiance to the High Priest, but was geographically separated from Judaea and Peraea. Since John Hyrcanus I had incorporated Idumaea forcibly into the Jewish community, this area continued as part of Judaea, ensuring the continuing influence of the Idumaean clan of Antipas in Jewish affairs. Furthermore, Antipater was soon able to make himself even more directly helpful to his Roman overlords and pave the way for himself and his family to supremacy in Judaea.

I

CHAPTER X

Antipater, the Idumaean Fox

The Judaean situation being for the moment resolved, the Romans under Scaurus were able to pursue their campaign against the Arabs. The Nabatean capital of Petra proved a difficult nut to crack, and for some time Scaurus ravaged the surrounding countryside, barren at the best of times. His army became short of food, and it seemed as though the Romans would have to withdraw and leave Aretas in peace for the moment in his rocky sanctuary. However, the Nabatean king's bosom friend and ally Antipater came to Scaurus's help by offering Judaean grain to sustain his troops, ostensibly at the direction of Hyrcanus, Aretas's other erstwhile confederate. Scaurus received the help graciously, and suggested that in view of the long-standing friendship between Antipater and the Arab king, he might like to negotiate a truce on the Roman's behalf. If Aretas would pay a substantial tribute, Scaurus would withdraw. We may imagine with what mixed feelings Antipater approached his old friend with this offer and with what lack of enthusiasm Aretas must have allowed him and his bodyguard through the Petra gorge for parley. That Antipater was successful and continued to draw breath says much for his resourcefulness and ready tongue, not to say courage. As far as the Romans were concerned, he had made a lasting impression of trustworthiness which was to stand him and his family in good stead in the years to come.

As we noted earlier, one of Aristobulus's sons, Alexander, had escaped whilst being carried as a prize of war back to Rome. In 57 BC, Alexander reappeared in Judaea and rallied the loyalists around the old Hasmonean standard once more. Clearly the few years of peace that had settled upon the country with the coming of the Romans merely cloaked the seething discontent within Jewry under Hyrcanus's rule. Josephus says that Alexander was able to fortify the strongholds of Alexandrium and Machaerus, and to collect no less than ten thousand heavily armed soldiers and fifteen hundred horses (*Ant* XIV v 2 § 83).

Despite the obvious exaggeration in numbers, it is clear that Alexander was able to count upon much financial support among the old "royalist" gentry of Judaea. We are told that he was even engaged upon restoring the walls of Jerusalem destroyed by Pompey before the Romans, under their newly appointed pro-consul of Syria, Aulus Gabinius, were able to offer Hyrcanus enough support to eject the intruder. Alexander was defeated just outside Jerusalem and withdrew with his remaining forces to Alexandrium, where he was besieged by the Romans.

At length, Alexander sent messengers to Gabinius, offering to surrender strongholds still under his control, including Alexandrium, in return for his free pardon. The Roman governor was assisted in his negotiations by Alexander's mother who had accompanied the Roman army to the Jordan plain. She had been left behind when Pompey took away her husband and their children as hostages to Rome, and was no doubt prevailed upon to act as peacemaker by the reminder that Aristobulus and the other children were still in Roman hands. Alexander was thus allowed to go free; Hyrcanus, on the other hand, was deprived of the kingship, despite his fidelity to the Roman overlord. He no longer had political authority over the areas owing religious allegiance to Jerusalem. Instead these were divided into five separate districts, administered overall by the provincial governor. Josephus reports that "the Jews welcomed their release from the rule of an individual and were, from that time forward, governed by an aristocracy" (*War* I viii 5 §170), that is, local priestly officials.

Gabinius's idea was presumably to separate religious from political jurisdiction among the Jews, a logical division of responsibilities more apparent to a Roman administrator than to a Jew. The Jewish State was merely an aspect of its religion, much as the quietist religionists on the one hand, and the "political" Jews, like Antipater and his successors, on the other, might have wished it otherwise. In any case, as it turned out the separation of religious Judaea into five independently administered districts was shortlived. Aristobulus and his other son, Antigonus, escaped from their Roman prison, and raised yet again the banner of revolt in Judaea. The ghost of Salome Alexandra must have rubbed her spectral hands with glee!

Of course, it was hopeless, but they made a brave show. Aristobulus headed for the ancestral refuge of Alexandrium and began to rebuild its fallen walls (*Ant* XIV vi 1 § 92ff.). Gabinius sent troops to the Jordan plain immediately, and Aristobulus promptly set off for Machaerus, on the other side of the Dead Sea. On the way, he took stock of his position and the patriots who had offered themselves to his cause. Unfortunately, that was all many of them had been able to bring, so he had reluctantly to send away all who were unarmed or lacking other equipment. With the remainder he turned to face the pursuing Romans, and suffered a heavy defeat. His followers scattered, while he himself managed to gain the temporary security of Machaerus. Those comparative few who had remained with him in his flight set to work restoring the fortifications as best they could. Still Aristobulus hoped to last out long enough to raise the country to his side, but after two days of siege, during which he was severely wounded, the Romans stormed through the walls and captured him and his son Antigonus (§ 96). Aristobulus was returned in chains to Rome, but on the intercession of his wife, his sons were permitted to remain in Judaea (§ 97).

One might have thought that the astute Romans would by now have learnt the mettle of the Hasmonean clan. The only good Hasmonean, they might have been expected to say, was a dead one. Hardly had Gabinius departed on an expedition against the Parthians—abandoned in favour of a more profitable operation to restore Ptolemy XI Auletes to his throne for ten thousand talents—than Alexander, Aristobulus's son, made another attempt to stir up a revolt. This time he was not directing the hatred of his Jewish followers against Hyrcanus and his Pharisaic supporters, but, more ominously, against the Romans. He and his cut-throats went through the country murdering every Roman they met, and finally besieging a party of them on Mount Gerizim in Samaritan territory (§100). This outbreak of vicious racialism was a foretaste of what was to come. Equally indicative of future events was Antipater's part in the affair. That ubiquitous helpmeet of the Romans, ostensibly acting for Hyrcanus, had already been of assistance to Gabinius on the Egyptian campaign to reinstate Ptolemy. He supplied food and money, and used his influence with the Jews above Pelusium (Fig. 6) to side with the Romans and, in their capacity of river-guards in Egypt, give them every help (§ 99). Now Gabinius asked Antipater to persuade the Jews with Alexander to put up their weapons and stop trying to resist the irresistible. He had some success, but his words were wasted upon Alexander who, with the remainder of his army, met Gabinius near Mount Tabor. The Jews never really had a chance, and the majority were cut to pieces, the survivors fleeing for their lives. Strangely enough, Alexander himself seems to have escaped punishment, and we hear of him marrying Alexandra, the High Priest's daughter, in the same year.

With such good service behind him, it is not surprising that Antipater was now able to emerge from behind the "front" of Hyrcanus and rule Judaea on his own account. Josephus says that "Gabinius then settled affairs at Jerusalem in accordance with the wishes of Antipater" (*Ant* XIV vi 4 § 103). Apparently these included cancelling the division of the Jewish community of Jerusalem into five independent districts and putting them once more under the control of the High Priest.

Gabinius was recalled to Rome and was succeeded by the triumvir, M. Licinius Crassus, in 54 BC. He took over the Syrian province in order to pursue the campaign against the Parthians, but first paid a call on the Jerusalem sanctuary to draw on its seemingly inexhaustible funds to finance the war. He took away the treasures that a wiser Pompey had left undisturbed. Josephus mentions particularly a bar of solid gold, which acted as a curtain rod supporting draperies of "admirable beauty and costly workmanship" (§ 107). The honest fellow whose task it was to supervise the Temple treasuries thought it best to buy off the Roman predator with the gold rather than risk his despoiling all the rich ornamentation of the sanctuary. In fact, it appears that nobody but the priest in charge knew of the existence of the golden bar since it was contained within a hollow wooden tube, which must have made it the more galling when the Roman broke his promise and carried off everything of value in the Temple (§ 109).

Josephus breaks off his story at this point to discourse on the wealth of the Jerusalem sanctuary:

"But no one need wonder that there was so much wealth in our Temple, for all the Jews throughout the habitable world, and those who worshipped God even in Asia and Europe, had been contributing to it for a very long time. And there is no lack of witnesses to the great amount of the sums mentioned (Josephus had said that Crassus stole two thousand talents of money, and gold amounting to eight thousand talents, as well as the gold rod worth 'many tens of thousands of drachmas'), nor have they been raised to so great a figure through boastfulness or exaggeration on our part, but there are many historians who bear us out . . ." (§ 110f.).

He adds further proof of the wealth that could be accumulated by popular Jewish donations to a common fund by pointing to the deposits on the island of Cos, the "Swiss numbered bank account" of Queen

Cleopatra III into which she had placed her personal wealth before her campaign against her erring son Ptolemy Lathyrus in 102 BC (see above, p. 111). He cites Strabo of Cappadocia as saying that Mithridates (VI, Eupator, who defeated the Romans in Asia Minor in 88 BC) sent to Cos and took the money that Queen Cleopatra had deposited there, "and eight hundred talents of the Jews" (§112). Josephus avows that this must have been public money of the Asian Jews donated for sacred purposes. It seems far more probable that the queen's Jewish generals Helkias and Ananias were following their regal mistress's good example and salting away their life savings for the rainy day that would certainly follow a failure to curb her son's ambitions.

That apart, it is certain that the Jerusalem sanctuary, for all its constant pillaging by foreign and native rulers, was an extremely wealthy institution. That alone should give more credence than has been fashionable among scholars to the famous Copper Scroll found in a cave near the Dead Sea in 1952 (Pl. 13ᵃ⋅ᵇ). On being cut open in 1955 and 1956, it revealed an inventory of sacred treasures, amounting to many tons of gold and silver, clearly referring to the deposits of wealth and ritual utensils of the Jerusalem Temple. These priceless objects, and the gold and silver bullion, had been deposited in various sites in and around the Holy City, and in fortresses and other locations in the area. One of the arguments offered against the inventory's validity (the work of a fanatic, as it was described by one interpreter) was that the amounts involved were too large to be credible. Perhaps a systematic search, or chance discovery, in one of the more outlying sites mentioned, will prove the scroll's list—and Josephus's estimates on this occasion— happily correct.

Crassus now took himself off to fight the Parthians and in the following year, 53 BC, was heavily defeated in the field, and perished along with most of his army. His quaestor, Cassius Longinus, managed to escape and returned to Syria to resist the Parthian invasion that followed their victory (§119). He had also to put down another Jewish rebellion, incited on the occasion of the Roman defeat by one Pitholaus who a year or two before had supported Aristobulus. He was captured and, on the advice of Antipater, Cassius put him to death. So we now have the Idumaean virtually acting as executioner of his own people on behalf of the national enemy. Of Antipater's standing with the Romans and his own people Josephus says: "he had at that time great influence with him (Cassius), and was then held in the greatest esteem by the Idu-

maeans also, from among whom he took a wife of a distinguished
Arab family, named Cypros, and by her had four sons, Phasael, Herod,
who later became king, Joseph and Pheroras, and a daughter, Salome.
This Antipater had formed relations of friendship and hospitality with
other princes, especially with the king of the Arabs, the same to whom he
had entrusted his children when making war on Aristobulus" (§ 121f.).

Antipater's political acumen was to be demonstrated within a few
years to even greater effect. He was obliged to make a sudden change of
loyalties and do it in such a way as to appear no less a friend to the new
despot than he had been to the old, and, above all, to be sure that the
successor had come to stay. His son Herod the Great brought this
political pirouetting to a fine art, as we shall see. But he had an excellent
mentor in his father.

In Italy, events were moving inexorably towards civil war. A
frustrated Senate declared Caesar a public enemy on 7th January 49
BC. Pompey's friends had thrust the sword of State into his not unwilling
hands, and four days later, Caesar crossed the frontier at the river
Rubicon (Fig. 6) to pose as the champion of an outraged constitution.

Caesar's speed of advance caught Pompey off balance and made him
despair of offering resistance in Italy. He decided to cross into Greece.
The capital fell without a blow to Caesar, who immediately took over
the reins of government. But the eastern provinces, scene of so many of
Pompey's earlier successes, with their seemingly inexhaustible reserves
of men, money and ships, were solidly pro-Pompey.

Aristobulus was still captive in Rome, and seemed to Caesar a useful
ally to deal with the Pompeians in that part of the world he knew best.
Caesar therefore put two legions at his disposal and thus gave him the
means to avenge himself on the man who had deprived him of his
office of priest-king in Jerusalem. However, before Aristobulus had a
chance to set out on his mission, he was poisoned by Pompey's friends in
Rome. To crown the career of this extraordinary man, who had spent
most of his life fighting the hated enemies of the Jews, and who at the
end was preparing to sally forth at the bidding of a Roman general to
harry his political opponent, he was given a royal interment in Jerusalem
at the behest of his gentile friends. His body was preserved in honey by
Caesar's partisans for a long while, an ancient and well-attested method
of conserving corpses, and eventually sent back on Antony's instructions
to be buried among the royal tombs of Jerusalem (§124). Salome
Alexandra must still be chuckling in her Hasmonean heaven.

Aristobulus's son Alexander was in Antioch, and had presumably been briefed for an important part in his father's campaign against Pompey in Syria. His removal from the scene followed quickly upon his father's death. Pompey's father-in-law, Q. Metellus Scipio, the proconsul of Syria in the years 49–48 BC, carried out an execution order already served on Alexander by Pompey for his previous offences against the Romans. Of his brother Antigonus and his sisters, still in the care of their mother in Ascalon, we have in our records some further information. It appears that a local prince of Chalcis, at the foot of Mount Lebanon, by name, Ptolemy, son of Mennaeus, resolved to take them into his custody, and sent his son Philippion to Ascalon to wrest them forcibly from their mother's side. We may imagine the anguish of mind suffered by this unhappy woman at the appearance of this foreigner at her last refuge, demanding the surrender of her children. She had already risked so much personal danger and public obloquy in her apparent siding with the Roman enemy to try to save her husband and sons from their suicidal challenges to an alien authority. Surely now it might have seemed she could live out her remaining days in peace, in the hope that the Hasmonean madness had burnt itself out with the death of her husband and her son Alexander. Here, in the warm coastal plain of Palestine, she must have hoped to enjoy the company of her remaining son and daughters, and let the world go by.

It was not to be, but the story had an even more poignant sequel. Part at least of Ptolemy's plan was to marry the younger of the daughters, Alexandra. But Philippion fell in love with the girl himself, and perhaps to save her from an older man's embraces as much as to fulfil his own passion, he married her in defiance of his father's command. Ptolemy had his son executed for his presumption and took the girl to his bed. Whatever favours she was able to bestow upon her lover's murderer, Ptolemy wheedled from her by promising to act as a faithful guardian to her brother and sister (§126; cp. *War* I ix 2 §185f.).

Antipater must have watched events in Rome and the eastern empire with some anxiety. When in August 48 BC, Pompey was defeated at Pharsalus (Fig. 6), and afterwards murdered on the coast of the Egyptian Delta, he knew that the time had come to show his allegiance to the new master in no uncertain way. The opportunity soon offered. Mithridates of Pergamon had the task of taking the important frontier post of Egypt at Pelusium, on the eastern side of the Delta, to assist Caesar, himself engaged on the other side at Alexandria (Fig. 5).

Resistance by the local inhabitants of Pelusium necessitated a full-scale attack for which Mithridates was insufficiently supported by his auxiliary force. Antipater appeared on the scene with three thousand heavily armed Jewish soldiers, and used his influence with his Arab friends to lend their support also. None showed more bravery in the field for his new-found Roman master than the Jewish Antipater. He was the first to pull down part of the wall of Pelusium and force an entrance for others to follow. Having thus broken through into Egypt, the allies pressed on to meet Caesar, only to find that the Jews of a place called Onias, not far from Memphis, resisted their passage. Antipater managed, however, to win them over, not least by brandishing a letter from their High Priest in Jerusalem, Hyrcanus, urging them to be friendly to Caesar and to furnish supplies and hospitality to his armies (§131). Besides, Antipater pointed out, were they not all Jews, and so must stick together? The success of this appeal to their common race in Caesar's name also won over the Jews around Memphis itself, who not only invited Mithridates into their city, but even joined his army (§132).

Having passed round the Delta, Mithridates and Antipater were heavily engaged at a place of uncertain location called the Camp of the Jews, the one commanding the right wing, the other the left. Mithridates found himself in difficulties during the battle, when the right wing collapsed. Antipater's men had been more successful and now came to his ally's rescue, running along the river bank and routing the common enemy. He pursued them to their camp, and sent off a party to relieve Mithridates himself who had become separated from the main body of his troops. This officer was so grateful for the help thus afforded by his Jewish friend that he sat down there and then and composed a letter to Caesar, full of praise of Antipater, declaring that he had been responsible for the victory and their safety. The Roman general was much gratified and, as a mark of his appreciation, gave Antipater all "the most dangerous tasks throughout the entire war". "The natural result", Josephus adds, "was that Antipater was wounded in some of the battles" (§136). Nevertheless, having survived, and helped Caesar to final victory, the Roman showed his gratitude rather more profitably for Antipater by making him a Roman citizen and exempting him from taxation everywhere (§137). It is interesting to note that Antipater's use of Hyrcanus's authority to win over the Egyptian Jews was so pronounced as to give rise to the unlikely tradition that Hyrcanus himself was engaged in the fighting with Mithridates (§138f.). At all events, Caesar acceded to Antipater's request that he confirm Hyrcanus in his high priesthood (§137; cp. *War* I ix 5 §194).

Antigonus, Aristobulus's surviving son, watched the rise of Antipater in Caesar's esteem with growing resentment. It was, after all, in Caesar's service that his father and brother Alexander had lost their lives, the one by poisoning on the eve of his campaign against Pompey in Syria, the other by execution in Antioch by Scipio. Yet here was this Idumaean and his weakling protégé, Hyrcanus, Antigonus's uncle, receiving all the honours at Caesar's hand. Antigonus made his protest to the Roman along these lines and launched into an attack on the morals and perfidy of Caesar's newfound friends, Antipater and Hyrcanus, who had banished Antigonus from his native land, done violence to their own people, and, furthermore, had only at the last moment offered their support to Caesar when they saw the futility of continuing their previous allegiance to Pompey and were afraid for their own safety (*War* I x 1 §196).

Josephus suggests that Antigonus would have done better confining his words to lamenting for his dead father and brother and pleading a hard-luck story, rather than attacking the wily Antipater, at least to his face. The Idumaean sprang to his feet, and with a wonderful gesture of injured innocence and complete irrelevance to the charges laid against him, flung aside his robes and displayed his honourable scars of battle before the astonished company. His loyalty, he said, needed no words from him; his body cried it aloud, were he to hold his peace (§197).

Having thus captured the sympathetic attention of his audience, Antipater then turned to the wretched Antigonus, his voice rising in simulated disbelief and scorn. He professed himself utterly astounded by the audacity of this man. His father had been an avowed enemy of Rome, a fugitive from Roman justice, and Antigonus had inherited all his father's vices, among which his love of rebellion and sedition was foremost. And now, here he was, asking for preferment over the loyal Hyrcanus. Why, he ought to be thankful to be allowed to live, let alone plot for power simply in order to sow more trouble among the Jews and arouse them against the authority he was now petitioning! (§198).

Antigonus had lost. Caesar decreed Hyrcanus to be the more deserving claimant to high-priestly office. To Antipater he left the choice of his own position in the imperial administration. With downcast eyes and deferential manner, the faithful Idumaean demurred: "it rested with him who conferred the honour to fix its degree", rather as the modern taxi driver in that part of the world will leave it to his fare's generosity to fix the price, and express astonished disbelief if the proffered amount is less than twice the norm. Such demonstrations of disappointment were not called for from Antipater, however. Caesar gave him no less than the procuratorship or principal administrative post of all Judaea. He was further authorized to rebuild the walls of Jerusalem, and, that all men should know the favour in which he and Hyrcanus were held by Caesar, "these honours were to be engraven in the Capitol, as a memorial of his own justice and of Antipater's valour" (§ 200). The Idumaean had arrived at the corridors of imperial power.

Josephus quotes a whole series of decrees made by Caesar in the Jews' favour which, if true, are quite astonishing, and go far beyond mere rewards for military help in the Egyptian campaign. It is clear that the Roman was intent on offering this strange and rebellious people a status in the empire and a self-respect which would make them loyal subjects and upholders of peace and order in the eastern lands. He seemed to believe that, given the chance of achieving political adulthood, the Jewish nation would identify their continued well-being with that of the empire as a whole, and with that of their immediate neighbours in particular. To emphasise that degree of responsibility, the Jews were no longer a *demos*, a community of citizens of Jerusalem, but an *ethnos*, a tribal race under their own native ruler. Thus Hyrcanus was now the Ethnarch of the Jews, as well as their High Priest, and that office was hereditary. Furthermore, he and his descendants were technically "allies" or "confederates" of Rome. This meant, in effect, that his rule no longer depended upon the assent of his people, still very much divided in their attitude to the monarchical rule of the High Priests and of the Hasmoneans in particular. From now on, rule was given and sustained by Rome itself, to whom Hyrcanus and his successors could make direct appeal for help.

Similarly, Antipater, by being made a citizen of Rome, also had direct access to Caesar and could call upon the protection of the empire in the event of dispute between himself and the high priesthood or the Jews themselves. As for the nation, its borders were extended in Galilee, and Joppa was once more included in Jewish territory, so that she again had her outlet to the sea. The land was exempted from compulsory billeting of Roman troops in winter and the Jews excused from military service because of the restricting nature of their religious customs. Complete religious freedom was allowed to Jews of the Jerusalem community, that they be in no way hindered from performing their worship and rituals. Furthermore, and most significantly, other peoples in the vicinity were informed of the existence of these decrees, inscribed tablets being set up for this purpose in the sanctuaries of such traditionally hostile cities as Sidon, Tyre and Ascalon. Jews here and, indeed, anywhere in the Diaspora, could now count upon the advice and support of the high priesthood in their cult centre of Jerusalem, whose decrees were to be considered as having the authority of Rome. So, whereas Jews in different parts of the civilised world had before been linked merely by their common religion and veneration of the Temple of Jerusalem, but were subject to varying attitudes and treatment from the gentiles among whom they lived, now they became an ethnic group with political rights all their own, enforceable by Rome on intercession from their own central authority. The pressing need for Jews, say in Egypt, more fully to integrate with their non-Jewish neighbours for their own security no longer prevailed. The Chosen Race now not only had the special blessing of God, but of Rome. Let ordinary mortals beware: to be a Jew was second only to being a Roman citizen! At a single stroke of the pen, Caesar had destroyed for ever the one hope that Jewry would eventually be merged with non-Jews in the world at large, or that Jews would sink their racial and religious differences from gentiles for the sake of living together in harmony. The terrible revolts of AD 66 and 132 and their aftermath of anti-Semitism, and the largely self-imposed ghetto existence of so many millions of European and Asian Jews thereafter, were now inevitable. Caesar, like imperial rulers before and after him, had succumbed to the fatal error of believing that the Jew of the post-exilic period sought only religious freedom within a politically stable society. Give him leave to worship his tribal god in his own quaint fashion, and allow him the self-respect of a mature citizen of someone else's empire, and he will remain a loyal servant of his political master, and resist all temptations to rebel against the hand that feeds him. But the Romans were to learn, as the Persians and Greeks learnt to their cost before, that to the Jew, Yahweh is not just a tribal deity, but the God of the Universe. His Chosen People are not just another *ethnos*: they are the Sons of God, destined to rule the world. Jerusalem is not only the cultural centre of the Jews, it is the City of God, from which His rule will reach out to embrace all men.

Worship of the one God would only be complete for the Jew when all men bent the knee in adoration of his Saviour. Caesar, no more than Cyrus, was but a divinely appointed servant, a tool in the hands of the Creator, destined to be cast aside when the fashioning of His kingdom on earth was complete. Then real power would lie in the hands of God's Anointed, the Jewish priest-king to whom all man-made institutions would be subject.

Viewed in such terms, the weak Hyrcanus was a pitiable creature. He was never more than the puppet of Antipater, a respectable "front" for the Idumaean's political manoeuvring. As soon as Caesar had left Syria, Antipater returned to Judaea to take over the reins of government with an iron hand. He set in hand the rebuilding of Jerusalem's walls, and then toured the whole area making his presence felt, "suppressing disorders therein by both threatening and advising the people to remain quiet" (*Ant* XIV ix 1 § 156). He warned them that if they remained loyal to Hyrcanus, they could live undisturbed in enjoyment of their own possessions, but if they clung to the hope of achieving something by rebellion, they would find in Antipater "a master in place of a protector, and in Hyrcanus a tyrant in place of a king, and in the Romans and Caeser bitter enemies in place of rulers" (§157).

The time had now come to replace Hyrcanus as wielder of any real power. Antipater found him, as Josephus says, "indolent and without the energy necessary to a king" (*War* I x 4 § 203), which is, of course, why he had proved so useful to the Idumaean in the past. Now Antipater brought control of civic affairs in Jerusalem more firmly into the family by appointing his own son Phasael as governor of Jerusalem and its environs (§203). And to Galilee he sent another son, as yet only a stripling, but "a young man of spirit, who quickly found an opportunity for showing his prowess" (*Ant* XIV ix 2 §159). His name was Herod. Another evil genius had been launched upon the Judaean scene.

CHAPTER XI

The schooling of Herod

The young Herod started well. Hearing that the Syrians were being plagued by a gang of bandits terrorizing the villages, he routed them out and killed most of them, including their leader. This action brought Herod not only the gratitude of the local inhabitants, who could now feel safe in their beds at night, but the approval of the Roman governor of Syria, Sextus Caesar, a kinsman of the great general. Herod's brother, Phasael, sought also to win popular acclaim in his toparchy of Jerusalem. Not having any bandits to liquidate, he achieved his aim by exercising his power over the inhabitants with the maximum consideration for their feelings, so that "they felt very friendly towards him" (*Ant* XIV ix 2 §161).

Such wide popularity accorded the sons enhanced Antipater's own position, but it also brought inevitably the envy and discontent of Jewish leaders, Pharisees and Sadducees. It was now only too obvious that Hyrcanus was nothing more than a tool of Antipater and his sons, in whom alone real power rested. They therefore seized upon Herod's summary treatment of the bandit leader in the north to arraign him before the Sanhedrin, the supreme legislative and judicial body of the Jewish state, convened at Jerusalem. The charge was that Herod had killed men in supposed violation of the Law, without their first having been condemned by the Sanhedrin (§167). Clearly the real intention was to test the respective authorities of the high priesthood of Hyrcanus and the civil government of Antipater and his filial designates. The mutual arrangement hitherto prevailing, whereby Hyrcanus allowed himself to be manipulated by his stronger-willed confederate and to serve as the Idumaean's cloak of religious respectability, had turned sour. The real state of affairs was too blatant to serve any more as a blind, and the Jerusalem leaders were determined to force a challenge between the two arms of the State. They were, of course, far too late. Hyrcanus was but a figurehead, and had been for some time. Antipater had not only the Jewish army but the authority of Rome behind him.

The summons was issued, and on the advice of his father, Herod made a grudging appearance before the Sanhedrin. He had taken the wise precaution beforehand of posting garrisons around his toparchy of Galilee, to dissuade any take-over during his absence. He arrived in Jerusalem with a bodyguard, sufficiently strong to deter the execution of adverse court decision, but at the same time not so large as to give the impression that he had come to unseat Hyrcanus from the throne (§ 169). The worthy councillors were overawed by his appearance and somewhat at a loss on how to proceed. As one spokesman is reputed to have said, "I cannot myself recall, nor I suppose can any of you, ever seeing someone summoned before the Sanhedrin present himself in such a manner. Normally an arraigned person appears in the garb of a suppliant for mercy, with unkempt hair and wearing black garments. But this fine fellow Herod, who has been accused of murder no less, stands here clothed in purple, with his hair carefully arranged, and surrounded by soldiers ready to kill us if we judge against him . . ." (§ 172f.). He went on to warn the company that if Herod were acquitted and allowed to leave, it would not be long before he returned, intent on seizing absolute power himself—a remarkably accurate prophecy, as it turned out.

Just how and why he was, in fact, released, is variously explained in Josephus's works. It is said that Hyrcanus acquitted Herod because he "loved him" (War I x 7 § 211); elsewhere, that, for the same reason, he postponed the trial for another day and in the meantime urged Herod to escape with his troops while he had the chance (Ant XIV ix 5 § 177). Probably the real incentive to letting Herod go unscathed lay in a firm directive from Sextus Caesar, the Syrian proconsul to Hyrcanus, threatening him with dire punishments if anything happened to his young friend (§ 170). In any event, Herod left Jerusalem without more ado and made straight for Damascus and his Roman protector. In return for money, the proconsul conferred upon Herod the governorship of Coele-Syria and Samaria. Rightly or wrongly, Herod took this as moral support to take vengeance on the Jerusalem leaders and their king, Hyrcanus. Still burning under the insult he had suffered in being brought to stand trial like a common criminal, he marched upon Jerusalem with an army. His father and brother rushed to head him off before his impetuosity brought ruin on himself, the family and the whole country. At the tender age of twenty-five, Herod had not yet learnt to temper his rash courage with discretion. The days would come when no man would be able to calm his paranoiac rage, nor stay his hand from maniacal acts of blind vengeance, but before he could exercise such despotic power with impunity, he had to climb higher on the ladder of tyranny.

Antipater and Phasael managed to calm Herod down. Leave the matter where it is, they urged. By your presence at the gates of Jerusalem you have struck terror into the craven heart of Hyrcanus. After all, he is king and High Priest, at least in name, and commands the sympathies and allegiance of the people by virtue of his office. For all you know, he might even have the support of God who orders the fortunes of war, and you might conceivably lose the battle. As it is, you have shown your strength, you have escaped the power of the Sanhedrin; be thankful and go home (§ 181ff.). Herod went, snarling his defiance. For the time being he would wait, but his craving for revenge remained unsated and the day would come when none should restrain him from its bloody satisfaction. However, before then, greater events abroad were to convulse the eastern empire.

On the Ides of March, 44 BC, Caesar was murdered, and those responsible moved to take over the eastern parts of the empire. Among them was one, C. Cassius Longinus, who had been a previous administrator of Syria from 53–51 BC. For two years he was proconsul of this area, and made his prime object the ruthless milking of Judaea of seven hundred talents in taxes. He looked, naturally enough, to his procurator to organise the exaction of this vast sum, and Antipater had no option but to obey. But no one knew better than the rich Idumaean that there is no surer way of courting disfavour among one's subjects than by heavy taxation, and that in a situation already fraught with tension and general distrust of himself and his sons, to have to set about this unwelcome task could only cause more trouble. He was at least able to unload part of the opprobrium on one of Hyrcanus's supporters named Malichus, whom he ordered to collect a proportion of the money. But the remainder fell to the lot of his sons. It went especially hard on poor Phasael who had been all along courting favour in Jerusalem by trying not to lean too hard on the citizens in such sensitive matters of tax-collection. Herod, on the other hand, worried not at all. He raised his hundred talents from Galilee before all the others, "and became especially friendly with Cassius" as a result (*Ant* XIV xi 2 § 274). As Josephus says, he bought Roman esteem with other people's money.

Other city governors were not so fortunate—or ruthless. A number

11 The old road from Jerusalem to Jericho, where it debouches on to the Jericho plain.

12   The south-eastern corner (The Pinnacle) of the Temple area, seen from the other side of the Kidron Valley.

were sold as slaves for not fulfilling their quota, and Malichus so incurred the wrath of Cassius by his tardiness that he was on the point of being executed, when Hyrcanus, supposedly at Antipater's instigation, saved the situation by sending along a hundred talents of his own money to buy his safety. If the Idumaean really was instrumental in saving Malichus's life, he was ill-rewarded, for the ungrateful fellow began eliciting support for a rebellion against Antipater immediately Cassius had left Judaea. It was not difficult to play on the outraged emotions of those who had suffered badly in the tax levy and to find Jews willing to try and oust Antipater from office. The intended victim heard of the plot in time, however, and immediately sought help from his Arab friends across the Jordan. As it turned out, he had no need of their military assistance, since Malichus, realising the plans had been compromised, cancelled the operation, and denied under oath before Antipater and his sons that he had contemplated rebellion. How could he have entertained such a notion, he protested, "with Phasael guarding Jerusalem and Herod having the custody of the arms?" (§ 287). He was given the benefit of the doubt, but Malichus was too confident of popular support to let the matter rest there.

One day, when Antipater, Malichus, and Hyrcanus were dining together at the High Priest's house, Malichus bribed the butler to slip poison into Antipater's cup. In the uproar that ensued, Malichus busied himself restoring order in the city, and again later emphatically denied any knowledge of the affair before Herod and Phasael. Herod was characteristically minded to take vengeance straight away and lead an army against Malichus, despite his considerable following in the country. Phasael, however, as on the previous occasion, tried to restrain his younger brother. He did not want to spark off a civil war, and suggested that they should seem to accept Malichus's denial of complicity and quietly seek another way of taking their revenge.

There then followed a cat-and-mouse game between Herod and his intended victim which, if it does not redound to the moral credit of either party, illustrates vividly the need for circumspection in dealing with the popular heroes of a country needing little to push it over the edge into civil war. It shows, too, that the young and impetuous Herod was growing up and learning that guile can be the handmaid, and at times the equal, of naked violence.

When, at the next Feast of Tabernacles in October 43 BC, Herod came to Jerusalem, he arrived suitably guarded with his retinue of

K

armed mercenaries. Malichus took fright and urged Hyrcanus to bar
them entry. Hyrcanus, who wanted no trouble, and particularly at such
a time when patriotic emotions and religious sensibilities ran high,
acceded to his friend's request on the grounds that foreigners in a state
of ritual impurity could not be allowed entry into the Holy City during
the Festival. Herod took not the slightest heed. When night fell he led
his men into the city, and made sure that Malichus knew of his presence.
The man was petrified with terror, and went nowhere without a bodyguard. Still he protested his innocence of Antipater's murder, and
redoubled his demonstrations of lamentation for the good man's
passing. For his part, Herod masked his hatred behind a show of
friendliness; but the hand that grasped the arm of his father's murderer
in greeting was icy. Malichus shivered and drew his robes more tightly
about him.

It is the measure of Herod's newly acquired self-control that he was
able to keep up the pretence during that visit, and laid his plans carefully for making the murder he intended the responsibility of the
Roman proconsul. He reported the death of his father to Cassius who
sent back the answer he wanted: "Take revenge on the murderer."
Having himself no love for Malichus, Cassius commanded his tribunes
to give Herod every possible assistance in the execution (*War* I x 6
§ 230). A suitable occasion arrived when, later in 43 BC, the nobles of
Syria crowded around Cassius in Tyre to offer their gifts and congratula-
tions on his taking Laodicea (Fig. 6). Malichus himself had a desperate
scheme to carry into operation. His son was a hostage in Tyre at the
time, and he planned to effect his secret escape and flee with him back
to Judaea. There he intended raising a popular revolt against the
Romans as soon as Cassius became preoccupied with his war against
Antony. A more prudent—or less courageous—man would have stayed
well away from Tyre and left his son to his fate.

Herod arranged a dinner party. This gave him a pretext for circulating
those tribunes whom Cassius had commanded to afford Herod assistance
in killing Malichus. Ostensibly handing our invitations, the messenger
was in fact conveying the time and place of the planned execution.
Herod, Hyrcanus and the conspirators foregathered on the sea-shore
that evening and awaited the arrival of their fellow-guest. As the time
approached, Herod drew Hyrcanus, apparently ignorant of the plot,
aside from the tribunes, who silently unsheathed their swords beneath
their cloaks. Malichus arrived and the tribunes moved forward to greet

him. Then they struck together, plunging their blades repeatedly into their victim's body, sharing thus the honour of carrying out their Roman master's command. Herod smiled in the darkness ; revenge was doubly sweet when the blood-guilt lay on the heads of others.

Poor Hyrcanus was terrified, and swooned on the spot. When the company managed to bring him round—not without difficulty, as Josephus remarks (§ 234)—he asked by whose authority Malichus had been killed. A tribune proudly replied that it was done on Cassius's orders. "Then", said Hyrcanus, "Cassius has saved both me and my country, by destroying one who conspired against both" (§ 235). Our historian expresses some reasonable doubt whether he thus expressed his real opinion or merely acquiesced in the deed through fear. Equally unclear is how far Hyrcanus had been party to Malichus's planned anti-Roman revolt. When Cassius left Syria the following year, 42 BC, for what was to be his final encounter with Mark Antony (Pl. 15a.) and Octavian at Philippi, a certain Helix, a partisan of the dead Malichus, rose against Phasael in Jerusalem. The troops at his command were Hyrcanus's, left under his charge to look after the High Priest's interests while he was away in Tyre. Furthermore, Malichus's brother took over certain fortresses in Judaea, including the mighty Masada by the Dead Sea. The whole revolt was thus on a large scale and well planned in advance, and Hyrcanus must have known something of it. Phasael managed to put down the revolt by himself—Herod was sick at the time in Damascus— and then turned on Hyrcanus demanding to know how he could show such ingratitude to his Idumaean friends in abetting the rebels (§ 237).

It would seem also that Antigonus, of the other branch of the Hasmonean family, was involved in the move to oust the Romans and their Quislings. Upon his restoration to health, Herod set about clearing the rebels from the fortresses, among them the ruler of Tyre, one Marion, whom Cassius had appointed to his post. Marion had conspired, along with Fabius, the Roman general at Damascus, and Ptolemy, son of Mennaeus, to promote the interests of Antigonus, the dead Aristobulus's surviving son. It will be remembered that Ptolemy had married his sister Alexandra, and at the time had promised to look after her family. The conspirators now brought Antigonus forward to rally support from the Jewish malcontents, smarting under combined Idumaean and Roman domination. However, Herod and his brother were too firmly in command just then to offer much chance of success to a patriotic uprising of this kind. Antigonus was defeated in battle before he was able even to get beyond the Judaean frontier (*Ant* XIV xii 1 § 299), and retired once more to the sidelines.

At this point Herod again demonstrated his growth in political acumen. This last effort to re-establish Hasmonean suzerainty over the country reminded Herod of the psychological weakness of his position. He may have had the goodwill of the Romans and an effective mercenary fighting force, but he never deluded himself into believing that the bulk of the Jewish people loved him or his brother. The Edomites had always been the political enemies of Israel; their latter-day representatives were no less hated. Everyone knew that the present High Priest-King, Hyrcanus, was merely a tool of Idumaean power, howbeit of recent times a somewhat restive one. He was too closely linked to the Herod clan to offer the religious Jew any hope of a resurgence of the old Maccabean glory, a fulfilment of the messianic dream of a Jewish-dominated world order. Herod realised that he must make a bid for the affections of the people if he was to continue in power; he must become somehow more identified with Judaism and the Jews, even though it meant suppressing his traditional Arab contempt for the race. Much of his subsequent extravagant glorification of things Jewish, particularly in his grandiose building schemes like the reconstruction of the Jerusalem sanctuary, stems from his trying to be more Jewish than the Jews, another David, Solomon, and Judas Maccabeus, rolled into one. It was perhaps his failure in this regard that, more than any other cause, drove him eventually to the homicidal mania that destroyed his family and himself.

His first move to win for himself some of the old Hasmonean charisma was to become one of the family. He announced his betrothal to a daughter of Alexander, Aristobulus's son, Mariamne by name, although he was, in fact, already married to a Jerusalemite, called Doris. The announcement brought instant favour, we are told: "even those who had hitherto stood aloof were now reconciled by his marriage into the family of Hyrcanus" (*War* I xii 3 § 240). The marriage itself was not destined to take place for some five years, and then in circumstances that aborted its purpose of reconciliation. Just as Herod was about to break into Jerusalem at the end of a devastating siege, he took advantage of a lull in the operations to rush off to Samaria and consummate the union he had planned, and by which he fondly hoped to win popular acclaim amid the smoking ruins of his capital city. Such was the extent of the man's need to be accepted as a Jew, and his almost pathetic incapacity to understand the mind of Jewry.

The victory of Mark Antony and C. Julius Caesar Octavianus at Philippi in 42 BC upset the whole system of alliances in the East. Control of Asia now fell to Antony, and the local rulers hastened to Bithynia to declare their new allegiance. Among them were spokesmen for the Jews and with them their rulers, each accusing the others of perfidy. Particularly outspoken were the opponents of Herod and Phasael, saying that they had deprived their High Priest, Hyrcanus, of all but the trappings of power. But they were cut short in their entreaties by the appearance of Herod himself, who won Antony's favour with large bribes, and this induced the general to deny the Jewish complainants further audiences. Later, near Antioch, a hundred Jewish officials approached Antony and laid accusation against the Idumaean brothers. On this occasion Herod and Phasael had the active support of Hyrcanus, who now considered Herod one of the family. When asked by Antony for his opinion, the High Priest affirmed that Herod and his brother were best fitted to rule the Jews. Antony forthwith created them tetrarchs, entrusting to them the whole of the territory of Judaea (§ 244), and was pleased to do so, not least because of the friendly relations he had already enjoyed with their far-seeing father, Antipater.

The deputation gave vent to their indignation and fifteen of the more outspoken were clapped in chains and condemned to death. Only Herod's intervention saved them (*Ant* XIV xiii 1 § 326). At the time, Antony was even less inclined to bother with the wrangling of the Jewish antagonists since he had entered upon his fatal relationship with the Egyptian queen Cleopatra (Pl. 15b.), whom he had summoned in the late summer of 41 BC to answer an unfounded charge of aiding Cassius. He showed even less patience with the Jewish malcontents when a second embassy of a thousand waited upon him in Tyre, where he had broken his journey to Jerusalem. On this occasion he could not bear the clamour of their demonstration, let alone listen to their pleas, and he told the governor of Tyre to chase them away and flog any his men managed to catch. Above all, he had to make them understand that his newly appointed Idumaean tetrarchs had Antony's full support, and that was to be an end to the affair.

Before the governor could set his riot squad to work, Herod and Hyrcanus met the deputation on the sea shore, and urged them to disperse before they brought more trouble on themselves and those they represented. This only roused them to more noisy anger, and Antony ordered his troops to break up the crowd and cut down any who resisted. Despite the casualties in dead and wounded and the hostages taken by the military, the disturbance continued throughout the city. Thoroughly exasperated, Antony put the prisoners to death (§ 327ff.).

Behind the seething discontent of a large faction of the Jewish people there stood, of course, the heroic figure of Antigonus and those who supported his claim to the high priesthood. As long as Antony remained in Syria and lent his authority to Herod and Phasael, Antigonus had no chance of taking effective action. However, a surprise element was entering Asian affairs which would give the Hasmonean his opportunity of temporary success. While Antony dallied in Alexandria with his regal mistress, leaving his army in Syria to look after itself, the Parthians appeared once more on the scene. They invaded Roman provinces in the Near East, occupying Syria in 40 BC. Antigonus, with the support of Ptolemy's son, Lysanias, who had by now succeeded to the throne, offered the Parthians a handsome bribe of a thousand talents and five hundred women, if they would deprive Hyrcanus of power, destroy Herod, and make Antigonus High Priest and King of the Jews. They agreed, and while his new allies were still in North Syria, Antigonus collected supporters in Judaea and marched upon Jerusalem. First an advance force, then the larger party engaged Phasael, Herod and Hyrcanus in the city. There was much street fighting, intensified as pilgrims, many of them armed, flocked in from the country for the festival of Pentecost. Then the Parthians arrived on the scene, ostensibly to calm the situation, but actually to carry out their side of the bargain with Antigonus.

An official with five hundred horsemen sought admission to the city as a mediator, and, urged to do so by Antigonus, Phasael let him in and even agreed to go with him to see his general and discuss a means of resolving the conflict. Herod was suspicious, and warned his brother not to trust the barbarian, whose race, he assured him, was noted for its perfidy. Nevertheless, Phasael, accompanied by Hyrcanus, departed with the official, who left some of his cavalry behind. On their arrival in Galilee, they found the district in turmoil. The Parthian general, however, received them cordially enough, gave them presents, and had them escorted to Achzib, halfway between Tyre and Carmel (Fig. 7). It was there that the secret bargain made between Antigonus and the Parthians was revealed to Phasael. His informant quietly pointed out to him the guards that were never far away. As soon as word came that Herod had been taken in Jerusalem, Phasael and Hyrcanus would be arrested. There was still time to flee, and help was at hand. A local man of means had promised assistance and a boat was waiting on the shore to take the prisoners—for such they really were—out of harm's reach.

Phasael had now to choose between ensuring his own and Hyrcanus's safety, or face the Parthian general and demand an explanation for this outrageous violation of his territory and their safe-conduct guarantee. He was afraid that their escape, which must necessitate some violence, would jeopardise his brother's position, since Herod was presumably unaware as yet of the true purposes of the Parthian company in the city and unprepared for a treacherous assault on his person. Phasael chose, with much courage, to face the general, who vehemently denied any plot or secret understanding with Phasael's enemy. He brusquely terminated the interview. Returning to his quarters, Phasael walked into the arms of the already alerted guards and was put, with Hyrcanus, under close arrest. Nevertheless, Phasael managed to get word to Herod of the existence of the plot, and he immediately confronted the Parthian officer left in Jerusalem.

Vehemently protesting his innocence of any such perfidy, the Parthian tried to persuade Herod to come outside the city walls and meet the messengers now approaching from Achzib with the latest despatches. Then he would learn the real position there and receive news of Phasael's successful mission to their general. Herod hesitated, more than ever suspicious of the Parthian's motives, and convinced of the truth of the reports he had received of treachery against his brother. Hyrcanus's daughter Alexandra, mother of the girl to whom he had become betrothed, Mariamne, also urged him to suspect the Parthians. We are told that others thought her a silly woman, but Herod had come to respect her judgment (§351). The Parthians also hesitated. They did not want to attack Herod openly within the city, protected as he was with his own men. They postponed matters until the next day, which gave Herod time to prepare his escape. That night, he gathered members of his family who were in the city, set the women on beasts of burden, surrounded them with his bodyguard and as many of his followers as he could muster, and led the party away unseen. His plan was to make first for the Judaean Wilderness and the Dead Sea fortress of Masada, and then to find their way ultimately to the safety of Herod's own country of Idumaea.

Josephus has left us a long and moving account of that journey across some of the most barren and difficult country in Palestine. Derived no doubt from one of his main sources, Nicolas of Damascus, an intimate friend of Herod, we may reasonably suspect a strong bias in favour of the hero of the tale. Nevertheless, the overall account of this harrowing journey is probably correct and worth recounting here in some detail, if only for an insight into the opposition Herod had to face in the country and among his supposed allies in time of adversity.

"No enemy", says Josephus, "would have been found so hard of heart that, on witnessing what was taking place at that time, he would not have pitied their fate as the wretched women led their infants, and, with their tears and wailing, left behind their native land and their friends in chains; nor did they expect anything better for themselves" (§ 354). When we consider the brutality of Herod in his dealings with those he considered his foes, particularly later when confirmed in absolute power, we might wish to restrain our sympathy. All the same, this reversal in fortunes to one of such pride and high ambition as Herod, must have had a traumatic effect which time did nothing to obliterate. It had seemed so short a time ago that nothing could halt his progress to the councils of the mighty; he was the friend and confidant of kings and generals, who repaid his attentions with rich gifts and unlimited trust. He knew that he had played his cards well earlier, and that Rome needed him in the eastern marches of the empire almost as much as he needed her favour and continued support. And now, here he was, fleeing from the Parthian invader of Roman territory like a beaten dog, while his lord and master fawned upon an Egyptian harlot and wallowed in the sumptuous delights of her palace. Herod was no stranger to the lusts of the flesh, and was to pay dearly in the years to come for his over-indulgence. But he could keep his women in their place, and would behave as ruthlessly to those of his own household as to any man who dared to cross his path. Now Antony dallied in Alexandria, while the Herod men would one day call "Great" could do no more than stumble through the desert and nurse his hatred and contempt for enemy and so-called friend alike.

Still, Herod found it in him to offer encouragement and a spirited demeanour to his disconsolate band of refugees. He rode along the straggling trail, urging them on, promising safety once they reached his fortress by the Salt Sea. He knew that the Parthians would follow as soon as daybreak revealed their flight. Certainly by then the fugitives might hope to hide in the caves and deep gorges of the craggy wilderness, but food and water must eventually drive them on, an easy prey to ambush in narrow defiles. Added to this, Herod knew well that the difficult terrain and the Parthian pursuers were not his only enemies. For all his betrothal into the Hasmonean family, Herod could have had no delusions about the unpopularity of the Roman-sponsored Idumaean rulers of Judaea. His foes were all about him while he remained in that country; he must press on to Idumaea and seek help from his own people.

Herod's tormented state of mind is poignantly illustrated by an incident early on in the night journey. The track the party was taking southwards, avoiding villages as far as possible, was unsuitable for wheeled traffic. The waggon in which Herod's mother was travelling overturned, severely injuring the old woman. It was desperately necessary to right the vehicle and continue as quickly as possible, since any delay now would give an advantage to the Parthian followers. The accident must have occurred at a particularly awkward place, or the party's feverish haste hindered the efficiency of the workmen. Even Herod's bravado temporarily deserted him, as his mother's cries grew fainter and he feared for her life. It seemed as though fate were against him and he and his party were doomed to be overtaken and caught like rats in a trap. He drew his sword and would have cheated the enemy of their prize and ended his own shame there and then had his companions not held his arm and begged him to remember those who depended upon him in their extremity. He pulled himself together, took renewed command of operations, revived his mother and made her as comfortable as possible, and urged the party forward.

With daylight, the Parthians were soon upon them, and Herod and his men fought running battles to hold them off while the baggage train and women and children were ushered to positions of relative safety. No sooner had the Parthians been driven off to regroup for further attempts than local Jews now showed their hatred for the Idumaean and his family by swooping down on the band from every side. At one place in particular, some seven miles from Jerusalem and four miles south-east of Bethlehem, his men were engaged in hand-to-hand battles with local Jewish residents. Later Herod celebrated his success in holding them off by erecting a magnificent palace-fortress on the spot, called Herodium, the modern *Jebel el-Fureidis* (Fig. 7, Pl. 14).

Arriving in Idumaea, at a place known in the Bible as Horesh

(I Sam 23^{15}; modern *Khirbet Khureisa*: Fig. 7), six miles south of Hebron, Herod was met by his younger brother Joseph. They immediately held a council of war to decide how best to proceed. The party of refugees had now become unwieldy, having been joined by villagers fearful of a Parthian invasion. It was essential to keep those making for the rocky fastness of Masada as mobile as possible, and not to over-strain the resources of that fortress. Most of the people were thus dispersed, and told to fend for themselves in whatever places of refuge they could find in Idumaea. Herod's immediate relatives, and the mercenaries he still retained in his service, he then led to Masada, and installed the women-folk in quarters there with sufficient food and water and armed men to offer them security for some time. Herod himself then pushed on to Petra to seek the assistance of his Arab allies.

Back in Jerusalem, when the Parthians woke to find their quarry gone, they promptly ran amuck, looting the palace and everything else in the city that seemed of value. It seems they were disappointed as far as Herod's possessions were concerned, since he had already seen to it that they had been salted away in Idumaea for just this kind of eventuality. What drove the Parthian despoilers even more frantic was the realisation that they had lost that part of the reward for their perfidy which they considered of even greater desirability than the money. The women they had been promised were to have come from Herod's own house-hold (§ 379), perhaps implying that ladies of such refinement of breeding were especially coveted as sexual partners by the barbarians from the east. In any case, the Parthians' lust for spoil cost them time and gave Herod's party a better chance of effecting their escape.

The Parthians, despite their being denied the cream of their reward, brought Antigonus back to the city and gave him the throne and high priesthood. If some factions among his subjects now found cause for rejoicing at the enthronement of another Hasmonean, others will have ruefully acknowledged the bitter fact that he had been brought to power by an alien no less hateful than those who previously dominated Jewish affairs. Phasael and Hyrcanus were brought in chains to Jerusalem and handed over to Antigonus. The new spiritual head of Jewry made his first contribution to his sacred office by going up to the miserable Hyrcanus and chewing his ear off. This unfriendly act, besides being extremely painful, removed for ever the possibility of Hyrcanus again holding the office of High Priest, since the Law required that "none of the descendants of Aaron who has a physical blemish should approach to offer the bread of his God" (Lev 21[17ff.]; *War* I xiii 9 § 270). The Parthians carried off the ear-less Hyrcanus to Parthia. Later he was allowed to go to Babylon and was there cordially received by the Jewish community and even, despite his embarrassing mutilation, for some time acted as their spiritual leader (*Ant* XV ii 2 § 14ff.).

Phasael had no illusions that he would be treated so leniently, either by Antigonus or the Parthians. Nor could he hope for any deputation from his erstwhile Jewish subjects to plead for his life. Rather than give his captors the satisfaction of executing him, he dashed his head against a rock, his bound hands preventing other more effective ways of self-destruction. The desired result was nevertheless achieved, though whether directly from the wound so inflicted or from the "medication" Antigonus ordered his physicians to apply (as currently rumoured), is uncertain (*Ant* XIV xiii 10 § 368). Before Phasael breathed his last, a woman whispered to him that his brother Herod had escaped from the enemy, and he died cheerfully contemplating the fact that he was leaving behind one who would certainly exact a terrible vengeance for his death if ever the opportunity offered. His trust was not misplaced.

CHAPTER XII

Herod, King of the Jews

Even Herod's Arab friends denied him help in his hour of need. King Malchus, who had now succeeded to the Nabatean throne, refused him entry into Petra, sending messengers to order him out of the country. Whether he was genuinely afraid of reprisals from the Parthians if he helped Herod, or, as Josephus says, merely that the money Herod sought was largely his own, left on deposit previously, and the king hoped to avoid repayment, is not certain (*Ant* XIV xiv 1 § 370ff.). Herod made a suitably picturesque reply to Malchus's messengers ("the reply which his feelings dictated"—*War* I xiv 2 § 277), and pressed on south to Egypt. Part of his present concern for money was to ransom his brother from the Parthians, since he was as yet unaware of his fate. To that end he had with him Phasael's seven-year-old son whom he had intended leaving in Petra as a deposit against any additional money he might have to borrow from his friends. Now that they had failed him, he aimed to seek assistance from the Egyptian queen to speed his way to Rome. It was from this quarter alone that any restoration of his fortunes could be expected. Rome would have to act soon and decisively to save her eastern possessions and would then need her staunch Idumaean ally to govern the restored territory of Judaea. In this correct reasoning Herod once more showed his flair for thinking in terms of world politics, and setting local issues into their larger perspective. A lesser man might have returned to Masada and sat tight waiting for the tide of events to change, hoping to emerge when the Romans returned and seek anew their favour. A weaker man might have succumbed even to the temptation to end his own life, as we saw he almost did earlier. The country he had ruled was now enemy territory, the local inhabitants as much his foes as the eastern invaders; his home-land was no more hospitable, denying him even the opportunity to retrieve his own possessions. Yet Herod's eyes turned to Rome, and his mind was even then planning his return to power at Antony's side.

The night after his rebuttal at the gates of Petra, he rested in a wayside shrine, and while there heard the news of his brother's death. His very real grief (§ 277) cannot have been entirely unmixed with relief. In some measure his immediate responsibilities were lessened in that he need not now negotiate a ransom for Phasael, but could concentrate on reaching Rome and instituting action there. Similarly when eventually he arrived in Egypt and was cordially welcomed by Cleopatra, he resisted her attempts to enlist his support in an expedition she was planning, possibly to help Antony who had at last bestirred himself to action against the Parthians. Here again Herod demonstrated remarkable foresight and political acumen. It would have been all too easy to indulge in the pampered luxury of the Egyptian court after his trials in Judaea and Nabatea, and then immediately to have assumed command of an expeditionary force and assuaged his lust for violent revenge upon his enemies. Instead, despite the inclement weather of winter and reports of disturbances in Italy, he insisted on setting sail for that country without delay.

The ship in which he was travelling ran into a violent storm and only just managed to limp into Rhodes. There two friends helped him to equip a new trireme, and in their company he set sail for Brindisium, and thus travelled to Rome.

Antony listened with sympathy to Herod's tale of misfortune, indulging, we are told, in philosophic reflections on the wilful actions of Fate even against those she had previously favoured (*Ant* XIV xiv 4 § 381). Impressed perhaps by his supplicant's fortitude in bearing patiently even this further ordeal, and recognising Herod's potential worth as an ally in clearing and holding Judaea for the Romans, Antony there and then determined to make Herod King of the Jews. Octavian, too, was readily won over, remembering the part Herod's father Antipater had borne with his own father in the Egyptian campaigns (§ 383). The Senate was convened, and Herod's suitability for succeeding to the rule now held at Parthian behest by Antigonus, an avowed enemy of Rome, was acclaimed by his champions, and generally agreed. Thus, at the end of 40 BC, Herod was appointed King of the Jews by the Roman Senate. We are told that the new monarch left the Senate chamber between Antony and Caesar, the consuls and other magistrates leading the way, to offer sacrifice and deposit the decree in the Capitol. Festivities continued at Antony's expense, marking this supremely happy first day of Herod's reign, hardly a week after he had arrived nearly destitute in Rome (§ 387ff.). Only the Jews remained to be told of their good fortune.

Herod's chroniclers tell us that he was taken aback by being given the kingship. He had not come to Rome to claim such honour, not least because he was aware that the Romans customarily ensured that regal office among their subject peoples continued through legitimate succession within the reigning family. Herod actually meant to press the claims to the crown of the brother of his betrothed Mariamne, Aristobulus III, being a grandson of Aristobulus on his father's side, and of Hyrcanus on his mother's (§ 387). We should perhaps be a little more inclined to give Herod credit for this honourable intention did we not know that four or five years later he had the youth, then eighteen and but recently appointed by Herod to the high priesthood, drowned by his companions whilst sporting in a pool at Jericho (*Ant* XV iii 3 § 55f.). He was a comely lad and so great a favourite with the common people that Herod feared they might want him to be their king (§ 52).

It was, however, one thing to be proclaimed King of the Jews by the Roman Senate, and another actually to take over the kingdom. Herod sailed from Rome in the winter of 40/39 BC, and after some six months had collected a force in Ptolemais with which to wrest his kingdom from Antigonus. The Roman governor in Syria, P. Ventidius, had already driven the Parthians from the country, but Antigonus was still firmly in control of Judaea. While he may have gained his regal position with the help of the Parthians, he was, nevertheless, a Jewish king commanding the allegiance of the majority of his Jewish subjects. There were few who welcomed the return of Herod, a non-Jew by race and completely dependent upon his Roman masters. The Idumaean had thus to fight his way back every inch of the way, and it was only after two years of bitter struggle, largely against his intended subjects and with the aid of the Romans, that Herod reigned triumphant in Jerusalem, or what was left of it.

Joppa was the first city to fall to Herod's forces, and then he made for Masada to relieve its defenders, of whom many were his own family. The fortress had been under continual pressure from Antigonus, and during the early part of the winter the cisterns had run dry. At one stage, Herod's brother Joseph had planned to break out with two hundred of his people and make for Petra. Word had reached them that King Malchus had afterwards regretted his churlish treatment of Herod and might be prepared to offer his family sanctuary. At the last moment,

however, a heavy rainstorm filled the tanks, and thus encouraged by
what was evidently a sign of divine goodwill, the beleaguered garrison
sallied forth on a number of raids against the besiegers.

Ambushed at every turn by Antigonus's men, Herod made his way
south to the Dead Sea and relieved Masada, took Horesh, and came up
to Jerusalem. There he joined the Roman army already besieging the
city, and made a public proclamation to the citizens that he had come
"for their own good and the welfare of the city" (§ 402). The reply
offered by Antigonus on their behalf to the Romans is doubtless
apocryphal, but nevertheless sums up the chief objection to Herod's
assumption of royal office:

". . . it would be contrary to their own notion of right if they gave the
kingship to Herod who was a commoner and an Idumaean, that is, a
half-Jew (*hemi-ioudaio*), when they ought to offer it to those who were of
the (royal) family, as was their custom. And, he argued, if they were now
ill-disposed toward him and were determined to deprive him of the
kingship on the ground that he had received it from the Parthians,
there were at least many of his family who might lawfully receive the
kingship, for they had committed no offence against the Romans, and
were priests; and thus they would be unworthily treated if they were
deprived of this rank" (§ 403f.).

For some reason the Romans were reluctant to press home the attack
on Jerusalem at that time. Josephus suggests their leader, Ventidius's
second in command, was bribed by Antigonus, and that he persuaded
his men to grumble about short rations and the approach of winter
(§ 406ff.). In any case, despite Herod's urgent reminders that their
presence there was on orders from Antony, Caesar, and the Senate, the
Romans withdrew and Herod was obliged to do likewise. Nevertheless,
he did not remain inactive, but returned to Galilee and carried out some
operations against more companies of "brigands" hiding in caves and
terrorizing the neighbourhood. We may suspect that, as on the previous
occasion when Herod campaigned against similar troglodytes in this
area, the "brigands" were in fact religio-political rebels, part of the
underground resistance movement constantly in action against foreign
oppressors. Of particular interest in the long account given by Josephus
of this operation, certainly compiled from contemporary military
records or reminiscences, are the methods used to effect entry into caves
set high in vertical cliff faces. Of such are the caves recently explored in
the Judaean Wilderness, whence have come in recent years manuscripts

and other relics of similar religio-political revolts of the first and second centuries AD. Standing in the entrance of such caves, one has often wondered how the Romans could have obtained access, since they could be so easily defended. With this in mind, the relevant passage in *War*, supplemented by the parallel account in *Antiquities*, is worth quoting in full:

"These caves, opening on to mountain precipices, were inaccessible from any quarter, except by some tortuous and extremely narrow paths leading up to them; the cliff in front of them dropped sheer down into ravines far below, with water courses at the bottom . . ." (*War* I xvi 4 § 310).

"In such dens did they lurk with all their people. Thereupon, the king, whose men were unable either to climb up from below or creep upon them from above because of the steepness of the hill, had cribs built and lowered these upon them with iron chains as they were suspended by a machine from the summit of the hill. The cribs were filled with armed men holding great grappling hooks, with which they were supposed to draw towards them any of the brigands who opposed them, and kill them by hurling them to the ground. The lowering of the cribs was proving to be a risky business because of the immense depth that lay beneath them, although the men within them had everything they needed. But when the cribs were let down, none of the men standing near the entrances of the caves dared come forward; instead they remained quiet out of fear. Then one of the soldiers, in irritation at the delay caused by the brigands who dared not come out, girded on his sword, and holding on with both hands to the chain from which the crib was suspended, lowered himself to a cave entrance. When he came opposite an entrance, he first drove back with javelins most of those who were standing there, and then with his grappling hook drew his opponents towards him and pushed them over the precipice. After that, he attacked those within and slaughtered many of them, and then returned to the crib and rested. Fear thereupon seized the others as they heard the shrieking, and they despaired of their lives. All action, however, was halted by the coming of night . . .

"The same method of attack was used the following day, when the men in the baskets fell upon them still more fiercely, and fought at their entrances and threw flaming fire inside, so that the caves, which contained much wood, were set on fire.

"Now there was an old man shut up in one of the caves with his seven

13(a)   The Copper Scroll from Qumran: an inventory of sacred treasure:
before opening.

13(b) A cut segment showing
part of the text.

14   Herodium from above the roofs of Bethlehem.

children and his wife; and when they begged him to let them slip
through to the enemy (to surrender), he stood at the entrance and cut
down each of his sons as he came out, and afterwards his wife, and after
hurling their dead bodies over the precipice, threw himself down upon
them, thus submitting to death rather than to slavery. But before doing
so, he bitterly reviled Herod for his meanness of spirit (*War*: 'upbraiding
him as a low-born upstart'), although the king—for he was a witness of
what was happening—stretched out his right hand and promised him
full immunity . . ." (*Ant* XIV xv 5 § 422–430).

The last incident is a revealing reflection on the nature of these
"brigands". The rebels of the Bar-Kocheba revolt, whose caves have
yielded archaeologists such treasures recently, similarly took their
families into the deserts with them, and many of their relics, clothing
and toiletries as well as legal records, have witnessed to their use of
such caverns as homes and refuges from the war (Pls. 16ᵃ, ᵇ; 17ᵃ⁻ᵉ).

In the year 38 BC, the Parthians again invaded Syria and the Romans
were too fully occupied on this front to afford Herod further help to
regain his kingdom. The king took the opportunity to contact Antony,
then besieging Samosata on the upper Euphrates. The siege came to a
victorious conclusion soon after his arrival—though hardly, as Josephus
would have us believe, because of it! (*War* I xvi 7 §322)— and before
the Roman himself left for the west, he appointed his general Sossius
governor of Syria and ordered him into Judaea with two legions to assist
Herod assert his claim to the crown.

During the visit to Antony, Herod's brother Joseph, whom he had
left in charge of a restricted holding operation against Antigonus in
Judaea, was killed in battle at Jericho. Herod made but a brief lamentation for his loss at the time. After recruiting more men from Lebanon,
he pressed on into Galilee and crushed a revolt against his partisans by
the local people. They had signified their disapproval of their Idumaean
king's return by drowning his representatives in the Lake of Galilee
(*Ant* XIV xv 10 § 450). In Judaea also there was a general uprising
against Herod, who now marched into the country to take a terrible
vengeance for Joseph's death, "burning for a fight . . . with memories of
his murdered brother, risking all to be avenged on his murderers"
(*War* I xvii 6 § 336). In a village called Isana, near the frontier between
Judaea and Samaria, he butchered the inhabitants, pulling their houses
down upon them: "there was such a heap of corpses that the streets
were impassable to the victors" (§ 338). It needed then only to cut off

L

the head of Antigonus's general, Pappus, who had been responsible for killing and similarly dishonouring the body of Joseph, for Herod's revenge to be complete. He could now turn his attention to the more earnest business of taking Jerusalem, his royal city.

It was now the spring of 37 BC, two-and-a-half years after Herod's proclamation by the Roman Senate as King of the Jews. During a lull in the three months' siege of Jerusalem that followed, Herod took the opportunity to consummate his marriage with Mariamne, as previously mentioned. He returned to the fray, vainly hoping that his even closer alliance with the Hasmonean family might make him more acceptable to the people he was now preparing to beat into submission. Sossius, the Roman general, had now arrived from the north, to add his weight to the Idumaean's forces, so that they now totalled eleven divisions of infantry, six thousand cavalry and a body of auxiliaries from Syria. The net they drew round the city prevented any but the most daring of its inhabitants from attempting foraging expeditions, and the population was reduced to famine. The physically weaker members of the community could do no more than gather around the sanctuary, "indulging in transports of frenzy and fabricating numerous oracular utterances to fit the crisis" (War I xviii 1 § 347). This recourse to biblical prophecy and ritual lamentation was a common feature of popular reaction to attacks upon the Holy City by aliens. Since Jerusalem, and the Temple in particular, was the seat of Yahweh, it followed that God would defend its integrity against the invader by sending his angelic warriors from on high. Thus false hopes were engendered in an atmosphere already tense with religious emotion and militarily dangerous situations became inevitable disasters. It was so on this occasion, and again, even more calamitously, in AD 70.

The first to break through the defences were twenty men of Herod's mercenaries, and Sossius's centurions followed on their heels (§ 351). The city environs were first secured and the citizens driven like sheep to the slaughter inwards towards the Temple mount. "The Romans were infuriated by the length of the siege, and the Jews of Herod's army were determined to leave none of their opponents alive. Masses were butchered in the alleys, crowded together in the houses, and flying to the sanctuary. No quarter was given to infancy, to age, or to helpless womanhood" (§ 352).

We are told that Herod tried unsuccessfully to stop the wholesale slaughter, and when Sossius's men ran amuck, pillaging and destroying, expostulated "that if the Romans emptied the city of money and men, they would leave him king of a desert, and that he would count the empire of the world itself too dearly bought with the slaughter of so many citizens" (§ 355). In the end he was obliged to buy off his plundering allies with liberal rewards "from his own resources" (§356). They left at last, dragging Antigonus with them in chains. Herod watched him go with some reluctance. While Antigonus lived he could not feel safe. The Hasmonean would always be, in the eyes of the majority of Jews, the rightful wearer of the crown, scion of a line which, with all its faults, was at least Jewish. Furthermore, Herod was afraid that if he were allowed to reach Rome, he might find an opportunity to plead his cause before the Senate, perhaps prevailing upon them to revoke their former grant of kingship to Herod on the grounds that Antigonus, despite his former enmity to Rome, was the natural heir to the crown.

The Idumaean therefore sent a messenger to Antony in Antioch, whither he had come from Italy and Greece in the winter of 37 BC, requesting that Antigonus should be executed. He accompanied the request with the customary fat bribe, and thus the last of the Hasmonean kings died. One ancient authority adds the detail that he was scourged on a cross and then had his throat cut, a punishment "no other king had ever suffered at the hands of the Romans" (Dio Cassius xlix 22). Josephus concludes his account of the episode: "and when this was done, Herod was freed from his fear" (*Ant* XIV xvi 4 § 490), one of the most profound untruths to be found anywhere in the chronicler's writings. Herod's fear and moral disintegration were just beginning.

CHAPTER XIII

Herod's womenfolk

Herod's greatest failing was not to have been born of the Chosen Race. He was a brilliant soldier, politician, administrator and architect; but he was not a Jew. Those deplorable traits of his character like cunning, avarice, viciousness and overweening pride would not of themselves have called forth the opprobrium of his people; rather might they have earned their admiration. The Bible abounds with stories of ancient heroes of Israel displaying no less dubious qualities in the service of their god. The Maccabees were no saints, but they were Jews, and Herod was an Idumaean, an Arab. Even his wife Mariamne despised him.

The marriage which he had consummated under such dramatic circumstances proved to be the greatest personal tragedy of Herod's life. By his betrothal into the Hasmonean house he hoped to find the acceptance in the eyes of his people denied to him by his inferior birth. All it did was to create a deep rift in his own family circle which the passage of time only widened and which culminated in the violent death of those he loved best. Mariamne was a granddaughter of Hyrcanus, who had been High Priest until 40 BC, when the Parthians carried him off to the east. Her mother Alexandra, a daughter of Hyrcanus, had been the wife of her cousin Alexander, executed by Pompey in 49 BC at Antioch. In the eyes of the common people these representatives of the Hasmonean house were the cream of Jewish aristocracy, proud members of a family whose forebears had withstood the tyranny of Antiochus Epiphanes and his imperial successors. The opposition they had faced within the country from their co-religionists, who wanted only freedom to worship and resisted their attempts to seize political independence at the cost of so much human suffering, tended to be forgotten with the years. The agonies they had inflicted on Jewry in the cause of their dream of a racialist empire faded before the Jews' present hatred of their Idumaean king and his Roman sponsors. Much could be excused of a Jew that was intolerable in an alien despot.

Mariamne was beautiful, and Herod adored her. Her disdain and periodic coldness roused him to even greater passion and insane jealousy. Their frequent quarrels were violent, but their subsequent reconciliations were equally intense, and left to themselves the pair might have contrived a compromise which found a mean of mutual happiness between the emotional extremes of love and hatred. But behind the lovely Mariamne stood a ruthless mother whose hatred for her Idumaean son-in-law was matched only by her ambition for her children, and particularly for her son Aristobulus.

With the now aged Hyrcanus physically disfigured, thanks to the mutilation inflicted on him by Antigonus, the high priesthood should legitimately have fallen to the young Aristobulus, Alexander's son. Herod was by birth ineligible, of course, and at first he thought to assuage the religious sensibilities of Jerusalem's priesthood by bringing home from his honourable retirement in Babylon the ageing Hyrcanus II. For a time the old priest demurred as the Jewish community there tried to persuade him to remain as their spiritual leader. Whether he eventually relented and came to Jerusalem with an idea of attaining to his old office despite his physical handicap, or, more probably, because he wanted to live the last years of his life in the company of what remained of his family, we cannot be sure. He would, in any case, have done better to have stayed where he was. He was not acceptable as High Priest in Jerusalem, and before long was to become involved in a tangled plot against Herod woven by his ruthless daughter Alexandra, and was sentenced to death for treason.

Herod tried to fill the high priestly vacancy by appointing another of the Babylonian exiles, a priest by the name of Hananel. Historically this man's lineage gave him a better claim to the post than any Hasmonean, for he came of a priestly line that stretched back to the days before the Maccabees dubiously snatched the sacred office for themselves. But Alexandra saw Hananel's appointment as a deliberate insult to her family, and to herself and her young son in particular. She looked around for allies for her cause, but knew that the only person Herod feared was Antony. On the other hand, the Roman was open to influence from his Egyptian mistress, Cleopatra, who herself had reasons for wishing Herod dispossessed of his kingdom. There thus developed an extraordinary conspiratorial relationship between the ladies of the royal courts of Judaea and Egypt which was to have profound consequences on Herod's home and foreign policies.

Alexandra contacted Cleopatra in the first instance through the medium of a "a certain singer" (*Ant* XV i 5 § 24), asking that the Egyptian queen use her influence with Antony to procure the high priesthood for Aristobulus. Antony saw no immediate reason for acceding to this request, and the matter might have ended there, at least for the time being, had Alexandra not found another ally in one Dellius, a "lover" or "favourite" of the Roman general (Dio Cassius xlix 39: *paidikia*). This worthy, who apparently acted as a procurer for his master, happened to be in Judaea on some other business, when he saw Mariamne and her brother, now in his late teens. He was struck by the beauty of the pair, and suggested to their proud mother Alexandra that through her offspring—"surely of divine conception!" (§ 27)—she might influence Antony more directly. If she would have their portraits painted and sent to the general, his desire for both as sexual partners would ensure his granting her every wish.

The pictures had their desired effect upon the susceptible Antony, but he hesitated to send for Mariamne, partly because he did not want to upset his Idumaean ally at a time when storm clouds were gathering on the Roman horizon and he needed every friend he could keep, and partly because he was afraid of what Cleopatra might say. So he invited the lad to visit him "in an outwardly respectable way" (§ 28). Herod, however, who was well aware of his Roman friend's weaknesses, thought it unwise to send the sixteen-year-old Aristobulus, whose beauty and careful breeding would have made him particularly desirable, and who might find it impossible to resist the sexual advances of so powerful a suitor. He therefore wrote apologetically, saying that the lad's absence from the country might provoke civil disorders at a time when seditious talk of an overthrow of the present monarchy was already rife. To foil his patron's designs for good in that direction, and also to give himself relief from his mother-in-law's constant nagging, Herod appointed the handsome youth High Priest without more ado. He sent Hananel packing, thus displeasing the Jewish lawyers who denied his authority to dismiss High Priests so summarily. At the same time, he spelt out to his mother-in-law a firm warning to desist in the future from interfering in affairs of the State. He arraigned her before a council of advisers on a charge of conspiring with a foreign ruler to overthrow her rightful king, inferring—probably quite correctly—that she was after the crown as well as the high priesthood for her son. This Alexandra vehemently denied, saying that she had only wished to right the wrong done her son by Herod's overriding his legitimate claims to the sacred office. She expressed profound regret if her natural concern for her family had led her to impulsive action and unwarranted outspokenness. Herod answered that he had only appointed Hananel as High Priest until such time as Aristobulus should reach the statutory age for the post. And so, amid a welter of insincerities and mutually empty assurances of good faith, the meeting broke up. Herod instituted a constant watch upon Alexandra, instructing that her every action should be reported back to him, and she retired to brood darkly on her ignominy and plans for revenge.

Somehow, despite Herod's spies, Alexandra managed to send another message to Cleopatra, this time lamenting her virtual imprisonment and humiliation. The queen urged her to escape with her son, and she would give them sanctuary in Egypt. There they could formulate a plan for overthrowing Herod. Apart from any womanly sympathy Cleopatra might have felt for Alexandra, the Egyptian ruler was not averse to stirring up trouble in Judaea for her own ends. For a long time she had wanted to restore Egyptian sovereignty over the land of Palestine, so long part of Ptolemaic territory. When Herod entered upon his kingdom in 37 BC, the area under his control was virtually that left by Pompey to the religious community of Jerusalem after the elimination of Hasmonean rule; that is, Judaea with Idumaea, Peraea and the interior of Galilee. To this had been added the coveted sea-port of Joppa and the villages of the Jezreel plain ceded by Caesar to Hyrcanus p. 139 Cleopatra had already managed to persuade Antony to give her the Palestinian coastal cities including Joppa, and even the balsam groves of Jericho whose produce was world-famous and extremely valuable. He had refused her the whole of Judaea in deference to his friend and ally Herod, and now she saw an opportunity for removing Herod and exercising control through the stripling Aristobulus and his doting mother.

With Cleopatra's assurance of support, Alexandra devised a desperate plan of escape. She had two wooden coffins made in the palace, and placed herself and her son in them, giving orders that they should be carried thus to the sea where a ship lay ready to transport them to Egypt. As few people as possible knew of the ruse, but unfortunately one of them confided in a friend called Sabbion under the mistaken impression that he was included in the number of the confidants. Sabbion, who happened to be in disfavour at the time with Herod, thought to regain the king's esteem by telling him of Alexandra's plot. Thus apprised, Herod waited until the coffins were sealed and being carried from the palace, and then captured the whole party.

However strong his first inclinations may have been to make an immediate end of his troublesome mother-in-law and her potentially dangerous son, Herod held his hand. He was old and wise enough now to beware of precipitate action in affairs of State, particularly as he was aware of the part being played by Cleopatra in the background. He knew her influence with his patron Antony and the repeated demands she had made for Herod's removal from control of Judaea. He had therefore to step carefully in any matter in which the queen had taken an active interest, lest she add a complaint of high-handed treatment of her personal friends to her other real or imagined charges against him. Herod therefore, with as much good grace as he could muster, forgave Alexandra and Aristobulus, and bided his time. At least for the present he had the satisfaction of knowing that his display of magnanimity towards the culprits must have offended the proud woman's vanity almost as painfully as the executioner's knife. She must have known, too, that her involvement of her son in treasonable associations with Herod's most bitter enemy, had sealed his fate, if not her own.

Herod let a decent interval elapse before he took decisive action, since he hoped to disarm suspicion that whatever happened to Aristobulus was of the king's design. The annual Feast of Tabernacles came round, and the young High Priest carried out his duties before the altar, clad in the full regalia of his sacred office. The hearts of all the onlookers went out to him.

His youth and grace of movement seemed to speak to them of the glory of a renewed Israel, combining the traditions of her past with the ever-springing hope of the messianic age to come. In this handsome youth the Jews caught a glimpse once more of the ideal to which their prophets had called them when they promised that all mankind would look to Jerusalem to lead them; in Aristobulus they saw the light to lighten the Gentiles. Herod saw only a flame which could too easily kindle a conflagration of revolt that would sweep all Jewry. The time had come to quench the spark.

The religious ceremonies over, the royal party proceeded down to Jericho where entertainment had been arranged by Alexandra. Herod encouraged the young man to indulge himself with wine, and generally to give vent to his youthful high spirits as relaxation from the considerable strain of the previous week's cultic celebrations. Even in October, the heat of the Jordan valley is oppressive, and the fresh waters of Jericho offer welcome relief at the height of the day. In the palace gardens were pools, and the younger members of the party were soon splashing around in the water. Herod urged Aristobulus to join them, and to forget for a moment the responsibilities of his high office. Nothing loath, the youth jumped in and for the afternoon he and his friends sported together, scooping water over one another, jumping on each other's backs, ducking one another. The shadows lengthened quickly, and one of Aristobulus's companions, looking up to the side of the pool where Herod stood benignly surveying the happy scene, caught the sign he gave and in turn signalled to others in the pool. A number of them turned on Aristobulus and ducked him under, as they had been doing all afternoon, but this time kept his head down until they felt his body grow limp.

Herod was, of course, among the first to help them bring the body to the side. The womenfolk shrieked, and the cry of lamentation was caught up outside the palace walls. Soon all Jericho and then Jerusalem, and all Judaea mourned the tragic end of their young High Priest, the symbol of so many renewed hopes. Alexandra, her heart bursting with pain and hate, looked on the body of her son, and then at the weeping Herod, knowing full well how and why the "accident" had happened. Thus Josephus:

"But Alexandra was most deeply affected of all because she understood what the death of her son meant. But although she had the greater pain for knowing how it had been brought about, she believed it necessary to bear up bravely in anticipation of a still greater evil. Often she came close to ending her life with her own hands, but still she held back, hoping that if she lived she might help to avenge the son who had been treacherously and lawlessly killed. For that reason she was all the more encouraged to live and thought that by giving no indication of her suspicions that her son's death had been premeditated, she would have opportunity for revenge" (*Ant* XV iii 4 § 58f.).

Herod arranged a lavish funeral for the dead Aristobulus, sparing no expense in the grandeur of the tomb or the rarity of the anointing perfumes, and thus assuaging to some extent the grief of the female mourners. Alexandra took her place among them, but the time for pain was past. She was already composing her letter of complaint to her

Egyptian friend, urging Cleopatra to use every female wile to prevail upon her lover to bring the murderer Herod to justice.

During that winter of 35/4 BC, Cleopatra never ceased to lay the burden of Alexandra's complaint before Antony, stressing that Herod had been brought to his high office by the Romans, thus overriding the more legitimate claims of others to the crown, and they were thus more than usually responsible for acts of lawlessness carried out by their creatures. At length, Antony agreed to interview Herod and since he was setting forth himself for Laodicea on his way to a campaign in Armenia, he sent word to the king to meet him there and clear himself of the charges that had been brought against him regarding Aristobulus.

Herod could do nothing but obey, and for a moment he felt a chill of apprehension. Antony he could handle, but when behind his Roman master there stood the sinister figure of his Egyptian concubine, and alongside her that of his mother-in-law bent on vengeance for her son, his nerve nearly failed him. He called Joseph, his sister Salome's husband, and charged him with the care of the kingdom during his absence. Furthermore, he secretly instructed him that should the worst befall and Antony were to condemn him to death, Joseph should immediately have his beloved Mariamne killed, so that no man should bring disgrace upon Herod's name after his death by taking his wife and violating her beauty. By this, Josephus adds, he was referring to his friend Antony's known desire for Mariamne (§ 67). Perhaps, too, he feared that his forthcoming trial before the Roman might have this element also weighing the scales against him.

It was thus with some considerable uncertainty of his future that Herod left for his appointment with his Roman patron. Joseph busied himself about State affairs, in the course of which he was in constant contact with Mariamne and her mother. Alexandra questioned Joseph about Herod's state of mind, in the hope of discovering some new weapon to use against him. The ever loyal Joseph assured the ladies of one point: Herod was very much in love with Mariamne, and nothing, not even death itself, would break that union. Come, come, the ladies expostulated, let us not exaggerate. No man, let alone the mighty King Herod, could so allow his affections to be engaged to a mere woman; and what precisely did he mean about death not breaking the bond of love?

Poor Joseph was no match for Alexandra's guile. In his anxiety to prove to the women the depth and sincerity of Herod's great passion for his wife, he blurted out the substance of his parting instructions. Mariamne and her mother were staggered—not at the strength of Herod's passion for Mariamne that should have wished no other man to hold her in his arms, but that he should have been so cruel, "reflecting that not even by his death would they escape the doom of tyrannical murder" (§ 70).

To make matters worse, rumour reached the city that things had gone ill with Herod, and that Antony had put him to the torture and killed him. There were many in Jerusalem for whom these were glad tidings indeed, among them Alexandra, who suggested to Joseph that the three of them should escape while there was yet time and seek protection from one of the Roman legions stationed near the city. She thought that not only would this give them greater protection from any civic disturbances that might follow Herod's death, but that she might prevail upon Antony to grant her family the crown by playing on his lust for her daughter. Unfortunately for Alexandra, not only was the rumour of her enemy's death untrue, but word of her suggested flight to the Roman standards and her intended offer of Mariamne to Antony in return for his support of her claim to the kingship, reached hostile ears within the court.

Hasmonean antagonism for Herod extended also to his family. In particular, there was bitter rivalry between Mariamne and her mother on the one hand, and Herod's sister Salome and his mother Cypros on the other. Again, at base it was a matter of the disdain of the Hasmoneans for the Idumaeans, Jew against Arab. Since Joseph was Salome's husband, report of Alexandra's intentions could hardly be kept from her, and she lost no time in letting her brother know what treason the false rumour of his death had inspired in the minds of his mother-in-law and wife.

Herod had fared a good deal better at his interview than he was afraid might be the case. In a letter back to Jerusalem, which arrived shortly after the spurious news of his death, the king detailed the honour accorded him by Antony, how he had sat with the general in the courts of judgment, and been entertained at dinner every day. Thanks to their long-standing friendship—and the rich gifts Herod had brought with him—Cleopatra had not won her case, nor the land of Judaea she coveted. Antony had given her Chalcis in the Lebanon region as compensation, but that was all. According to Herod's report, Antony had gone so far as to tell the Egyptian queen to mind her own business, that "she would be better off if she did not meddle in the affairs of the ruler" (§ 76).

All in all, Herod returned to his kingdom well pleased with himself, only to hear from the lips of his sister and mother the news that his wife and mother-in-law had been planning to make a bid for power the moment they had heard of his death. There was an even uglier side of the gossip. It was being said that Joseph's relations with Mariamne during the king's absence had been much closer and more personal than was necessary. In fact Salome directly accused her husband of having had frequent sexual intercourse with her sister-in-law. Herod's nerves had already been frayed by recent events, and they were in no condition to stand further abrasion in respect of his wife's fidelity. A moment's reflection might have pointed to the absurdity of the accusation, and the improbability that either Salome herself or Mariamne's mother Alexandra would have permitted the affair to have reached such a stage without taking drastic action earlier on to bring it to an end. He would also have taken more note of who was telling him the tale and allowed for the inter-tribal hatred that might have engendered it. But, mad with jealousy, he stormed off to confront Mariamne with the charge. The proud Hasmonean was no less incensed that her husband should have given any credence at all to the story, but being an intelligent woman she was also alive to the delicacy of her position. Her mother had done nothing but provoke the king to anger since he came to the throne, and the Hasmonean fortunes were not so well favoured at the time that either of the women could afford to challenge the king's authority and rely upon help from the people. Besides, for all Herod's love for her, his present rage would let no fear of the consequences in the country hold him back from killing her there and then if he had a mind to.

Mariamne, therefore, simply affirmed her innocence of the charge on oath, and with such sincerity and tears that the couple were soon in each other's arms, making love as fervently as moments ago they were seething in their mutual hatred. In the intensity of emotion Herod babbled his undying love for Mariamne and urged her to tell him she loved him too, and that she forgave him for ever doubting her. Yes, of course, but was it the act of a lover to leave orders that if he should die his wife should be killed too, though innocent of any wrong? It took a moment before the full import of her sweet chiding penetrated Herod's consciousness. Then suddenly he stiffened, and flinging her aside, sprang to his feet.

"Joseph told you!"

It seemed inconceivable to Herod in his present emotional state that his lieutenant could have divulged his secret charge save in the intimacy of the bed-chamber. This was damning proof of the truth of Salome's report. He was on the point of killing Mariamne immediately, but stayed his hand and ran choking with rage from the room. He issued orders for Joseph's immediate execution, without a chance of appeal, and for his mother-in-law's imprisonment in chains and under close guard (§ 85ff.).

If Herod's relationships with the women of his court had come to a head, he was also no less bedevilled by the activities of his female adversary in Egypt. Cleopatra prevailed upon Antony to give her parts of Judaea and Arabia, denying their control to Herod and King Malchus, the Nabatean. She demanded they rent them back from her, and added insult to injury by making Herod her agent in the collection of his and Malchus's revenues (*Ant* XV iv 2 § 96). But even that failed to provoke Herod to rebellion against his Roman overlord, as she had hoped. For then her repeated charge to her lover that Herod was untrustworthy and should be removed from office would have seemed justified and she could enter into the suzerainty of the whole of Palestine-Syria that had been her aim from the beginning. Perhaps Herod had already read the writing on the wall regarding his friend Antony's future. The day of the final clash between him and Octavian was drawing near, and Herod was astute enough to know that there was always the possibility that he might have to make a sudden change in loyalties. He could not afford to run the risk of being ousted from power now for the sake of pride or payment of tribute, even if it was to his enemy for his own land.

Cleopatra tried a further desperate ploy to trap Herod. In 34 BC, after she had accompanied Antony as far as the Euphrates on his expedition against Armenia, she returned via Judaea and confronted her Idumaean enemy. She treated him as the bailiff of her Judaean possessions, almost as a messenger-boy, and then, quite unabashed, tried to seduce him. Josephus says she "attempted to have sexual relations with the king, for she was by nature used to enjoying this kind of pleasure without dissembling" (§ 97). The historian admits the possibility that she might have found herself sexually attracted to Herod, but thinks it more possible that she was setting a trap for him. Herod carefully evaded her invitation, and sought the counsel of his friends on whether he should take the opportunity of her presence in his kingdom to have her killed, "in this way ridding of many evils all those to whom she had already been vicious or was likely to be in the future" (§ 99). In particular, Antony would be the chief benefactor, since her offering herself to Herod in this wanton manner showed what her friendship to the Roman general was really worth. His friends urged him to do nothing so rash: Cleopatra was still a powerful woman, and they thought it doubtful whether Antony would view his beloved's assassination in quite the same objective light: "his love would flame up the more fiercely if he thought she had been taken from him by violence and treachery" (§ 101).

Herod let himself be persuaded by his friends' sound advice, and presumably resisted Cleopatra's advances successfully, thereby adding to her determination to destroy him and seize his kingdom. Although not the beauty that popular tradition has pictured her, this Macedonian princess, still only thirty-four or so, must nevertheless have had the power of attracting men of action and holding their love. Josephus records the popular belief that Cleopatra's influence over Antony was at least partly due to drugs (§93). Nevertheless, she cannot have been overpleased that the Idumaean had managed to resist her wiles, and the honourable escort and rich presents with which he accompanied her to the Egyptian frontier would have done little to salve her wounded pride.

Cleopatra's next move in her feud with Herod was to try and weaken his position by manipulating his Arabian ally, the Nabatean king Malchus, into a position of antagonism towards him. This she contrived through Herod's ignominious role as rent collector for her revenues from Nabatean as well as Jewish properties. Malchus defaulted on his payments, so that Herod was obliged, on Antony's orders, to prepare a force to march against him. One suspects that behind the Arab king's recalcitrance lay Cleopatra herself, since we find in the account of the decisive battle that followed that one of her generals was present, holding locally recruited troops in reserve. When, at one stage, it seemed that the Arabs were about to be defeated, he fell on the Jewish forces unexpectedly and gave their enemies a chance to recover and eventually to win a decisive victory (§ 115ff.). For some time Herod could do no more than launch a series of raids on Arab territories, avoiding open battle and seizing as much booty as he could in an attempt to make good some of his losses. In the spring of 31 BC, a particularly violent earthquake occurred in Judaea which caused considerable damage around the Jericho area. Traces of the convulsions are to be seen today in the cracks that appear within the Essene settlement by the Dead Sea, recently excavated in connection with the famous Scrolls (Pls. 6, 18). The Arabs were apparently misled into believing that the whole of Judaea lay in ruins and was an easy prey to attack. Herod rallied his troops (Josephus provides us with two different and quite incredible accounts of his speech in *Antiquities* and *War*) and led them to inflict a humiliating defeat upon his erstwhile allies.

However successfully Cleopatra's strategy had set Herod against the Arabs, it probably saved him from worse trouble elsewhere. To support his Roman patron in the forthcoming struggle with Octavian, Herod had enrolled and equipped an auxiliary force on his own account to fight on Antony's side (*Ant* XV v 1 § 109f.). It had seemed to the Roman general, however, that Herod's army would do better staying in Judaea to ward off any Parthian attack that might develop, and that the Idumaean could in the meantime carry out his punitive mission against the Arabs as Cleopatra had requested. Thus Jewish forces were not directly involved in Antony's defeat before Octavian at the crucial battle of Actium (Fig. 6), on the 2nd September 31 BC.

Nevertheless, the outcome of the battle placed Herod in a dangerous political position as the known ally of the vanquished Antony. The realisation that before long he would be called to account by Octavian sadly marred his triumphal homecoming from victory over Malchus. There were not a few, however, who viewed the future with renewed hope in the light of Herod's discomfiture. Among them was Alexandra.

Herod's estrangement from his Arab neighbours had given his mother-in-law a potential new ally in her struggle against the king. Doubtless the irony of a situation which allowed the possibility of her using an Arab king to foster a Jewish rebellion against a leader of his own race was not lost upon Alexandra. She prepared the ground by nagging her poor old father, Hyrcanus, now in his seventies, into believing that the time had come to exert his authority as a Hasmonean and true heir to the Jewish crown. With Herod's downfall certain following on Octavian's victory over Antony, Hyrcanus, with the surviving members of his family, must be prepared to take up the royal sceptre. Jew would once more rule Jew.

The old man needed much persuading. Life for him had been a succession of bitter disappointments, not the least being that he had not been allowed in his younger days to retire on a pension and leave to others the rough and tumble of power politics, and the hardly less dangerous and exhausting role of High Priest. But Alexandra assured him that this time there was no danger since they had an ally in Malchus. He would, if asked, arrange a safe escape from Jerusalem and would look after them in Arab territory until Herod met his just deserts. They could then return in triumph to lead the Jewish nation. Reluctantly, Hyrcanus allowed himself to be persuaded and wrote as instructed to Malchus. The arrangement was that the Arab should send a posse of horsemen to carry him and his family to the Dead Sea and thus to safety.

Hyrcanus entrusted the fateful letter to an old friend of the family, Dositheus, who had no cause to love Herod since he was a relative of Salome's husband Joseph whom Herod had summarily executed on suspicion of committing adultery with Mariamne. However, once the letter was in his hand, Dositheus began to have doubts about the wisdom of treason while Herod was still very much alive. He therefore took the missive to his king, who, commending the honest fellow for his loyalty, performed the ancient equivalent of steaming open the envelope. Having read the contents, perhaps not without a certain amount of grim satisfaction, Herod handed the letter back and told Dositheus to re-seal it, deliver it as instructed to Malchus, and bring him back the reply. The man hastened to obey, and the answer came back from Malchus assuring Hyrcanus of his fullest support. Not only would he and his family be brought to safety, but as many Jewish sympathisers as he could muster would similarly be made welcome in Arab territory to await their day of liberation.

It was probably a matter of deep regret to Herod that his mother-in-law had kept in the background of this affair, and that the illicit correspondence he had intercepted offered no proof of her complicity. It was thus only the luckless Hyrcanus whom he arraigned before the Sanhedrin. On being presented with the damning evidence, they could do no other than assent to his execution. Alexandra and Mariamne Herod had imprisoned in the Alexandrium fortress in the Jordan valley, with instructions that should he not return from his forthcoming interview with Octavian, they should both be put to death. His own mother Cypros, his sister Salome, his brother Pheroras, and all his children, he had taken to Masada. In the event of Herod's death, Pheroras was to make every effort to secure the kingdom for the king's children and thus to continue Idumaean control of the Jewish State. This done, Herod prepared to meet whatever fate offered at the feet of Octavian, the new master of the empire.

15(a) Mark Antony, at the age of 42, from a gold coin struck at Ephesus in 41 BC.

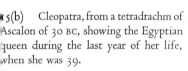

15(b) Cleopatra, from a tetradrachm of Ascalon of 30 BC, showing the Egyptian queen during the last year of her life, when she was 39.

16(a)   The "window" of a cave used by insurgents of the Second Jewish Revolt, set in cliffs in the lower Kidron Valley.

16(b)   The   Judaean Wilderness: site of the cave in the above picture.

CHAPTER XIV

Plot and counter-plot

There was little point in Herod's denying before Octavian that he had been Antony's friend. Crown in hand, the Idumaean took the only stance open to him, that of a humble suppliant for mercy, offering the victor in return for his life a loyalty no less true than that he had given Antony. The vanquished general had trusted him, and, in all but one matter, his calamitous infatuation for Cleopatra, had accepted and acted upon Herod's advice. Were Octavian now to accept his friendship, he, too, could count on his good offices and support in all State affairs. And as a token of his esteem, Herod offered a few trinkets which the Roman general might be gracious enough to accept . . .

Whether it was the suppliant's air of humility, mingled with pride that he had remained loyal to his friend in his adversity (not strictly true, since he had deliberately thwarted attempts to send Antony gladiatorial reinforcements after Actium—*Ant* XV vi 7 §195), or simply that Octavian needed an ally in Palestine, the Roman accepted the gifts and heaped honours upon the king. He asked him to be as great a friend in the future as he had been to Antony in the past, and Herod gave an earnest of his goodwill by giving every assistance to Octavian's army on their way to settle accounts with his former benefactor in Egypt. A grand welcome was arranged for the troops in Ptolemais, where Herod had the honour of riding with Octavian when he reviewed his men. When the army reached the southern deserts of Judaea, it was Herod who supplied water, and even wine, to sustain the thirsty soldiers on their vengeful mission.

Octavian entered Alexandria as conqueror on the 1st August 30 BC. He found Antony already dead, killed by his own hand—though not very efficiently, from all accounts—on hearing that his royal mistress had previously committed suicide. In fact, she had refrained from doing so before she had made at least one attempt to come to terms with the young Caesar. Barely forty, Cleopatra must have felt that life surely had much yet to give, and, according to popular tradition, offered her

M

charms to Octavian as she had done so successfully with Antony and less so with Herod. The Roman general found his would-be seducer resistible, however, and dreamt rather of parading her before the street mobs of Rome in his victory procession. Despite his precautions against her cheating him of this happy prospect, the proud queen killed herself with the aid of one (or two) asps secretly conveyed to her and pressed against her bosom.

Cleopatra's death brought more to Herod than grim satisfaction at the downfall of an enemy. All the possessions in Palestine that she had received from Antony were restored to the Jewish crown, with the addition of such prizes as the cities of Gadara, Hippos, Samaria, and the maritime centres of Gaza, Anthedon, Joppa and Straton's Tower, the later Caesarea (§ 217: Fig. 7). Thus, far from meeting a just retribution at the hands of his previous patron's enemy, Herod came away from the affair with a territory as large as that controlled by the mighty Alexander Jannaeus at the height of his success.

Not everyone was so pleased, of course. In particular, Mariamne and her mother, confined within the fortress of Alexandrium, had hoped for a different outcome. True, they had managed to prise from their jailor Sohemus the secret of Herod's parting instructions to put them to death should the worst befall him. Doubtless they planned by flattery and bribery to stay their executioner's hands in the same way as they had extracted from him the king's command. Now Herod was back, well pleased with himself, and still passionately in love with his wife, to the disgust not only of that lady and her mother, but of his sister Salome and their mother Cypros.

For a year this rancour persisted in the royal household, the Hasmoneans making no secret of their contempt for the low birth of the Idumaeans and their hatred of the whole family. Slanderous rumours flew thick and fast, and both sides watched each other, constantly seeking fresh material for impugning the characters of members of the other faction. One day, late in 29 BC, Herod retired to his room at noon and, as was his wont, called for Mariamne to come and make love with him. Whether she was feeling more than usually disgruntled with her husband, or was simply in an irritable frame of mind, the queen refused to join her husband on the couch. She stood instead by his side, spitting contemptuous remarks about him and his family, and reminding her pleading lover that he had killed her father and brother (§ 222). At length, Herod's frustrated sexual desires turned to no less passionate hatred, and their quarrelling was heard throughout the palace. Salome, never far away when trouble seemed to be brewing, decided the time had come for her to put into action a long-prepared plan involving the king's cup-bearer.

At her bidding, the man went to his master while he was still fuming with anger, and told him that Mariamne had tried to bribe him to give the king a love-potion. Not unnaturally, since an aphrodisiac was probably the last thing he needed, Herod suspected foul play and demanded to know the nature of the drug. The butler played his part and said he did not know; Mariamne had simply said that it was quite harmless and if his master showed none of the usual signs of stimulation, he was not to worry but to forget all about it. As Salome intended, the king was by now certain that his wife intended to poison him. He tried to force more information out of the servant by torture, but the poor fellow could give him no more than the additional fact that part at least of Mariamne's hatred for her husband was due to the instructions he had left with Sohemus for her execution if Herod himself should die at Octavian's hands. Again Herod went berserk with rage and jealousy, asserting that the hitherto faithful Sohemus would only have betrayed his secret trust in a moment of sexual intimacy with Mariamne. He ordered his immediate execution without trial, as he had done on the similar occasion with his brother-in-law Joseph. Mariamne herself was tried on charges of conspiring to poison her husband, and found guilty. By now, however, some reason had returned to the distraught king, and he would have merely imprisoned her in one of his fortresses had his sister Salome not prevailed upon him to have her killed immediately. Salome insisted that while the Hasmonean was still alive she would attract the loyalties of a large number of his dissident subjects proclaiming her the innocent victim of a tyrant. Mariamne was therefore put to death, but to judge from the obituary given by Josephus, was no less regarded popularly as a Jewish martyr, tragically murdered by barbarians for no more cause than the nobility of her birth and haughtiness of her demeanour:

"Thus died Mariamne, a woman unexcelled in self-discipline and in greatness of spirit, though deficient in reasonableness and having too contentious a nature. But in beauty of body and in dignity of bearing in the presence of others she surpassed her contemporaries beyond reckoning. And this was the chief cause of her failure to please the king and live with him in peace. For being constantly courted by him through his love, she came to expect no harsh reprisals and allowed herself an unreasonable licence of speech in his presence. Furthermore, her natural distress at the misfortunes that had befallen her relatives led her to express her feelings to Herod so unrestrainedly as eventually to incur the enmity of the king's mother and sister and that of Herod himself, from whom she had mistakenly expected never to suffer any harm" (§ 237ff.).

Our historian dwells at some length on the effect that Mariamne's death had upon Herod. This "divine madness" (*enthousiastikos*), as he calls the king's passion for his wife, continued to assail him after her execution, driving him to a depressive mania which threatened his life. He would call out for his beloved, and indulge in soul-racking lamentations. Then he would devise all manner of distractions, such as wild parties and banquets, to drive his loss from his mind. He neglected his administrative duties, and would sometimes command his servants to call Mariamne to him, as if she were still alive.

About the same time, a plague of some kind swept the country and carried off large numbers of the people including some of his best friends. By common consent this visitation from heaven was a direct result of Mariamne's unjust execution, and the accusation drove the king even further into decline. On the pretext that he was going hunting, Herod went off on his own and gave way to such extremes of depression that whilst in Samaria he succumbed to some organic disease which defied all the remedies prescribed by his doctors. In despair, they decided to let him have whatever he asked for and leave the "faint hope of his recovery to Fate" (§ 246).

When news of the king's supposed mortal illness reached Jerusalem, Alexandra moved swiftly to secure the kingdom for the Hasmoneans, or what remained of them. Her hopes now lay in Herod's sons by Mariamne, Alexander and Aristobulus, and she argued with the defenders of the fortresses that controlled the city and the Temple, that if they were now to hand their control over to her, she would see to it that the lads succeeded to their father's throne and thus a disruptive hiatus in government might be avoided. She professed herself concerned that when the king died "others" might seize power, meaning, presumably, Idumaean interests headed by Herod's mother and sister (§ 249). One of the fortress commanders was a cousin of Herod's, and all were "old friends" of the king (§ 250), and, we may suspect, related to him. It would have been unlike Herod to have left control of vital strategic installations in his capital city in the hands of other than persons of proved loyalty who knew that their interests coincided with those of the king. They were well aware that Alexandra's intent was to restore Hasmonean, that is, Jewish rule to Judaea, in which case they would hardly be likely to survive. Her plea, therefore, fell upon unsympathetic ears; indeed, its content was immediately made known to the sick Herod. He needed no other excuse to rid himself at last of his old enemy, and gave orders at once for his mother-in-law's executon.

Doubtless Herod's illness made him more than normally irrascible and suspicious. But the purge that now followed among even his friends cannot be laid simply at the door of "his ugly mood", or that "being afflicted in mind and body at once, he found fault with everything and was quick to use any and every pretext to inflict punishment on those who fell into his hands" (§251). His apparent nearness to death revealed once more the strains within his kingdom, and in particular the inevitable antagonism between the Idumaean ruling party and the Hasmonean faction who claimed the loyalties of Judaism at home and abroad. Interestingly, the conspiracy that is next recorded in Josephus's account involves an Idumaean noble as its chief character. He had formed too close an alliance with the Hasmoneans and thus, from Herod's point of view, compromised his allegiance to the crown.

The Idumaean's name was Costobarus, of an ancient Edomite family of priests of the days before Hyrcanus forcibly converted the inhabitants of the southern territories to Judaism. On his assumption of royal power, Herod had appointed Costobarus governor of Idumaea and Gaza. He honoured him even further by giving him the hand of his sister Salome after the execution of her husband Joseph. However, before long, Costobarus began to grow restive under Herod's rule. It rankled that this Idumaean king should perpetuate the humiliation of his fellow-countrymen imposed by his Hasmonean predecessors, obliging them to adopt the religion of the Jews and forsake their traditional deities. Costobarus looked round for possible sources of help in his effort to rid his people of the Jewish yoke, and made diplomatic overtures to Cleopatra. Her Ptolemaic ambitions to incorporate Judaea into her territory were well known. The Idumaean governor reckoned that if his country were to come once more under Egyptian suzerainty, the queen might at least give the people freedom to worship their own gods, and perhaps offer them also a greater degree of autonomy.

Cleopatra gladly consented to the idea, and put forward this Idumaean plea for secession from Jewish control and political integration with Egypt as a further reason for Antony's giving her Herod's southern territory. The Roman refused to jeopardise his friendship with the king by giving Idumaea to Cleopatra, but thought it right to warn Herod of the treasonous intentions of one of his most trusted lieutenants. Naturally, the king's immediate reaction was to have Costobarus killed, and he was only restrained from doing so by the combined pleas of his sister and his mother. However, thereafter Herod watched his brother-in-law with particular care.

It seems probable that the women's concern for the Idumaean's safety was more politically inspired than humanitarian or even familial. They appreciated the harmful effect his execution would have in their own homeland perhaps better than the king, who had found it necessary to identify himself religiously with the majority of his subjects. For Herod, an Idumaean ancestry was a barrier to his acceptance by the Jews; for his family it was still a matter of deep pride. Nevertheless, Salome and her mother would not tolerate treachery in their midst, however popular Costobarus's cause back home. Probably, Salome's marriage to the Idumaean had never been more than a political gesture, and when Herod's life seemed to be in danger, she took steps to end the alliance.

The immediate cause of the rupture was her discovery that her husband had for some years been giving sanctuary to some well-known Hasmonean sympathisers, named the Sons of Baba. They had come into prominence during the time of Antigonus and had spared no effort in using their considerable influence with the common people to denigrate Herod and promote the Hasmonean cause. At the time of the capture of Jerusalem by Herod, Costobarus had been given the task of sealing the exits from the city and preventing known Hasmonean partisans from leaving to cause trouble elsewhere in the country. Knowing the considerable following among the people enjoyed by the Sons of Baba, and hoping for some personal political advantage therefrom, the Idumaean governor offered them the sanctuary of his own estate and had kept the secret of their refuge ever since. Herod had from the beginning had his doubts about the assumed escape of the Sons of Baba and the effectiveness of his lieutenant's blockade, but had accepted Costobarus's assurance that he knew nothing of their whereabouts.

On learning the truth, Salome could no longer feel justified in perpetuating even the form of her marriage with a traitor. Clearly

Costobarus was not a wholehearted supporter of his king. He had taken into his care known enemies of Herod, and had made surreptitious advances to a foreign ruler with an offer to transfer his allegiance. All along his aim had been to safeguard his own position in any future eventuality, rather than to promote the present interests of his fellow-countryman and ruler. Salome thus took the unusual step of formally divorcing Costobarus. According to Jewish law, the right of divorce lay with the husband only: "When a man takes a wife and marries her, if then she finds no favour in his eyes because he has found some indecency in her . . . he writes a bill of divorce and puts it in her hand and sends her out of his house . . ." (Deuteronomy 24¹). One may suspect that in a possibly matriarchal Idumaean society, the wife had equal rights of divorce, and that Salome was here following her native practice and deliberately flouting Jewish law. In this case, her action is an interesting sidelight on how readily Idumaean "Jews" threw aside the yoke of their enforced proselytism, and how little the Hasmonean policy of Judaising conquered peoples permanently affected their religious outlook and customs.

Salome reported to her brother the reason for her divorcing Costo-barus, and the king lost no time in arresting and executing his Idumaean governor, together with three of his fellow-conspirators, Antipater, Lysimachus and Dositheus. He ferreted out the Sons of Baba in their refuge and killed them. That these all had Hasmonean connections is implied by Josephus's concluding statement: ". . . none was left of the family of Hyrcanus, and the kingdom was wholly in Herod's power, there being no one of high rank to stand in the way of his unlawful acts" (§ 266).

In fact, things were not quite so simple, nor was power completely in Herod's own hands. The Hasmoneans had not been entirely liquidated; a daughter of Antigonus many years later married one of Herod's sons, Antipater (*Ant* XVII v 2 § 92). More serious, Herod's marriage to the Hasmonean Mariamne had produced five children of whom two sons, Alexander and Aristobulus, were his special favourites and earmarked by their father for high office. Yet they regarded themselves as primarily of Hasmonean stock, and were eventually to stand condemned of plotting against their own father, as avengers of their mother's blood. Herod's own Idumaean family hated the two youths as much as they had done Mariamne, and championed the cause of another of his sons, Antipater, born of his first Idumaean wife, Doris. Thus, far from eliminating all Hasmonean opposition, Herod had in fact merely created more from his own loins. For all the blood that had been and was to be spilt to secure Idumaean tenure of the crown, nothing could heal the rift between Arab and Jew, the ruler and the subject. The ill-starred marriage Herod had contracted with Hyrcanus's grandchild as a means of bridging that gulf brought only further dissension and ultimate tragedy.

To the dismay of most Jews and the relief of his Idumaean family, Herod survived his illness. Even his grief for Mariamne faded in a year or two before the dazzling beauty of a maiden of the same name, the daughter of a priest of Jerusalem named Simon. This new Mariamne was considered locally as the most beautiful woman of her time, and when the king discovered for himself how strikingly she justified her reputation, he set out to win the girl for himself. Since her father was too highly respected by the people for Herod to be able to ride rough-shod over convention and seize the maiden as his concubine, he was obliged to raise the family to a sufficiently noble rank to warrant his taking Mariamne to wife. This he did by dismissing the incumbent High Priest and appointing Simon in his place (*Ant* XV ix 2 § 322). One wonders whether he might not have done less violence to Jewish susceptibilities by simply making the girl his mistress. Merely to treat this most sacred office as a means of sleeping with the local beauty queen was to bring the high priesthood and himself into contempt.

The fact is that Herod never did understand the Jews, or their religion. True, he wished to appear as the promoter and champion of Judaism, and seemed at times, to be almost over-zealous in his attempts to win the admiration and confidence of the religionists among his people. His building activities in Jerusalem are a good example of how, from lack of understanding, he could seem to achieve his object in one respect, and yet simultaneously ruin any advantage he may have gained by his ineptitude in another.

Herod's reconstruction of the Temple was a brilliant demonstration of civil engineering, as the present-day visitor to the Muslim Haram in Jerusalem may judge for himself (Pls. 19, 20ª· ᵇ). The king announced the project as "the most pious and beautiful of our time", replacing the Temple built by "our fathers after their return from Babylon" (*Ant* XV xi 1 §385), a self-identification with Jewry which must have been as astonishing to his Jewish listeners as it was infuriating to his Idumaean friends and family. But for all his lavish expenditure on Judaism's most sacred shrine, and the care that he took to ensure that only priests should be engaged on the work to preserve its sanctity, he ruined the effect by enlarging and strengthening the old Hasmonean fortress at the north-western corner of the Temple area (Fig.8). Now, more than ever, its towers dominated the most holy place, and served as a perpetual reminder to priest and pilgrim that Big Brother Rome was watching them. To add insult to injury, this mighty citadel continued to bear the name of Herod's erstwhile Roman benefactor in its title "Antonia" (§ 409). Furthermore, the king had a secret passage constructed for himself, running underground from the eastern gate of the inner sacred court (beyond this point he could not penetrate since he was not a priest) into the heart of Antonia, for use as a means of escape "should there be a revolt of the people against its kings" (§ 424; Pl. 21). Thus, in such practical safeguards, however justified, this would-be "Jewish" ruler identified his interests far more with the hated foreign guardians of the sanctuary than its native worshippers.

The splendid edifice which now arose on the site of Solomon's and Zerubbabel's temples was never, of course, intended solely for Jewish eyes and admiration. It was meant to be one of the wonders of the world, a spectacle for men of all nations to come and adore. In that sense, Herod's architectural achievements helped to fulfil part of the eschato-logical promises of Israel's prophets, that the gentiles would one day flock to the Temple of the Jews. He intended that they should gape wide-eyed "at its wonderful stones and offerings" (Luke 21[5]), if not to worship its god.

But more was needed to attract the tourist than religious buildings, particularly as the most interesting parts of them were barred to alien eyes. Herod therefore supplemented the cultic attractions of the city with a racecourse and theatre, and instituted athletic and gladiatorial contests at regular intervals. He invited top-class performers from every land, offering large prizes to tempt them to this out-of-the-way corner of the empire: "and whatever costly or magnificent efforts had been made by others, all these did Herod imitate in his ambition to see his spectacle become famous" (*Ant* XV viii I § 271).

It was the old story of the Hellenization of Jerusalem of pre-Macca-bean times all over again. Doubtless now, as then, there were "modern-ists" among the Jews who were not averse to watching the games and condemned criminals desperately pitting their strength against wild animals in the arena. There were others for whom "it seemed glaring

impiety to throw men to wild beasts for the pleasure of other men as
spectators" (§ 275). The religionists focussed their disapproval on the
national trophies wrought in gold and silver with which Herod had
decorated the amphitheatre, symbolizing the victories won by Caesar,
to whom the games were dedicated. These Jews were convinced that the
trophies covered human statuary and thus the reverence traditionally
paid by the Romans to their standards and weapons and to these
trophies of war was a contravention of Jewish law against image
worship, and unacceptable in their Holy City.

Herod tried to reassure the religious leaders that the gold and silver
replicas were not covering human images, but they remain unconvinced
until he had brought them to the amphitheatre and had the attendants
strip off the trophies and reveal the bare wooden posts beneath. Roars
of laughter arose from the crowd who had witnessed the pietists'
discomfiture, and this only added more fuel to the smouldering fires of
resentment against the king's innovations. For the substance of their
complaint was not, of course, simply that these emblems of war
surrounding the theatre were being venerated like gods, but that Jerusalem itself was being converted into a pagan city. The Temple was just an
ornate adjunct to a capital largely given over to business, military and
amusement activities like any great provincial centre of the time. It was
true that the promises of old were being fulfilled, and the people of the
earth were streaming to Yahweh's Holy Hill, but they came not to
learn of the Jewish god and bend the knee at his shrine, but to teach
the Jews the delights of the gentile world and convert them to the
culture of "bread and circuses". And the real danger, as the pietists saw
it, was that the Jews were proving not unwilling converts. Like Herod
himself, many of the inhabitants were asking why they could not mix
piety with pleasure like any other people in the ancient world. The
answer they received from their religious leaders was that the Jews were
not "any other people"; they were the Chosen Race whose destiny was
to lead all men to the worship of the one God. The biggest hindrance of
the time to the realisation of that divine mission was their Arab king
and the corrupting influence he wielded.

Events now took a sinister and ominous turn. Ten men joined in a
secret pact, swearing to hazard their lives in an attempt to assassinate
the king. One of their number was blind, which suggests that he may
have been credited with occult powers and could thus offer his comrades
divinely inspired exhortation in their desperate plan. They carried

daggers beneath their cloaks and went separately to the theatre in the hope of surrounding the king in the press of the crowd. In the event of their failing to approach their victim close enough to strike, they agreed to choose a secondary target, such as a group of Herod's bodyguard, and by their act and inevitable self-sacrifice proclaim to all their opposition to the alien king's violation of the Holy City.

Herod had, however, already taken precautions against this kind of subversion, by infiltrating known dissident factions with his own spies. News of the plot thus reached his ears in time, as he was about to enter the theatre, and he returned unharmed to the palace. The spy had provided the authorities with the names of the ten, and they were rounded up and brought unprotesting to the king. They made no attempt to deny the charge of attempted assassination; rather did they proudly display their weapons, and boasted of their high resolve to uphold the faith of their forefathers. Then they were carried off to die under torture.

It is significant that the spy was later identified by friends of the ten martyrs, torn limb from limb and thrown to dogs. Thus it is clear that behind the desperate band of assassins there was a larger religio-political organisation working underground with the intention of ridding Judaism of Herodian and probably Roman control. It was symptomatic of a form of subversion with which the authorities had increasingly to deal, and which, in the end, was to bring disaster to the New Israel.

CHAPTER XV

Rome's tightening grip

Herod's failure in Jewish eyes was not in his ability to administer or enlarge his kingdom, but in his not appreciating its religious destiny. Through his friendship with the Romans and his own diplomatic and military prowess he had been able to increase the prosperity of the country and extend its frontiers in a way that had not been possible since the Hasmoneans took advantage of the decline in Greek influence in the area. The Jews had no cause for complaint in this respect, but mercantile success and territorial aggrandizement was only part of the blue-print for the New Israel. Political control and exploitation of neighbouring peoples was but a step towards their proselytizing, at least to the extent of their acknowledging the sovereignty of the Jewish god. Although the gentile could never share the privileges and responsibilities of a member of the Chosen Race, he must learn to worship Yahweh and accept the disciplines imposed by the Jewish Torah. It was in this respect that Herod failed to play the part of a Jewish king, fulfilling the dreams of the prophets and the expatriate planners of Babylon. Much as he may have wished to please his Jewish subjects, he could not forget that his own people had been compelled to adopt Judaism by Hyrcanus, and he had no wish to inflict such humiliation on others. In any case, his Roman masters would not have tolerated such an interference with the religious liberties of their subject peoples. Freedom of worship was a first principle in the government of the empire.

Thus, although Herod built for the Jews a magnificent temple in Jerusalem, he was no less ready to embellish other cities in his realm with costly monuments to their pagan deities. He crowned his lavish extension of the old city of Samaria with a temple dedicated to his patron Octavian, now known by the honorific title of Augustus, "the venerable, majestic one". The outside staircase of this great edifice is still visible today, and the name survives also in the modern *Sebastiyeh*, from the Greek *sebastos*, equivalent of the Latin *augustus*. Again, on the coast between Joppa and Dora, some twenty miles south of Mount

Carmel, Herod built a new city overlooking a vast artificial harbour, on the site of a place called Straton's Tower (Fig. 7). It was an almost incredible feat of civil engineering, to judge from Josephus's description (*Ant* XV ix 6 §331ff.; *War* I xxi 5 § 408ff.), although little remains of it today. On a mound facing the harbour-mouth Herod built a temple to Rome and Augustus, containing a colossal statue to the emperor, after whom the whole city was named Caesarea, modern *Qeisariyeh*. The harbour itself was called Sebastos. From a religious Jew's point of view, perhaps even more horrifying was Herod's honouring his Roman patron with a temple built over the pagan shrine to the god Pan at the source of the Jordan, by the foot of Mount Hermon (*Ant* XV x 3 §363f.). He called it Paneion (later Caesarea Philippi: Fig. 7).

In short, Herod attempted and failed the impossible task of fulfilling the religious aspirations of the Jews while at the same time allowing the non-Jews of Palestine to follow their own cultures. He wanted to be a leader acceptable to all people in the territories put under his hand by his political masters, like any other client king of the empire. Unfortunately, at the heart of his kingdom was a people who considered themselves a race set apart by their god for the dominion of all mankind. His capital city was the centre of a territory believed by the Jews to have been ceded to their forefathers by the same god, as their inalienable property for all time. The kind of cultural and cultic compromises that made the Roman peace possible throughout the rest of the empire, and which Herod tried to emulate in Palestine, were, just not possible then any more than they seem to be now. One result of this difficulty in reconciling two incompatible attitudes within the kingdom was that Herod seemed to swing between the extremes of over-indulgence and vicious suppression in his treatment of both Jewish and gentile subjects. Thus we are told that, about the time of his building the Paneion just mentioned, around 20 BC, he tried to buy off the natural resentment of pious Jewry by remitting a third part of all their taxes, "under the pretext of letting them recover from a period of lack of crops, but really for the more important purpose of getting back the goodwill of those who were disaffected" (*Ant* XV x 4 § 365). On the other hand, he was obliged to take the most severe measures to prevent subversion of the kind we have already noticed: "No meeting of citizens was permitted, nor were walking together or being together permitted, and all their movements were observed. Those who were caught were punished severely, and many were taken, either openly or secretly, to the fortress of Hyrcania and there put to death. Both in the city and on the open roads were men who spied on those who met together. And they say that even Herod himself did not neglect to play a part in this, but would often put on the dress of a private citizen and mingle with the crowds by night, and so get an idea of how they felt about his rule" (§ 366f.).

In respect of his attitude to his gentile subjects, we are told that Herod "had the reputation of being the most inexorable of all men towards those of his own people (i.e. the Jews) who had done wrong, but magnanimous in pardoning foreigners" (§ 356). The occasion of this remark was an outcry raised by the people of Gadara against Herod's rule, in the presence of Caesar when he visited Syria in 20 BC. They wished to revert to direct Roman sovereignty and, according to Josephus, thought to take advantage of Herod's known leniency towards non-Jews, even when they provoked him. In fact, this hardly accords with the sequel to the story which relates that, on seeing the case going against them, the Gadarenes cut their own throats, or, like their swine in the New Testament story, "threw themselves into the river" for fear of being handed over to worse things at the hands of their king (§358; cp. Mark 5[13]). Nevertheless, in his gifts to gentile cities, particularly of fine buildings which might for ever act as constant reminders to the inhabitants and visitors of his generosity, Herod did strive to keep their people content and thus secure his frontiers: "he also surrounded himself with security on the outside, as though making this a reinforcement for himself against his subjects, for he treated the (gentile) cities skilfully and humanely, and he cultivated their local rulers, making them the more grateful to him because of the nice timing of the gifts which he presented to each of them. And his natural magnanimity he used in a manner appropriate to his royal power, so that his position became strong in all ways as his affairs prospered . . ." (§327ff.).

Herod also appreciated that Jewish affairs in his kingdom were not controlled only from within. He was well aware of the power exerted by rich Jews of the Diaspora and that links between them and the Jewish hierarchy in Jerusalem were maintained continually by religious pilgrimages and a constant flow of messages and gifts. The more difficult such Jews made life for themselves among their gentile fellow-citizens by their separatism and insistence on special treatment, the more they sought moral support from their cult-centre. The maintenance of their spiritual home in Palestine became an essential part of their own security in the lands of their adoption. So while they were willing to send vast sums to Jerusalem to support the cult, they expected the king and citizens there to reciprocate in helping to obtain the special privileges they demanded as Jews.

Thus, around 14 BC, Herod used his good offices with Marcus Agrippa, close friend and son-in-law of the emperor, to help the Jews of Ionia (Fig. 4) secure special rights from their fellow-citizens. During a joint visit to Asia Minor, Ionian Jews came to Agrippa complaining "of the mistreatment which they had suffered in not being allowed to observe their own laws and in being forced to appear in court on their holy days because of the inconsiderateness of the examining judges. And they told how they had been deprived of the monies sent as offerings to Jerusalem and of being forced to participate in military service and civic duties, and to spend their sacred monies for these things, although they had been exempted from these duties because the Romans had always permitted them to live in accordance with their own laws" (*Ant* XVI ii 3 § 27ff.).

Herod asked his close companion Nicolas of Damascus, to whom Josephus is heavily indebted for much of his material on Herodian affairs, to speak for the Jews, and we have in *Antiquities* a supposedly verbatim account of his lengthy plea (§ 31–57). Its main tenor is that all the special privileges claimed by the Jewish citizens had been granted by the Romans and thus should not be overridden by the local inhabitants through envy or simply because they did not like the Jews "spreading all over their country" (§ 59). To justify their special relationship with Rome, by which as Jews they might reasonably expect to be relieved from taxes and from civic and military duties, Nicolas pointed on his client's behalf to their king, proudly seated beside Agrippa: "What act of goodwill towards your house has been left undone by him? What mark of good faith has he failed to give? What form of honour has he not thought of? In what emergency has he not shown foresight? What, then, prevents your favours from being equal in number to so many benefactions?" (§ 51). And if Herod's loyalty and generosity had not been so adequately demonstrative of the affection felt by Jews for their political masters, Agrippa had but to search the records for tribute to Herod's father Antipater who had helped Caesar to invade Egypt, and was rewarded with public honour and Roman citizenship by the Senate.

Not surprisingly, the Greeks could find no ready answer to this blatant piece of hypocrisy, which must have left them—and, indeed, anyone who had any appreciation at all of what Jews generally, and those of Palestine in particular, thought of the Romans and the Herodian clan—positively gasping in their seats. Nevertheless, the case for the Jews of Ionia was won, and the incident ended most touchingly with Agrippa and Herod in mutual fond embrace, and the Greeks left paying the Jews' taxes for them.

By such diplomatic horse-trading Herod managed to keep his kingdom at least ostensibly at peace for most of his reign. For over a generation Palestine was free of the serious battles for power that had marked its history until Herod's accession. Thanks largely to the power of Rome and the peace that Augustus imposed throughout the empire, Herod was left in undisputed control of his kingdom and could forcibly restrain those internal disruptive movements which would otherwise have asserted themselves. But this imposed peace was bought at a fearful cost to the nation after his death, and to himself in the tragedies which beset his own family life.

As already noted, Herod set great store by his two sons by Mariamne, Alexander and Aristobulus. In 22 BC, he sent them both to Rome for their education and they were privileged to stay at Caesar's palace. They won their way into the emperor's affections, and he promised Herod that whichever of them he should choose would receive Roman support when it came to deciding on succession to the throne. The right of primogeniture properly fell not to these sons of Mariamne but to Antipater, son of Herod's first wife, the Jerusalemite Doris. This son had been banished from the court to please the Hasmonean clan into which his father had married, and thus, needless to say, had the complete support of the rival Idumaean family represented by Herod's sister Salome and their mother Cypros.

After five years of their royal upbringing in Rome, Alexander and Aristobulus came home in the company of their father. They were now young men, well favoured in every respect, and with all the old Hasmonean charisma they were acclaimed by the Judaean masses as princes worthy of their Maccabean lineage. Herod saw the danger too well, and tried to avert it in the manner he himself had so disastrously chosen when he married their mother. He gave as wife to Aristobulus his sister Salome's daughter by Costobarus, Berenice, hoping thereby to assuage the jealousy already evident on the Idumaean side of the family for the brothers' preferment over the banished Antipater. For Alexander he arranged a union outside the family circle, with Glaphyra, the daughter of Archelaus, the king of Cappadocia. But the rift in the family was too deep-seated to be bridged by matrimonial arrangements, and no sooner had the young men returned from Italy to the cheers of the crowds than the plotting to destroy them had begun.

There were faults on both sides. Salome and her mother were afraid now, as they had always been, of a popular revolt to unseat the Idumaean ruler and his family. They rightly saw that the princes could easily become the focus of nationalist sentiment and could rally behind them a large measure of Jewish support, both at home and, thanks to their foreign education, abroad, among the powerful Diaspora. The women therefore set out to discredit them before their father, and to seize upon any pretext to inflame his jealousy and provoke his resentment at their lofty and condescending manner.

The princes were obsessed with their mother's death at their father's hand, and regarded themselves, perhaps with much prompting from Hasmonean interests, as her avengers. They could not wait to seize power from their tyrannical father, and rashly made no secret of their aspirations in this regard. Such treasonous outspokenness Salome and her brother Pheroras made sure was fully reported to the king. "Finally," says Josephus, "the whole city was filled with talk about these things, and, as is the case in such disputes, the inexperience of the youths aroused pity, but the carefully made schemes of Salome prevailed, and in their own actions she found an opportunity to avoid having to speak falsely about them. For they were so grieved by the death of their mother, that when Salome spoke ill of her as well as of them themselves, they made every effort to show how pitiable was their own condition, being forced to live with her murderers and to experience the same fate" (*Ant* XVI iii 1 § 71f.).

Herod returned home from his successful meeting with Agrippa in Asia Minor, and proudly proclaimed to the Jews of the kingdom the news that, thanks to his intercession with the Roman commander, their co-religionists in Ionia were henceforth to be unmolested in their special privileged existence. To drive home the careful regard their king had for his Jewish subjects at home as well as for their friends abroad, he remitted to them a quarter of their taxes for the previous year (§ 63ff.). It was thus, yet flushed with good works and warmed by the cheers of his grateful subjects, that Herod was confronted by Salome and Pheroras with dire talk of rebellion involving his favoured sons. Furthermore, the marriage made for Alexander with the daughter of the Cappadocian king was proving a source of potential danger. The princes were relying on Alexander's new father-in-law to bring their charges against Herod to the notice of Caesar.

Again misjudging the strength of feelings involved, Herod decided in about 14 BC to recall to favour his first-born, Antipater, Doris's son, more as a warning to the brothers that they could not count on a preferment as a matter of right than with any real intention of making Antipater his heir and successor. Not surprisingly, this action did nothing at all to heal the rift, nor to calm the emotions on either side. The princes merely added this humiliation of themselves to their grievances about the treatment of their late mother. They became even more outspoken, and every heated word was faithfully reported back to their father. Antipater himself was not averse to stirring up the situation since he now began to have real hopes of succeeding to power, and he gathered around him a faction of supporters who willingly contributed to the slanderous accusations against his half-brothers.

Herod's inevitable reaction was to show more and more favour towards Antipater, hoping to cow the princes into obedience and docility. He even brought Doris back into the household and reinstated her as queen. In 13 BC, when Agrippa was returning to Rome from Asia, Herod sailed from Judaea to meet him and took with him Antipater, with the request that the Roman commander take him along and introduce him to Caesar in Rome as Herod's heir apparent. He had already written of his qualities to the emperor and other friends in the city, so Antipater found the ground for his reception well prepared on his arrival, and was not slow to take every opportunity to advance his standing. He also continued in his correspondence with his father to exacerbate his feelings over Mariamne's sons, and his friends left in Jerusalem furthered the process.

At length, the sorely tried king decided to seek satisfaction at Caesar's judgment seat and, about 12 BC, he sailed for Rome with Alexander and, according to one account, with Aristobulus (*Ant* XVI iv 1 § 90ff.; cp. *War* I xxiii 3 § 452ff.). He met up with the emperor at Aquileia and at the first opportunity arraigned the princes before him on charges of treason and plotting to cause his overthrow and death. Despite all the affection that he, and indeed, Caesar himself, had shown to them, they seemed intent upon destroying their father, and life had become so unbearable that he had perforce to bring this whole sordid domestic strife to his emperor's notice that he might be rid of the danger they presented to the throne. Thus he, as a father, was setting his own natural rights of paternal discipline aside, and demeaning himself to approach the judgment throne of Caesar as a suppliant, presenting his case for consideration at the same level as any argument his sons might bring in their defence.

The whole incident is a remarkable commentary on Herod's own feeling of insecurity at home. The only way he could escape responsibility for doing away with Mariamne's sons, and the danger of open revolt the action would have aroused in Judaea, was to seek redress from his master, hoping that Caesar would order the execution and leave his client king's hands free from blood. As it turned out, however, Alexander showed himself a more skilful orator and psychologist than his father, and so played upon the emotions of all present, as one more sinned against than sinning, that the company was reduced to tears of compassion. It seemed to Caesar quite incredible that such handsome and well-favoured young men should conspire against their own father. Even Herod began to have doubts about the charges he himself had brought against the princes, and to find himself in need of some defence against the wave of antagonism which rippled around the assembly.

"After a brief pause, Caesar said that though the youths seemed to be wholly cleared of the charge brought against them, they were at fault in one respect at least, namely in not having behaved towards their father in such a way as to prevent this report from being made about them. He also urged Herod to put away all suspicion and be reconciled to his sons, for it was not right, he said, even to believe such things against his own offspring . . ." (*Ant* XVI iv 4 § 124f.).

Thus admonishing both parties, Caesar effected a tearful reconciliation between father and sons. Even as the youths were about to fall at Herod's feet in supplication, he gathered them in turn into his arms and embraced them, "so that no one who was present, whether free man or slave was left unaffected" (§126). Caesar decreed that Herod should have authority to dispose of his kingdom and to appoint his successor as he wished, even to apportion the rule among his sons, if that were his will, giving a share of the honour to each. But until his death Herod should reign supreme.

On the way home, the happy party called in to see Alexander's father-in-law, the Cappadocian king Archelaus, who professed himself overjoyed at the outcome of the affair, both that his son-in-law had been cleared of the charges and that the family was now reunited. Back in Jerusalem, Herod proclaimed the glad tidings to a general concourse of citizens on the Temple mount. He thanked God and Caesar for having brought about the reconciliation, and made a solemn declaration of his intentions regarding succession to the throne after his death. Antipater was to be heir apparent, followed successively by Alexander and Aristobulus. But, since he himself was still in good health, the reins of government would remain in his hands, and he would select his sons' advisers and counsellors, "and hold them responsible for keeping the peace, being well aware that factions and rivalries among princes are produced by the malign influence of associates, while virtuous companions promote natural affection" (*War* I xxiii 5 § 460).

Herod's friends must have allowed themselves a wry smile. The old fox had pulled things round to his advantage after all. True, Caesar had refused to rid him of his troublesome offspring, but in the reconciliation that he had sponsored and that Herod had so publicly and heartily endorsed, the king had after all appeared as the maligned but generously forgiving party. The emperor's call to friendship Herod directed towards his whole nation, asking for the loyal support of all his subjects no less complete and unswerving as Caesar had required it of his factious sons. As Caesar had confirmed his kingship during his lifetime, so now Herod stressed that he and he alone would rule the country. Whatever honour might now be accorded Alexander and Aristobulus, the substance of power would remain in the king's hands, so let the schemers and plotters on both sides take due notice and beware. As far as Hasmonean ambitions were concerned, Herod's previous instructions still stood: Antipater was first in the line, Mariamne's sons following in their order of birth.

The public meeting dispersed with mixed feelings. Some joined in Herod's prayer for an end to rivalries; others, says Josephus, "pretended they had not even heard him" (*War* I xxiii 5 § 466). Whatever tactical advantage Herod may have won over his rivals by his clever handling of the whole charade, there was little real change in the situation. Mutual distrust, scorn and disparagement, backbiting and slander, plot and counter-plot were all still as rife in palace affairs as ever. Salome found another object for her hatred and malice in Alexander's wife Glaphyra, who considered her proud heritage from Darius, son of Hystaspes, on her mother's side, raised her socially far above the other ladies of Herod's court, and particularly his wives. She implied they were little better than tarts, chosen for looks rather than breeding (§ 477). Aristobulus in turn was jealous of his brother's high-bred wife, and considered Salome's daughter a peasant compared with the haughty Glaphyra, and told her so to her face. Thereupon she ran in tears to her mother, and Salome stormed off to complain to Herod. Herod's own brother Pheroras, to whom he had entrusted control of a considerable part of the kingdom, upset the king by falling in love with a slave girl and rejecting one of Herod's daughters betrothed to him by royal command. Even Salome was caught up in some calumny involving a love affair and espionage with a diplomatic representative of Obedas III the Nabatean king. He had wooed her so ardently that the whole court knew of the matter, and when on a subsequent visit he asked Herod for his sister's hand, he assented, but demanded for the sake of the convention by which he felt himself bound as King of the Jews, that the young and handsome Arab should accept Judaism before entering the royal family. This the suitor rejected out of hand, saying that if he should assent, his fellow Arabs would stone him to death. So Salome saw her beloved charging off back to Arabia, while her enemies began suggesting that they had done more than hold hands under the dinner table, and even her brother accused her before Herod of signing a secret marriage contract and passing State papers to a representative of Herod's enemy (*Ant* XVI vii 6 § 220ff.; x 5 §322; *War* I xxiv 6 § 487; cp. xxviii § 534).

At the centre of much of this court intrigue was the rivalry between Antipater and Mariamne's sons. Eventually Herod's suspicions of the latter, justified or not, grew to such proportions that he placed the matter once more before Caesar. The emperor suggested that an impartial council be convened at Beirut, consisting of local officials and such friends as he thought necessary, to advise the king on how to treat his erring offspring. The majority verdict went against the princes, and not long after, in the winter of 7/6 BC, Alexander and Aristobulus were executed by strangling in Samaria and buried in the family tomb in the fortress of Alexandrium.

Two years later, Antipater was also executed on the grounds of having organised an attempt to poison his father. The legitimacy of the judgment was ensured on this occasion by having the trial enacted before the legate of Syria, P. Quintilius Varus (6–4 BC). Herod survived his son by only five days, dying in agony in Jericho of some dread disease whose symptoms included "a terrible desire to scratch himself ... an ulceration of the bowels and intestinal pains that were particularly terrible, and a moist, transparent suppuration of the feet. And he suffered similarly from an abdominal ailment, as well as a gangrene of his genitals that produced worms. His breathing was marked by extreme tension, and it was very unpleasant because of the disagreeable exhalation of his breath and his constant gasping. He also had convulsions in every limb that took on unendurable severity" (*Ant* XVII vi 5 § 168f.). All of which was decreed by the men of God as just retribution for his impiety (§170).

Herod's last will designated his sons by a Samaritan woman, Malthace, as his chief heirs: Archelaus to be king and (Herod) Antipas to be tetrarch of Galilee and Peraea, while Philip, the son of a Jerusalemite, Cleopatra, was to control Gaulanitis, Trachonitis, Batanaea, Auranitis and Panias, that is, the region north and east of Galilee (Fig. 7). These arrangements had to be confirmed by Caesar before they could be recognized by the Roman authorities, and Archelaus made arrangements to travel to Rome and present his claims to the kingdom. He was delayed for some time by a popular uprising, which his clumsy handling did nothing to quell, and when he finally arrived, it was to find his case challenged in person by his brother Antipas demanding the kingship. A little later a deputation of Jews arrived from Jerusalem asking that the monarchy should be abolished entirely, and the people placed under the direct rule of Rome. In this plea they were supported by a large number of expatriate Jews domiciled in Italy. The accusations they brought against the dead Herod ran the whole gamut of tyranny from the violation of their virgin daughters and the debauching of their wives, to lavishing gifts upon non-Jewish cities at the cost of their own. Such indeed was the spoliation of Judaea, they claimed, that whole cities had been ruined and even disappeared for the purpose of indulging foreigners. Indeed, "he had reduced the entire nation to helpless poverty after taking it over in as flourishing a condition as few ever know" (*Ant* XVII xi 2 § 307). Even the local Jewish "lobby" must have wondered if this were not going too far: the particular "foreigner" the deputation was addressing had been left ten million pieces of coined silver by the late unlamented "despoiler", besides gold and silver vessels and some very valuable garments, and his wife Julia and others of the family had benefited by a legacy of half that amount. Even while the various deputations were journeying to Rome, Caesar's procurator in Syria, Sabinus, was on his way to Jerusalem to pick up what treasures he could lay his hands on from the "poverty-stricken" city. And as the Jews argued the poverty of their country and its ruination at Herod's hands, Caesar had before him all Herod's accounts brought by Archelaus, as well as the independent estimates of the late king's properties and annual revenues from Varus and Sabinus (*Ant* XVII ix 5 § 228f.).

Philip next joined the litigants in Rome, supporting his brother Archelaus's case and the validity of his own legacy of the northern tetrarchy (*War* II vi 1 § 83). Caesar's judgment ignored the wishes of the Jewish deputation for direct rule under the Syrian governor, and allocated the regions of control more or less as Herod had decreed in his will. Archelaus, however, was, for the time being at least, denied the royal dignity and made only an ethnarch, with the promise that if he showed himself worthy of kingship, the crown would be granted to him. His suzerainty, then, covered Judaea and Samaria, and Idumaea to the south. Antipas was appointed tetrarch of Galilee and Peraea, and Philip tetrarch of Batanaea, Trachonitis and Auranitis, and part of the northernmost valley of the Jordan. The cities of Gaza, Gadara and Hippos that Augustus had given to Herod were detached from Jewish rule and made self-governing urban communities directly under the province of Syria.

Once more, the New Israel was back in small pieces, and already its chief native ruler, Archelaus, had demonstrated by his inept handling of the popular revolt that opened his reign-that he lacked the character and foresight to rebuild it into the unified State ruled by his father. In ten years his despotism had given the Jews sufficient cause to complain of his conduct to Rome, and he was deposed and banished to Gaul in AD 6. Judaea was thenceforth constituted a procuratorial province, governed by a Roman official living in Caesarea through military garrisons stationed throughout the country and, in particular, in the Antonia fortress overlooking the Temple. The prophetic dream of a Jewish Holy Land ruling the world seemed farther away than ever. Judaea was now a minor province of inferior status within the mighty Roman empire, ruled by a procurator domiciled outside its capital city. Jerusalem, the city of God, resounded day and night to the tramp of Roman boots, and the Sanhedrin had to rest content with minor judicial powers. Even those Jews it condemned to death had first to be arraigned before a Roman judge.

It was clear to every religious Jew that the grip that had now tightened over the Holy Land had come to stay. This ruling force was no single man, Hasmonean or Idumaean, to be cajoled, bullied, or manoeuvred by court intrigue into acceding to popular or religious pressures. Whoever now carried the sceptre of State was an instrument of Rome, bearing responsibility to his far-off masters for the peace of the province. He would have no affinity with the Jews under his control, and no sympathy at all with their racialist aspirations. The only way now to their fulfilment lay in underground movements of the kind that produced the ten assassins pledged to kill Herod. While this sort of subversive activity could not of itself bring down the Roman empire, it could pave the way for God's direct intervention in man's affairs when he established His kingdom. Thus the turn of the era saw a dangerous concentration of religio-political activity gathering under the surface of Judaism and erupting now and again in various guises and names. Chief among such movements at this time was that whose initiates were called "Zealots".

CHAPTER XVI

Zealots and Sicarii

Josephus implies that the origins of the Zealot movement, the "fourth philosophy", as he calls it (the other three relating to the traditions of the Essenes, Sadducees, and Pharisees; *Ant* XVIII i 1 § 9), lay in an extreme Jewish reaction to a census imposed on Judaea by a Syrian legate named Publius Sulpicius Quirinius in the year AD 6. The emperor Augustus had sent this highly respected senator to Syria to make a general assessment of property and to liquidate the possessions of the deposed Archelaus. This administrative measure, reasonable in itself, aroused the fiercest opposition among some Jews for reasons which are not entirely clear. Certainly, it implied Roman sovereignty and, as the equivalent of our annual submission of Income Tax returns, was a means of assessing liability to taxation, never a happy prospect. Nevertheless, the High Priest at the time, one Joazar, whom Archelaus had deposed at the commencement of his ethnarchy (*Ant* XVII xiii 1 § 339), and who had presumably by now been reinstated, argued the Romans' case for them and managed to assuage some of the outraged feelings of his people. These Jews, without more ado, registered their property as required, deeming it as one of the necessary evils associated with centralized government. But a certain Judas, called variously a Galilean (*War* II viii 1 § 118; cp. Acts 5[37]), and a Gaulanite, that is from Gaulanitis, east of the Jordan and the Sea of Galilee, of the city of Gamala (*Ant* XVIII i 1 § 4: Fig. 7), with the aid of a Pharisee named Zadok, made the census a cause of rebellion. They claimed that the assessment reduced them to the status of slaves (we should perhaps say "ciphers") and that the nation should make a stand against such inroads into their dignity, and revolt against its perpetrators. If they were successful they would have "laid the foundation of prosperity, while if they failed to obtain any such boon, they would win honour and renown for their lofty aim" (§ 5). This stirring cry, while it will doubtless find an echo in the hearts of hard-pressed tax-payers of every age, seems strangely insufficient as the inspiration of the "fourth philosophy" and the devastating revolt it fostered.

There are other indications that the Quirinius census may not have been the immediate cause of Zealotism in Israel as Josephus implies, but rather that the historical event merely recalled a "census" motif in old Israelite folklore and cultic practice where Zealotism had its roots. It is interesting to note how often "counting of heads" and its associated imposition of forced labour, just another form of taxation, appears in Old Testament stories. Thus the Israelites are oppressed by "hard service" in Egypt (Ex $1^{13\text{ff.}}$); king David institutes a census at Yahweh's behest and thereby encompasses his own downfall (II Sam 24); and his son Solomon brings eventual disruption upon the kingdom by his demand for forced labour (I Ki 5^{13}; 12^4). The same theme is imported into the Christian myth, where Mary and Joseph are brought to Bethlehem by the Quirinius census, since the husband had to be counted "in his own city", being of "the house and lineage of David" (Luke $2^{3\text{ff.}}$). No such "general post" was, of course, required by the Quirinius or any other Roman census, and would have been quite impossible to organize and execute in real life.

We have shown elsewhere, in *The Sacred Mushroom and the Cross*, that behind the "census" and "forced labour" motif is a word-play on a very old, and by now secret name of the sacred mushroom, source of so much biblical and classical mythology. In the case of the Egyptian and Davidic legends of the Old Testament, and the birth story of the New Testament, this name has been woven into myth. It seems possible that the same name and its attendant folklore was sufficiently attached to Zealotism to have induced Josephus to find in the actual historical census of Quirinius the mainspring of the revolutionary movement. Luke's making this same event of AD 6 the commencement of his story of the Christ-child's birth at Bethlehem (despite the glaring anachronism that "the days of Herod" (1^5) ended a decade or so previously), is a further indication that the two religio-political movements of Zealotism and Christianity are related, not by a common circumstance of history, but by similar cultic practices and nomenclature.

The name "Zealots", Hebrew *Qannā'īm*, is but a word-play on another of the names of the sacred mushroom. Our recent researches have demonstrated that behind the fungus word lies a Sumerian phrase meaning "arched canopy, stretched across the heavens", a reference to the characteristic "umbrella"-shape of the mushroom cap. The name reappears in other, hitherto unrecognised guises, and all are related to this "Holy Plant", as it was called. Thus, the so-called "Garden of Adonis" of classical and biblical sources (cp. Ezekiel 8^{14}), still connected as late as Jerome's time (fourth–fifth century) with Bethlehem, was from ancient times associated with some fertility rites of unknown origin and nature. We now know that this mysterious "Adonis planting" which was induced to grow quickly from the ground by the ritual lamentation of female worshippers, and as quickly shrank away before the sun, was none other than the sacred fungus. The name by which the god Adonis was otherwise known in the Semitic world was Na'iman, and we may now recognise that the Qur'anic "gardens of delight" (gannāti-nna'īmi), where the Islamic warriors are welcomed after death, is but another representation of the same theme. In the Old Testament, the equivalent phrase is "the Garden of Eden" where the "tree of life" grew, by which mortals could learn the knowledge of good and evil and become like the gods (Gen 3). The common element "garden" comes from a misunderstanding, or purposeful word-play for myth-making, of the old Sumerian word GAN, "arched canopy", improperly equated with the Semitic gan "garden".

Thus, from the lost Sumerian original, *GAN-NA-IM(-AN), "arched canopy, stretched across the heavens", popular nicknamers found a half-serious epithet for those religious fanatics whose "zeal" was to bring Judaism down in ruins around its shattered Temple, the Qannā'īm, "Zealots": "for so these miscreants called themselves, as though they were zealous in the cause of virtue and not for vice in its basest and most extravagant form" (War IV iii 9 §161).

The viciousness which characterized the Zealots and which made them feared and hated by Jew and Roman alike, probably owed much to the stimulation of the drugs they obtained from the cap of their sacred fungus. Our recent studies have enabled us to identify this mushroom as the well-known Amanita muscaria, or Fly-Agaric, denizen of the pine and beech forests of the world. We know it best in this country from its frequent illustration in children's story-books, the popular "toad-stool" of the fairies. Its religious use has been studied for some years past, particularly among Siberian tribes, and it has recently been suggested that it is this fungus which is given divine honours as the Soma plant of the Rig Veda hymns. The fungus was always held in awe by the ancients, not least because of the strange manner of its conception without seed (i.e. its "virgin birth") and its speedy expansion from the "vulva" in the form of the human phallus, erecting under sexual stimulus. In the case of the *Amanita muscaria*, its brilliant red canopy, spotted with white, was especially noticeable and gave its name to a number of ancient words for "red" and "purple". Furthermore, it was known that if two or three of the caps were eaten, the poisons contained under the white "warts" would give the subject a variety of strange sensations, ranging from mild euphoria and hallucinations, to a raging passion of sex- and blood-lust. We can now trace to the use of this mushroom the wild ravings attributed to the worshippers of Bacchus/ Dionysus, the Maenads or Bacchantes. The details of their strange rites have long been hidden in mystery, since a feature of this and related cults was their secretiveness over the source of their inspiration and the nature of their sacred meals. In fact, the Bacchus/Dionysus god the Maenads worshipped and ate was the red-topped mushroom, and the same identification can now be made of the original "Lord's Supper" of the equivalent rite of early Christianity. It is also the original "nectar", the food of the gods, and the verbally equivalent "mandrake", with which Leah bought a night's connubial bliss with Jacob (Gen 30[14ff.]).

In association with the Zealots, Josephus later names the Sicarii, "assassins", who created so much havoc during the revolt of AD 66–73. We might quote this passage in full as a description of the terror such religious fanatics spread among their own people during the first century:

"But while the country was thus cleared of these pests (by the procurator Felix, AD 52–60), a new species of banditti was springing up in Jerusalem, the so-called *Sicarii*, who committed murders in broad daylight in the heart of the city. The festivals were their special occasions, when they would mix with the crowd, carrying short daggers concealed under their clothing, with which they stabbed their enemies. Then, when they fell, the murderers joined in the cries of indignation, and through this plausible behaviour, were never discovered. The first to be assassinated by them was Jonathan the High Priest; after his death there were numerous daily murders. The panic created was more alarming than the calamity itself; everyone, as on the battlefield, hourly expecting death. Men kept watch at a distance on their enemies and would not trust even their friends when they approached. Yet, even while their suspicions were aroused and they were on their guard, they fell; so swift were the conspirators and so crafty in eluding detection.

"Besides these there arose another body of villains, with purer hands but more impious intentions, who no less than the assassins ruined the peace of the city. Deceivers and impostors, under the pretence of divine inspiration fostering revolutionary changes, they persuaded the multitude to act like madmen, and led them out into the desert under the belief that God would there give them tokens of deliverance . . ." (*War* II xiii 3 § 254ff.).

The name Sicarii is usually assumed to be a reference to the short sickle-shaped blade (Latin *sica*) carried by the Assassins under their cloaks. Josephus himself draws the connection thus:

"The so-called Sicarii—these are brigands—were particularly numerous at that time. They employed daggers, in size resembling the scimitars of the Persians, but curved and more like the weapons called by the Romans *sicae*, from which these brigands took their name because they slew so many in this way . . ." (*Ant* XX viii 10 § 186).

We may now more probably derive the name Sicarii from another name for the fungus. It has come down into modern Persian in *saqratiyun*, "mushroom", but it is more generally known in the form it assumes in New Testament mythology, as the name of Jesus's betrayer "Iscariot". Thanks to our recent researches, it is now possible to break through the "cover story" of the Gospels and Acts and penetrate to the very much more significant level of meaning beneath. For the whole of the Jesus story is quite fictional. It was widely disseminated for the dual purpose of conveying to the scattered members of the cult special, secret names of the sacred fungus, concealed in such nicknames as "Iscariot" and "Boanerges", and for laying a smoke-screen to deceive the authorities about the organisation's subversive activities. Despite the incredibly favourable attitude displayed in the New Testament towards the hated Romans, it does not seem to have allayed the suspicion of local governors, who were instructed to seek out participants in the mystic Christian rites, torture them to discover their secrets and then execute them by the vilest and most painful means. Contemporary Roman historians can hardly find words base enough to describe these worshippers of the "Chrestus".

We may also recognise today that the Gospel stories were no more successful in deceiving the Jewish authorities. Here and there in Jewish literature, there appear previously incomprehensible epithets applied to Jesus which relate to the sacred mushroom. Most rabbinic traditions about the Christian hero have been obliterated by the Church censors, through whose hands almost all such records have come down to us. Where, as in such cases, stories and epithets have been allowed to stand uncorrected, it is usually because the censors failed to understand their significance, and even Jews had long ago ceased to understand their original meaning, or had deemed it wiser to banish such traditions from their minds for fear of further persecution by the now dominant Church.

It would seem, then, that the "Zealots" and the "Sicarii" are one and the same, and that early Christianity was closely connected with this revolutionary movement. The disastrous revolt which ended in 73 with the capture of the rebels' last stronghold at Masada we shall deal with in greater detail later. But in Josephus's account of those tragic days, he includes a lengthy speech delivered by their leader Eleazar, a descendant of Judas who had opposed Quirinius's census, before carring out a gruesome suicide pact that left scarcely a handful of people alive to face the victorious legionaries. The speech is almost certainly fictitious, but it probably conveys accurately enough basic elements in the Zealots' "fourth philosophy":

"For from of old, since the first dawn of intelligence, we have been continually taught by those precepts, ancestral and divine—confirmed by the deeds and noble spirit of our forefathers—that life, not death, is man's misfortune. For it is death which gives liberty to the soul and permits it to depart to its own pure abode, there to be free from all calamity. But so long as it is imprisoned in a mortal body and tainted with all miseries, it is, in sober truth, dead, for association with what is mortal ill befits that which is divine.

"True, the soul possesses great capacity, even while incarcerated in the body; for it makes the latter its organ of perception, invisibly swaying it and directing it onward in its actions beyond the range of mortal nature. But it is not until, freed from the weight that drags it down to earth and clings about it, the soul is restored to its proper sphere, that it enjoys a blessed energy and a power untrammelled on every side, remaining, like God Himself, invisible to human eyes. For even while in the body it is withdrawn from view: unperceived it comes, and unseen it again departs, itself of a nature one and incorruptible, but a cause of change to the body. For whatever the soul has touched lives and flourishes, whatever it abandons withers and dies; so abundant is her wealth of immortality.

"Let sleep furnish you with a most convincing proof of what I say— sleep, in which the soul, undistracted by the body, while enjoying in perfect independence the most delightful repose, holds converse with God by right of kinship, ranges the universe and foretells many things that are to come . . ." (*War* VII viii 7 §343ff.).

We are reminded of what Josephus had said earlier about the Essenes:

"For it is a fixed belief of theirs that the body is corruptible and its constituent matter impermanent, but that the soul is immortal and imperishable. Emanating from the finest ether, these souls become entangled, as it were, in the prison-house of the body, to which they are dragged down by a sort of natural spell; but when once they are released from the bonds of the flesh, then, as though liberated from long servitude, they rejoice and are borne aloft . . ." (*War* II viii 11 §154f.).

Of course, one has to treat our historian's exposition of Jewish philosophies with some caution, since he habitually tries to state them in terms of current Greek thought. Nevertheless, this emphasis upon separate existence of the soul is particularly interesting since it lies at the root of the drug philosophy of the ancient world. The narcotics were thought to effect that release of the soul from its mortal "cage" so much desired by the prophet of old. In such a condition, the subject was considered better able to assimilate truth. Information gained whilst asleep, natural or drug-induced, was necessarily more accurate than any the brain could reason for itself under normal conditions. The soul was able to pass through the barriers that otherwise hindered it from perceiving the future, so that the Essenes were credited with powers of prophecy, "being versed from their early years in holy books, various forms of purification and apophthegms of prophets; and seldom, if ever, do they err in their predictions" (§159).

It was this confidence in their abilities to foretell the future, and the belief that their divine inspiration raised them above the level of ordinary mortals in the apprehension of truth, that made such mystic cults so great a menace to their fellow-men. While they remained in their monastic communities, muttering their incantations and prophecies to each other, little harm was done. But when others began to believe the stories of their occult powers and look to them for guidance, they became a positive danger to the political stability of the country. In the overheated atmosphere that prevailed in Judaea in the first century, when the old dreams of world domination seemed incapable of fulfilment without direct action by God, the presence of religious fanatics claiming they had special means of access to the divine counsels must inevitably lead to a breakdown in rational assessments of current political situations. In such circumstances Zealots-Sicarii could find large numbers of Jews willing to support them in their madness, confident in their leaders' assurances that God would not allow their Holy City to fall into barbarian hands. Before that could happen He would send his hosts of angels to lead them into battle, under the command of a new Davidic king-messiah, the power of whose breath alone would slay the wicked (Isa 11^4; II Thess 2^8).

The other appalling aspect of this religio-political frenzy is that, to those who have induced themselves into believing that God is directing their thoughts and wills, it follows that all who oppose them, compatriot or alien, is an enemy of God and must be ruthlessly swept aside. Thus Josephus describes the activities of the Sicarii as the revolt of AD 66–73 neared its bitter end and the fanatics plunged themselves and the whole of Judaism into an orgy of self-destruction:

"For in those days the Sicarii banded together against those who consented to submit to Rome and in every way treated them as enemies, plundering their property, rounding up their cattle, and setting fire to their dwellings; protesting that such persons were no other than aliens, who so ignobly sacrificed the hard-won liberty of the Jews and admitted their preference for the Roman yoke" (*War* VII viii 1 § 254f.).

Again, we must take into account the chronicler's avowed hatred for the Zealots in assessing the measure of local opposition to their cause, but the whole tenor of his account of their activities in Jerusalem, particularly during those last terrible years, is that they were opposed at every turn by moderate Jewish opinion. To such people the end of such rebellious activities against the might of Rome was inevitable catastrophe. That the fanatics could succeed at all was due to their own single-mindedness, their willingness to sacrifice themselves and their families to their cause, and to the fact that they were able to operate clandestinely through channels long established in Judaism. The so-called "fourth philosophy" was, in fact, a network of espionage and political intrigue woven from the stuff of the eschatological strategies and dreams of the New Israel. Zealotism in its later manifestation was but a continuance of the Exilic plans to create a racialist society dedicated to world domination. What the Hasmoneans had failed to do by open warfare, the Zealots and their friends thought to achieve by subversion of authority from within, and, by reducing the body politic to chaos, so make possible the creation of new order by the finger of God. The seemingly indestructible power of Rome had driven the strategists to

(a)

(b)

(c)

(d)

17 Relics left by insurgents of the Bar Kochebah revolt in a cave in the Judaean Wilderness:
(a) Ivory needle; (b) key; (c) spinning whorls and thread picker (a large tooth); (d) a wooden
comb; (e) a wooden kohl bottle with bronze spoon and applicator.

(e)

18   Plastered steps of a cistern in *Khirbet Qumran*, cracked probably in the earthquake of 31 BC.

look more and more to the need for direct intervention by heaven in human affairs. All Yahweh's servants could do in these circumstances was to upset the old dispensation and wait for the new. In this, the matter of timing was crucial, and knowledge of the divine counsels and the eschatological time-table was of paramount importance. Hence the emphasis placed within such groups on the powers of prophecy and preconception, and the so-called "knowledge of God".

What made the underground movement so authoritative within Judaism was that its claim to represent the true Israel, the most ancient Faith of their forefathers, had in it a very large measure of truth. For, as we can now recognise for the first time, the old mushroom cult was indeed at the very heart of ancient Yahwism. Its essence was fertility worship, whose manifestations in popular sexual cult practices prophetic reformations were for ever trying to eradicate. The life and death of the fungus was thought to represent a microcosm of the natural cycle of regeneration, and its phallic form was seen as the image of God, the heavenly penis. Now that we can decipher the old Hebrew names of the gods and heroes, we can understand their fertility and mushroom significance, and thus recover just those elements of old Israelitism that the post-Exilic religionists did their best to forget. Clearly, the old fungus cult was not so easily suppressed, but continued underground as a mystery religion transmitted secretly between initiates sworn to silence about the central features of their Faith. Thus Essenism and Christianity could claim to represent the True Israel, and, with some justification, accuse "orthodox" Judaism of having departed from authentic Yahwism. In the same way, the Christian "heresies" which caused the established Church so much trouble in the early centuries, with some justice maintained that they were the divinely-appointed recipients of the occult knowledge of God, and that the institution which was so intent on hounding them out of existence had lost, or never had, "the mysteries of Christ".

It is furthermore now plain that the cult of the sacred fungus was not confined to old Israelitism and its latter-day manifestations: it lies at the heart of many of the Asian mystery cults, like the Bacchic worship previously mentioned. The ground was already prepared, therefore, for Jewish-Christian cells to flourish in Asia Minor and the larger cities of the empire, and thus to provide a network of communication through-out the Mediterranean lands for the passing of information between dissident groups. A significant feature of such closely-knit religious

o

communities like the Essenes and Christians was the way members could pass freely between groups, with the minimum of money and luggage, always certain of hospitality and the free provision of the necessities of life and travel. It is small wonder that such societies were always the objects of great suspicion by the Romans, who rightly recognised that through their channels of information rebellions could flare up simultaneously in widely separated centres throughout the empire.

The fears of the authorities were amply justified by events in AD 66. Trouble in Jerusalem was simultaneously matched by uprisings in Caesarea, and soon spread like wildfire throughout Syria-Palestine. Then the large and influential Jewish community in Alexandria suddenly erupted in violent conflict with their gentile fellow-citizens.

Josephus may be right in dating the manifestation of Zealot influence to the period around AD 6. It was not, however, just the census of Quirinius of that year that brought the movement into the open, but the assumption of direct Roman control over the province under a procurator. Never had the Jewish dream seemed less likely to be realised by mortal means: it was the signal for the Elect to begin undermining the regime by guerrilla and terrorist tactics as the preliminary moves in the fore-ordained plan. We may see something of the fanaticism and unreality of this imagined apocalyptic war against the forces of darkness in the War Scrolls from the Dead Sea wilderness, discovered in 1947:

"On the day when the Kittim (used throughout the Dead Sea Scrolls as a pseudonym of the mortal enemies of the Elect, usually with reference to the Romans) fall, there shall be a battle and grievous carnage before the God of Israel, for that shall be the day appointed as of old for the war of annihilation of the Sons of Darkness. Then there shall be joined in battle for great carnage a community of gods and a concourse of men, the Sons of Light and the party of Darkness, warring together (to display) the might of God, with the clashing of a mighty host and a war-cry of gods and men, on the day of calamity. And it shall be a time of (great) affliction for the people, the redeemed of God. Of their afflictions, none shall be like this, from its sudden beginnings to its end . . ." (col. I, ll.9–12).

"The God of Israel has decreed war against all the gentiles, and by the saints of His people he will act mightily . . ." (col. XVI l. 1).

These first-century "saints" were now committed to a course of events which could only bring to painful reality the "affliction" their battle-hymn foretold. Of the Zealots, Josephus records mostly abuse and ascribes to them none but shameful motives, such is his low opinion of their actions and disregard for the well-being of their fellow-Jews. But seen in the context of the overall plan laid down by the Exilic dreamers for the establishment of the Jewish nation, owing allegiance only to its tribal deity, and charged with imposing his worship on all men of every race, the tragedy that followed was almost inevitable. The Zealots and their followers were simply instruments of Yahweh. If they spared no one, man, woman or child, in their preparation for the Day of the Lord, the suffering thus inflicted was no more than any Jew must expect before the dawn of the new Kingdom of God. In any case, death, according to their philosophy, was to be welcomed as a blessing, a means for the release of souls to experience the freedom of their proper existence.

The story of the Jews in Palestine over the next sixty years has all the stark inevitability of a Greek drama. But if we are prompted to cast judgment upon its chief actors, on the cupidity and callousness of local Roman governors, the blind indifference of Jewish leaders to religious emotions seething beneath the surface of their nation, and, with Josephus, to the ruthlessness of Zealot fanaticism, it is well to remember that the scenes of the tragedy had been painted long before in Babylon. Furthermore, what had there been planned by expatriate Jewry, dreaming dreams and seeing visions of a Jewish world-empire, was now activated by a sinister power that derived from the earliest origins of Yahwism. The madness that now drove the players in this awful tragedy to the final holocaust derived from a drug-fungus whose worship was older than history.

CHAPTER XVII

Herod Agrippa

Herod the Great had given his sister Salome's daughter Berenice to Aristobulus in marriage (see above, p. 192). Of that union was born Herod Agrippa, who was only three when his father was executed at Herod's command in the winter of 7/6 BC. The child's education was supervised by his grandfather, who sent him to Rome when he was six, in his mother's care. Whatever else he learnt in that city, the young Agrippa acquired the facility for indulging himself in luxurious living and surrounding himself with influential and extravagant friends. Whilst his mother lived, she was able to exercise some measure of control over her son's pursuit of pleasure, but after her death he soon ran through all his own money and borrowed heavily on all sides. Eventually he was obliged to leave Rome and fled to Judaea, hotly pursued by his creditors, among whom were the custodians of the imperial treasuries, to whom he owed 300,000 drachmas, some £29,000 (*Ant* XVIII vi 3 §158). With his wife Cypros, a grand-niece of Herod the Great, he took refuge in an Idumaean fortress, and in black despair contemplated suicide. Cypros, however, displaying more native resourcefulness, approached her sister-in-law Herodias, the wife of the tetrarch Herod Antipas. She begged help for her husband, and prevailed upon Herodias to persuade Antipas to offer Agrippa a post in his territory. As a result, Agrippa was made a market commissioner in Tiberias (Fig. 7), given a house to live in and a modest stipend, and left in no doubt that he and his family were poor relations and not particularly welcome.

Agrippa endured this humiliation for as long as he could. Finally, taunted beyond endurance at a dinner party at Tyre, he threw the job in his brother-in-law's face, and took himself and family off to visit a crony of his Roman days, one L. Pomponius Flaccus, who had been appointed governor of Syria in AD 32. In Antioch, Agrippa enjoyed the legate's hospitality for some time, but then quarrelled with his host and decided to try his luck once more in Rome. Only with some difficulty, and then at a punitive rate of interest, did he manage to borrow sufficient money to charter a ship. No sooner had he boarded her, than the hand of retribution gripped his shoulder once more in the person of the Roman procurator of Jamnia. This official reminded Agrippa that he still owed the treasury a large amount of money, and put the vessel and the fugitive under constraint. Agrippa gave his word that he would make no attempt to leave, and that night ordered the sailors to cut the mooring ropes and make for Egypt.

In Alexandria, Cypros prevailed upon the local Jewish leader, probably the tax administrator, one Alexander Lysimarchus, to lend her husband 200,000 drachmas, about £19,000, to enable him to continue his journey to Rome. The loan was made, somewhat cautiously, in two instalments: five talents (30,000 drachmas) were immediately handed over for the fare to Italy, and the rest was to be paid by the branch office of the Jewish bank in that country on Agrippa's arrival. The Jewish entrepreneurs doubtless had in mind the numerous Mediterranean pleasure beaches that lay between Egypt and Italy, and it must have been with no less misgiving that Cypros waved her husband farewell and returned with their children to Judaea.

Agrippa was received warmly by the emperor Tiberius. The happy atmosphere chilled only when a messenger arrived hot-foot from Jamnia with a complaint from the procurator there that the emperor's honoured guest had broken his bond and still owed the treasury a large sum of money. Tiberius immediately banned Agrippa from the court until the debt was paid. Undeterred, Agrippa turned for help to an old friend of his mother's, Antonia, mother of the future emperor Claudius, a companion of Agrippa's youth. Antonia lent Agrippa the whole of amount due to the treasury, so that he was able to renew old acquaintances, and in particular foster those friendships which promised rich rewards for the future. He cultivated especially the goodwill of Antonia's grandson, Gaius Caligula, and, at the emperor's request, became the constant companion of Tiberius Gemellus, successor to the imperial throne.

With such influential friends, Agrippa found no difficulty in borrowing a million drachmas, some £96,000, with which he repaid Antonia and lavishly courted the favours of his aristocratic acquaintances. It was money well invested. Life at the imperial court could be hazardous, particularly for a man with high ambition but no private capital. Some time later, loose talking in a chariot cost Agrippa six months of freedom. He had remarked to his friend Caligula, with whom he was riding at the time, that it was a pity the emperor was not already dead since his companion would thereby be enabled to succeed directly to the throne. The incautiously expressed wish was overheard by the charioteer and in due course conveyed to Tiberius. Agrippa was imprisoned, but not abandoned by his friends, so that he did not lack the luxuries of life to which he had become once more accustomed. When, six months later, Tiberius died and Caligula took his place, Agrippa was released and, by way of compensation for the indignities he had suffered, was made king of the tetrarchies previously held by Philip and Lysanias. These comprised the north-eastern districts of Palestine, on the far side of the Jordan, and the more northerly areas around Mount Lebanon.

Philip had died without an heir in AD 34, after an unremarkable but quiet rule of thirty-seven years. He seems to have gained a reputation for honest dealing, and a readiness to listen to the complaints of his subjects. He wisely maintained good relations with Rome, and generally "in his conduct of government showed a moderate and easy-going disposition" (*Ant* XVIII iv 6 § 106). When he died his province was annexed to Syria and ruled directly by the Roman authorities.

Agrippa did not hurry home to claim his new kingdom. Rome had much to offer an aristocrat, still in the prime of life, whose best friend was the emperor. After a year or so, however, he decided to make his triumphal return to Palestine, to exert his authority in his newly acquired dominion, and doubtless to enjoy the pleasure of seeing his sister and brother-in-law squirm with envy at his good fortune and superior rank. In this regard he succeeded beyond measure. Herodias was highly incensed that this wastrel brother of hers, who had left the country as a beggar with creditors hounding his footsteps, should have returned a king, lording it over herself and her husband. She began pestering her unhappy spouse to demand equal rank for himself from Rome. At last, unable to stand more of his wife's nagging, Antipas collected all the ready money he could lay his hands on and sailed in state for Italy, accompanied by Herodias.

When the suppliants arrived, it was to discover that Agrippa had sent urgent messages to his friend Caligula, accusing Antipas of treason and plotting with the Parthians to overthrow the emperor. As proof of the charge, he adduced the evidence that Herod's armouries contained sufficient equipment to furnish the needs of seventy thousand heavy-armed infantrymen. There was no denying this fact, but the idea that a man of Antipas's peaceable disposition would wish to join forces with the Parthians to rebel against his own patron was manifestly absurd.

Nevertheless, Caligula believed Agrippa's accusations, and banished Herod to Lyons in Gaul (or Spain, according to the parallel passage in *War* II ix 6 §183), whither Herodias voluntarily accompanied him. Caligula then gave his kingdom to Agrippa. Thus, by the end of AD 39, Agrippa's kingdom extended over all the land north of Samaria as far as the Lebanon, and over the regions north-east of the Jordan.

Agrippa's return in state to Palestine had done more than drive his sister to jealous anger and extend his own kingdom. It had also caused some disturbance in Alexandria, whither he had called on his way from Rome in AD 38. For the details we are indebted to the first-hand accounts of Philo, the Jewish philosopher, in his treatises *In Flaccum* and *Legatio ad Gaium*. It seems that Agrippa wanted his visit to cause as little stir as possible. It will be remembered that it had been Jewish money, advanced by the treasurer Alexander (actually Philo's brother), that had enabled the new king to return to Rome and pave the way to his present honour. Possibly he wanted now merely to repay his debt and make his acknowledgment of his Jewish patronage. The Jews, however, demanded that their protégé show himself in all his regal glory and to demonstrate to their gentile neighbours how well connected they were in having as a kinsman one so honoured by the emperor. In other words, the pipers, having paid the tune, were intent on having as good a show as possible in front of the Alexandrian Greeks with whom, over the years, they had waged a running battle of mutual intolerance.

Jewish settlements had existed in Egypt long before the Exile of the sixth century BC. In Roman times, the local Jews had shown themselves friends of the invaders, as in 55 BC, when Herod the Great's father, Antipater, had persuaded the Jewish garrison in Pelusium not to bar the way of the Roman army under Gabinius. Later, in 47 BC, Antipater had helped Caesar when the Roman general had been in some difficulties in an engagement around Alexandria. Then, too, the High Priest in Jerusalem, Hyrcanus II, had urged the Jews of Heliopolis (Fig. 4) to support Antipater in his pro-Roman policy, and the Jews of Memphis followed suit (see above, p. 137). Augustus had shown Roman gratitude for Jewish help in the past by confirming special privileges and rights they had previously enjoyed, including the appointment of their own ethnarchs, "desiring that the several subject nations should abide by their own customs and not be compelled to violate the religion of their fathers" (*Ant* XIX v 2 §283).

Not surprisingly, the local Greek population of Alexandria resented these favours granted to people who, in the eyes of many, were no better than traitors or fifth columnists. Rome, after all, was a foreign invader and the Jews had assisted her legions conquer the country. They could hardly expect to be loved. Furthermore, since their religion and customs were expressly ordained to set them apart from their fellow-men, social integration and intermarriage which might eventually have healed the old wounds and brought harmony to the city were rejected. The Greeks saw in their midst only a haughty, specially favoured, alien community of about a million Jews (Philo, *In Flacc.* § 6), continually expanding their commercial interests and their share of the city's living space.

The Jews had their own quarter in Alexandria, set apart for their convenience and not in the restrictive sense of a medieval European ghetto: "so that through mixing less with gentiles they might be free to observe their manner of life more purely" (*War* II xviii 7 § 488). It was, as Josephus remarks during his argument against the anti-Jew Apion of Alexandria, "by universal consent, its finest residential quarter" (*Contr. Ap.* II 4 § 34). The area was situated on the east of the harbour, on the side of the city farthest from the burial ground, extending along the coast and inland (Fig. 9). Its seaboard position gave the Jewish area commercial advantages as well as making it the most pleasant place to live in the heat of summer. However, the Jews were not confined merely to this part of Alexandria. Their synagogues were to be found in other parts of the city also, so that the Greeks were ever reminded of the Jewish presence and their special religious rights. There is some doubt, owing to conflicting evidence, about whether the Alexandrian Jews were, technically speaking, full "citizens", but they certainly enjoyed the same privileges of citizenship as the Greeks. At the same time they formed an autonomous civil community, with their own council of elders headed by a gerousiarch, or chief elder, possibly identical with the tax controller who financed Agrippa's enterprises.

When Agrippa made his grand entry into the city, as a king and friend of the emperor, the Greeks were provoked quite as deeply as the Jews intended. But their response was not a gratifying display of naked envy, but of disparagement. They mocked this beggar-turned-prince; they laughed at the high honours accorded him by the Jews as king,

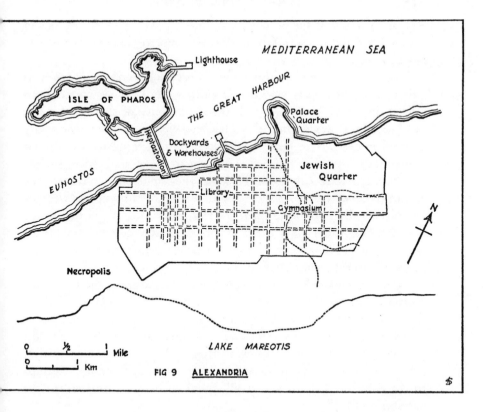

MEDITERRANEAN SEA

Lighthouse

THE GREAT HARBOUR

ISLE OF PHAROS

Palace
Quarter

EUNOSTOS

Heptastadion

Dockyards
& Warehouses

Jewish
Quarter

Library

Gymnasium

N

Necropolis

0   ½   Mile
0   Km

LAKE MAREOTIS

FIG 9   ALEXANDRIA

when not long before they had lent him the money to go to Rome to
fawn his way into imperial favour. The Greeks dressed a local idiot in
royal garb and paid mock homage to him in the streets, mimicking the
Jews acclaiming Agrippa in their quarter. Then they carted their
idiot-prince off to the gymnasium where, before a great crowd of
jeering people, they continued the mockery and coarse jesting at
Agrippa's expense.

The Greeks appreciated that the butt of their abuse was not only a
king but a friend of the emperor. Partly to rebut inevitable charges of
disloyalty to Rome, they began to raise a clamour against the Jews for
their refusal to acknowledge the recently-issued edict of the emperor's
divinity: "for while all the subject peoples in the Roman empire had
dedicated altars and temples to Gaius and had given him the same
attention in all other respects as they did to the gods, these people alone
scorned to honour him with statues and to swear by his name" (*Ant*
XVIII viii 1 § 258). On this occasion, the Greeks found an ally in the

Roman governor of Egypt, one A. Avilius Flaccus, who, for reasons of his own, wanted to curry favour with the emperor and restore his own favour at court.

Flaccus accordingly issued an edict against the Jews describing them as "aliens and interlopers" (Philo, *In Flacc.* § 8). Thus supported from official quarters, the Greeks took the opportunity of paying off a few of their old scores against their Jewish neighbours. The whole city erupted in riots. The Jews were driven into their quarter, and their houses and shops were pillaged and burnt to the ground. Men, women and children were cut down wherever they appeared on the streets, and in those synagogues not destroyed, statues of the emperor were set up. Flaccus did nothing to quell the riot, but rather added fuel to the fire by having thirty-eight elders of the Jewish council dragged into the theatre and publicly flogged. Jewish women were then brought there and made to eat swine's flesh or be cruelly tortured.

Agrippa seems to have been instrumental in affording the Jews some measure of revenge, at least upon the governor Flaccus. Before the riots, they had drawn up a declaration of loyalty to the emperor and put it into the hands of Flaccus to forward to Rome. He had failed to do this, and the Jews seized upon this dereliction of duty to lodge a complaint, which, together with a fresh address, they presented through Agrippa to the emperor. Flaccus was recalled and condemned to death in the autumn of AD 38.

The emperor's assumption of divine status elsewhere provoked trouble among the Jewish populations of the empire. In Jamnia (Fig. 7), around AD 39, the pagan inhabitants had set up an imperial altar which members of the religious community of Jerusalem high-handedly pulled down. When news of the outrage reached Gaius he commanded that the newly-appointed Syrian governor P. Petronius take two legions and, without regard for any local opposition, set up a statue of the emperor in the Temple in Jerusalem. The strength of the military force makes it clear that Caligula had in mind much more than pandering to his own vanity by setting his image in the Jewish sanctuary. He was clearly prepared for war on a large scale and must have had good reason to believe that behind the Jewish destruction of the imperial altar at Jamnia lay a much more serious revolutionary movement.

Petronius marched his legions and auxiliaries to Ptolemais, intending to spend the winter of AD 40/41 there, and begin the campaign in the following spring. Gaius approved the plan and commended his legate for his promptness. However, when Petronius arrived in Ptolemais, he was approached by a large deputation of Jews, who begged him to desist from an action which was bound to stimulate rebellion, or, at least, give the more violent factions of the community an excuse for a call to arms. Petronius summoned a further meeting of Jewish leaders in Tiberias to sound out their opinion, and received much the same response. He was approached also at this juncture by Agrippa's brother, Aristobulus, and one, Helcias, a prefect and friend of Agrippa, urging the legate to desist from all-out war which the erection of the statue would entail. Back in Rome, also, Agrippa himself used his good offices with the emperor to persuade him to exercise restraint. For a time, at least, Caligula allowed himself to be diverted from his firm intention of bringing the recalcitrant Jews to heel and demanding from them this outward act of loyalty to the imperial throne.

In this account of the affair Agrippa and his brother and prefect are portrayed as the heroes of the hour. Josephus says that Caligula was highly impressed with Agrippa's sincerity in braving the emperor's wrath, and pleading for the Jewish cause: "he admired the character of Agrippa in that he set little store on adding to his personal authority, either by increasing his revenue or by other privileges, but had regard to the happiness of the commonwealth, by giving precedence to religion of law" (*Ant* XVIII viii 8 § 300). Petronius, also, comes in for much praise as an instrument of the Jewish god in holding back the mad vengeance of his imperial master. In fact, when the legate's report reached Caligula, it convinced him that the Jews were indeed planning a revolt, and he is supposed to have written immediately to Petronius ordering him to take his own life for daring to have delayed immediate punitive action. The denouement, which proved beyond doubt that Yahweh was still guarding his own people and even his gentile servants like Petronius, was that the messengers carrying the emperor's orders to the Syrian governor were delayed by storms, and Gaius had been murdered by the Praetorian guards (on the 24th January AD 41) before they arrived. For the moment a full-scale Jewish war had been averted. The question remains how far Agrippa did in reality persuade the emperor against asserting his authority over the dissident elements of Judaea. One is tempted to wonder also, in retrospect, whether a spring campaign by Petronius as planned might not have aborted the more serious rebellion of AD 66, by bringing the underground forces out of concealment in premature self-identification and destruction.

Agrippa's known friendship with Caligula could have proved dangerous for him after the assassination. However, his early companionship of Claudius gave him entry into the confidences of that diffident classical scholar. Agrippa used his influence to persuade Claudius to accept the imperial crown, and as a result was rewarded, not with the ignominy he might have expected as the confidant of the murdered Caligula, but with the addition to his kingdom of the territories of Judaea and Samaria. He was now king over all the lands formerly ruled by his grandfather Herod the Great, plus the territory of Abilene in the Anti-Lebanon (Fig. 7), and lacking only the coastal plain about Gaza and those areas around Gadara and Hippos in the north, to the east of the Jordan.

Agrippa was now about fifty years of age, and he returned to his kingdom to play the part of a pious Jew, careful for all the Pharisaic ordinances, and generous in the extreme in his bequests to the Jerusalem cultus. He was also watching carefully for impending trouble. When on one occasion he had word that some young hotheads in the Phoenician city of Dora (Fig. 7) had placed an image of Caesar in a Jewish synagogue, Agrippa went immediately to consult with Publius Petronius, the Syrian legate who had so miraculously survived his late master's command to take his own life. The leading men of Dora were given clearly to understand by the governor that the Jews were still to be regarded as privileged persons, maintaining their own customs and relieved from the obligation of bending the knee before the emperor's image. Just how conscious both Agrippa and Petronius were of the underlying tensions and the need for caution is expressed in the decree sent by the governor to the magistrates of Dora:

"For both King Agrippa, my most honoured friend, and I have no greater interest than that the Jews should not seize any occasion, under the pretext of self-defence, to gather in one place and to proceed to desperate measures" (*Ant* XIX vi 3 § 309).

Another precaution taken by Agrippa in this regard was his refortification of Jerusalem, and his building a new third wall to the north of the city. It was massively planned and begun, but the Syrian governor reported the matter to Claudius who ordered Agrippa to desist, "suspecting that a revolution was afoot" (*Ant* XIX vii 2 § 327). As Josephus says in *War*, "had the wall been completed, it would have rendered ineffectual all the efforts of the Romans in the subsequent siege" (II xi 6 § 218). As it was, the unfinished north wall delayed the Roman legions hardly at all. But one can hardly believe that the faithful Agrippa was preparing for possible defence of his capital city against the *Romans*. It is far more likely that he was looking to the time when it might be necessary to retreat behind strong bulwarks from hordes of fanatical *Jews*, intent on taking over the Holy City in the name of their god.

It may be significant, also, that Agrippa was assiduous in cultivating the friendship of his non-Jewish neighbours. He spent vast sums on building projects in pagan cities, and particularly in Beirut, where he gave the people a magnificent theatre, an amphitheatre, baths and porticos, and was no less lavish in the spectacles displayed in the places of entertainment. On one occasion he lined up seven hundred condemned criminals against seven hundred more, and set them to massacring each other to the joy of all present. Thus not only did the community save the cost of executions, but they were regaled with gladiatorial combat for nothing, so that "the feats of war might be a source of entertainment in peace-time" (*Ant* XIX vii 5 § 337).

Of more importance was Agrippa's calling together of several vassal kings of the area at Tiberias. It seems evident that more than mere courtesy was involved for the gathering aroused the suspicions of the Syrian governor Marsus, and he promptly broke it up. "He took it for granted that a meeting of minds among so many chiefs of state was prejudicial to Roman interests" (§ 341). Again, it seems hardly likely that Agrippa was really planning an anti-Roman coup, but more probable that he was organising a mutual defence pact against subversion from within. However, just what his ultimate intentions were we shall probably never know, since he was taken suddenly ill at the spectacles at Caesarea in AD 44, and died after five days of agony with some abdominal complaint (§ 343ff.; cp. Acts 12[21ff.]). It is not unlikely that the reference in Acts 12[1ff.] to Agrippa's attack upon the Christians, despite the general legendary nature of the rest of the story, has at base the king's precautions against internal disorders by revolutionary groups. Undoubtedly, the authorities were well aware of the nature and extent of the storm that was brewing.

CHAPTER XVIII

Agrippa II and the Procurators

The emperor Claudius was dissuaded by his counsellors from appointing Agrippa's seventeen-year-old son, then at Rome, to his late father's throne. Their argument was that the young man was too young to bear such heavy responsibilities. It seems more probable that they wanted the central government to exercise a firmer and more direct control over this politically sensitive area. Claudius therefore incorporated the kingdom into the Syrian province once more, under the governorship of procurators living in Caesarea. The official title of the area was Judaea, and, although now larger in size, its legal position was the same as that obtaining after the deposition of Archelaus in AD 6.

The young Agrippa, however, had too many friends at court to be left entirely out in the cold. After the death of his uncle Herod in AD 50, he was given his kingdom of Chalcis, between the Lebanon and Anti-Lebanon, and not long after, the territory formerly included in Philip's tetrarchy, with Batanaea, Trachonitis and Abilene (Fig. 7). Later still, Nero added to his domain parts of Galilee and the Peraean city of Julias, with its fourteen villages. Furthermore, as a concession to the religious susceptibilities of the Jerusalem Jews, Agrippa II took over the responsibilities held by his late uncle Herod of Chalcis for the guardianship of the cultus. He had power to appoint and depose the High Priest, and to supervise the Temple fabric and treasuries, as well as its worship.

Agrippa II had already demonstrated his usefulness as a mediator on Jewish religious affairs. In AD 44, the newly-appointed procurator, Cuspius Fadus, had incensed the Jerusalem priesthood by requiring that the high priestly vestments should be placed in Roman care in the Antonia fortress, bordering on the Temple. When the Romans took over the direct rule of Judaea, after the reign of Archelaus, Herod the Great's successor, they made a similar provision, presumably to give the local garrison some measure of control over the ordering of the Jewish festivals. These were too often the occasion for popular anti-Roman demonstrations. By refusing to release the rich robes and other regalia from custody, the garrison commander could halt preparations for major services, even if he could not keep the potential trouble-makers out of the sanctuary. In AD 36/37, the Roman governor of Syria, Vitellius, had agreed to concede the right of custody of the vestments to the Jews once more. Now, with the situation becoming more and more menacing, Fadus wanted a closer control over the cultus.

The Jews sent a delegation to Rome to plead their case for maintaining their ability to order Temple affairs, and found on arrival that they had a friend at court, in the person of the young Agrippa. Claudius granted the request, adding that the people of Jerusalem had Agrippa to thank for the concession: "My friend Agrippa, whom I have brought up and now have with me, a man of the greatest piety, brought your envoys before me" (*Ant* XX i 2 § 12). Thus, even at that early stage, Claudius was grooming the young man as an important link between the central government and the religiously sensitive Jerusalem community.

As it turned out, Agrippa failed on a number of occasions to measure up to the high expectations of piety raised by this early concern for Jewish institutions. Somewhat later, in Jerusalem, he extended his palace facilities so that diners at the royal table might find their meal enhanced by a superb view across the Temple area to the Mount of Olives beyond (Fig. 8). The priests objected to this arrangement since it meant that Agrippa and his guests could watch the sacred ritual in progress, an offence to their cultic laws (*Ant* XX viii 11 § 189ff.). On another occasion, Agrippa gave the Levites permission to wear the linen costume customarily reserved for a higher class of priests, and this, too, was regarded by the pietists as a contravention of ancestral customs (§ 216ff.). Added to this, the priests could not reconcile themselves to the idea of a Herod manipulating the high-priesthood at will, although the conception of the sacred office as in any sense a charismatic appointment must have worn thin long ago. It had become a political and financial prize, a bargaining counter, since the time of the Maccabees, and High Priests cannot have commanded much respect from the ordinary religious Jew of the time. Agrippa's private life was also the subject of lively speculation, it being rumoured that Agrippa was living incestuously with his sister, Berenice, after the death of her husband (and uncle), Herod of Chalcis (*Ant* XX vii 3 § 145; cp. Acts 25[13]; Juvenal's *Satire* vi 156–60). But it is more probable that she was merely presiding over the court of her brother, who never married.

In any case, Agrippa had little real effect on the central issues involving Jews and Romans during his lifetime. Although he had a palace in Jerusalem, he lived most of his time in Caesarea Philippi, the capital of his province. The real struggles were to take place between the Roman officials of Judaea, particularly the procurators, the moderate Jewish leaders, and the subversive elements, now coming more and more into the open.

Among the disturbances with which the first of the new series of procurators, Fadus, had to deal was that involving a self-styled Messiah called Theudas. Seeing himself as a second Moses, this prophet proclaimed that the waters of the Jordan would divide at his command, a sure sign that the re-entry of the Chosen People into the Holy Land was about to take place (*Ant* XX v 1 § 97ff.). This event, of about AD 45 or 46, is placed by the New Testament storytellers anachronistically before the time of Gamaliel (i.e. before AD 37), and even before that of Judas the Galilean of the Quirinius census (AD 6)! But in connecting the Christian movement with these revolutionary incidents the writer of Acts is probably correct (5[36ff.]).

Fadus was succeeded in AD 46, interestingly enough, by an Alexandrian Jew, son of that communal banker who sponsored Agrippa's profitable enterprise in Rome, whence he returned with a kingdom. The son, Tiberius Alexander, now in Roman employment, was less religiously inclined than his father, and "did not stand by the practices of his people" (§ 100). During his time, the two sons of Judas the Galilean were arraigned before him and crucified at his command, the recognised punishment of a rebel against the State. Ventidius Cumanus then followed as procurator, probably in AD 48, and a more serious incident took place in Jerusalem. It was on the occasion of a Passover festival, when, as has been said, the military were accustomed to taking special precautions against riot (cp. Matt 26[5]). Soldiers were stationed on the roofs of the porticos surrounding the sanctuary, giving them excellent vantage-points from which to watch for signs of impending trouble. On the fourth day of the feast, for some reason perhaps connected with a detail of the ritual, one of the soldiers crouched down, raised his robe as if to defecate, and made a noise suitable to the posture. The crowd screamed for his punishment, and some of the young men began hurling stones at the soldiers. Cumanus immediately brought more troops in through the porticos and the crowds within the sanctuary panicked. More died under the feet of their countrymen than

19   The east wall and Sanctuary of Jerusalem, from the Mount of Olives.

20(a) Herodian Jerusa[lem]: the great marginally dr[essed] stones of the lower cours[es of] the wall around the Sanct[uary] (at the "Wailing Wall")

20(b) Herodian Jerusa[lem]: the south-west corner o[f the] Sanctuary, showing the s[pring] of the arch that once bri[dged] the Tyropoean Valley.

on Roman swords (§ 105ff.; cp. *War* II xii 1 § 223ff.). It was just this kind of trouble that the procurators and garrison commanders in Jerusalem most feared, since it was the least controllable. During the festivals the city was full of excited people from all over the country, and the Assassins were able to strike and vanish into the crowd. Within the Temple area the crowds were thickest and constrained by the surrounding walls, barriers and porticos. The air was thick with pungent smoke from burnt flesh on the altar, fresh blood streamed through the gutters from the shambles where the sacrifices were ritually slaughtered, and through the din came the incessant, mesmeric chanting of the Levitical priests. Small wonder that these emotive occasions were times of agonising concern for the Roman commanders, and that they should tend to play safe and seal off the Temple area with troops the moment anything untoward happened within the sanctuary.

Outside Jerusalem, the procurator had continually to watch for disturbances between the Jewish and non-Jewish populations. In AD 52, Cumanus was involved in such an incident which, in the end, cost him his post and earned him banishment into exile. Some Galilean Jews journeying to Jerusalem for a festival were set upon and suffered some casualties at the hands of villagers in northern Samaria. The aggrieved pilgrims called upon Cumanus to take action against the Samaritans but, for variously explained reasons, he refused, or was dilatory in doing so. When the survivors reached Jerusalem with their story, feelings ran high. The Zealots took charge of the situation and immediately launched a punitive raid against the Samaritans, firing and sacking a number of villages and putting their inhabitants, young and old, to the sword.

More responsible leaders in Jerusalem viewed the proceedings with horror, calling their people back from their madness whose end could only be the destruction of Judaea and its Holy City. The Samaritans demanded protection from the Roman guardians of the peace, and were given arms to defend their homes. Cumanus took a squadron of cavalry and four units of infantry, and combed the area for the Jewish insurgents, killing and capturing all he could find.

The voices of moderation in Jerusalem had their effect eventually and the people returned to their homes. The Zealots had tasted real blood, however, and the Samaritans were well aware that the vicious reprisals the Jewish guerrilla bands had carried out had little to do with the alleged ambush of a few Galilean Jews. There was systematic genocide

P

in the air, and all the protection Rome could offer was going to be needed by the non-Jewish populations of Palestine if they were to survive the next few years. The Samaritans, therefore, took their complaint to the governor of Syria, Ummidius Quadratus, who was at that time in Tyre. The burden of their complaint was not just that the Jews had attacked their villages, but that, in doing so, they had taken the law into their own hands instead of lodging any complaint they may have had against the Samaritans with the Roman authorities. They had thus shown their contempt for their lawful governors (*Ant* XX vi 2 § 125ff.). The Jewish leaders claimed that the rioting began with the Samaritans and it was they and Cumanus who must bear the responsibility. Quadratus tried to restore the situation by having the Samaritan and Jewish captives crucified. When this failed to settle the argument, and a further investigation in Lydda adduced more evidence, the governor decided the time had come for the whole matter to be reviewed in Rome, and despatched thither the Jewish and Samaritan leaders, together with the procurator Cumanus, to argue their cases before the imperial court. At first things went badly for the Jewish delegation, but Agrippa II, who happened to be in Rome at the time, was able to influence Agrippina, the emperor's wife, to persuade Claudius to favour the Jews and find the Samaritans guilty of inciting the trouble. Three of the Samaritan delegation were executed, Cumanus was sent into exile, and a certain tribune, somehow connected with the affair, was ordered to be dragged around Jerusalem as a spectacle, to assuage the outraged piety of the Jews, and then put to death. Thus, it was vainly hoped, honour would be avenged, and the country could be restored to peace.

In place of the exiled Cumanus, the emperor sent one of his favourites, Antonius Felix, as the next procurator, and he held the position for eight years, from AD 52 to 60 (cp. Acts 24). By now the whole of the Judaean countryside seems to have been in the grip of roving bands of Zealots—"brigands", as Josephus habitually calls them. Felix managed to catch one of their leaders, Eleazar, who had taken a prominent role in the punitive expeditions against the Samaritans, and he was sent to Rome to stand trial. The popular hero had been captured by treachery on Felix's part, having been called to parley under a dishonoured pledge of safe conduct. It was probably in revenge for this act that the High Priest Jonathan, a friend and supporter of Felix, was assassinated by the Sicarii in the press of the crowd in Jerusalem. Josephus would have us believe that the murder had been arranged by Felix himself, who was tired of his Jewish friend's continual lectures on how he should run the country (*Ant* XX viii 5 § 162ff.). He is said to have bribed Jonathan's most trusted friend, a Jerusalemite named Doras, to hire the Assassins to kill the High Priest. But our chronicler consistently denigrates the Zealots-Sicarii as mere blackguards. They were not paid assassins; if they murdered the High Priest it must have been for some more serious reason than bribery.

In all that Josephus says about this religio-political movement, he displays his hatred of their methods and their arrogant belief in their divine calling. We have therefore to adjust his opinions with a more balanced appreciation of the religious nature of the Zealot movement. We may deplore, with Josephus, the viciousness and inhumanity of their actions, and the spiritual pride that led them to believe they should rule the world. But Zealotism, as we have seen, was but the logical outcome of racialist policies formulated long before in Israel's history. We should not then, with our historian, place all the blame for the disaster which befell Judaism on the impiety of the Zealots-Sicarii:

"This is the reason why, in my opinion, even God Himself, for loathing of their impiety, turned away from our city and, because He deemed the Temple to be no longer a clean dwelling-place for Him, brought the Romans upon us and purification by fire upon the city, while he inflicted slavery upon us together with our wives and children; for He wished to chasten us by these calamities" (§ 166).

Again, those whom Josephus calls "impostors and deceivers" who, in these last desperate years, aroused popular support with such apparent ease "to follow them into the desert", were the Messiahs or "Christs" who were expected and whose coming had been foretold in Scripture. "They said they would show them unmistakable marvels and signs that would be wrought in harmony with God's design" (§ 168). Such men may have deluded themselves, and thus tragically misled simple folk, but their intentions were sincere. At a time when revolution was in the air, and wild-eyed men were preaching sedition at every street-corner, proclaiming the imminent approach of the Kingdom of God and the end of the present world order, every unusual event was reckoned an omen, a "sign of the times". Old men dreamed dreams and young men heard voices and believed themselves prophets and even Messiahs. In such an overheated emotional atmosphere it was not difficult to convince others of the genuineness of one's calling and lead large numbers of people, particularly the poor who had nothing but their lives to lose, into the deserts around Jerusalem, to await some greater sign from heaven that the time was at hand.

Thus we learn of a certain mysterious "Egyptian" who took a large crowd of people out on to the top of the Mount of Olives. He told them that at a divine command the walls of Jerusalem would tumble down and the way would be open to a triumphal entry and the establishment of the Christ's rule. It would appear that he was referring to the prophecy in Zechariah of the coming Day of the Lord: "On that day his (the warrior god Yahweh) feet shall stand on the Mount of Olives which lies before Jerusalem on the east; and the Mount of Olives shall be split in two from east to west by a very wide valley . . . and you shall flee as you fled from the earthquake in the days of Uzziah, king of Judah. Then Yahweh your God will come, and all the holy ones with him. . . . And Yahweh will become king over all the earth . . ." (14$^{4-9}$).

This Messiah from Egypt is presumably the one referred to in the New Testament story of Paul's encounter with the tribune on the steps of the Antonia fortress. The Roman asked him if he were not "the Egyptian who recently stirred up a revolt and led the four thousand men of the Sicarii out into the wilderness" (Acts 21^{38}; cp. Matt 24^{23ff}). Josephus adds the sequel that most of the Egyptian's followers were captured or killed by troops sent out by Felix, but that the prophet himself escaped from the battle and disappeared (§ 172; cp. *War* II xiii 5 § 261ff.).

The advent of the "Egyptian" seems to have been the signal for more open rebellion. Zealot bands roamed the countryside, demanding that villages show their allegiance to the rebel cause and take up arms against the Romans. Where they met a cold refusal, the villages were systematically destroyed, and their richer inhabitants were robbed and killed. Money and arms were thus procured for the holy war, and fear of sudden attack by bands of fanatics drove even the the most hesitant and peace-loving Jews into affording the marauding gangs food and shelter.

The Romans could do little at this stage to contain the revolt. They had in the whole of the Syrian province only two legions, some twelve thousand men, mostly based on Caesarea. The Zealots gangs avoided pitched battles and the terrain gave their guerrilla tactics an advantage over the more orthodox warfare of the legionaries. Again, the Jewish underground could organise diversionary outbreaks of trouble wherever they wished, and so distract the attention of the authorities from any area under too intense pressures. In the larger cities there were not only cells of subversion, but Jews with money to bribe officials and to finance operations. We have already seen that a well-organised complaint of maltreatment, like that against the Samaritans, pressed home with sufficient weight of civic authority, could be carried to the highest courts of Rome and result in the removal of one procurator and appointment of another, more favoured official. In the case of the Samaritans, thanks largely to Agrippa's influence in high places, Cumanus was dismissed and Felix, a friend of the High Priest's, appointed.

About AD 59, following the Egyptian Messiah incident and Felix's breaking up of that concerted effort, an uprising in Caesarea by the Jews against their gentile fellow-citizens similarly resulted in the procurator's removal from office. The quarrel was ostensibly about equal civic rights, the Jews claiming that since Herod their king had built the city they had precedence over non-Jews. The Syrian inhabitants argued that the place was there long before Herod had enlarged and rebuilt it, and in those earlier days there were no Jews at all dwelling there. Therefore, on the grounds that they more truly represented the original inhabitants of the city Herod had called Caesarea, the Syrians should have precedence over the Jews. The magistrates, confronted by the quarrelling parties, took the sound course of knocking their heads together and telling them to be quiet. The Jews, however, would not let the matter rest, and the richer among them began openly to disparage their poorer Syrian neighbours in such a manner as to draw forth inevitable retaliation, which was soon whipped up into displays of violence on both sides. The Syrians felt that, since the Roman army stationed there consisted largely of natives of their own city and of non-Jewish Samaria, they could count on official support to counter the weight of Jewish wealth. Felix responded in the manner both sides expected, and quelled the discord with force, largely against the Jews. This now gave the rich Jewish citizens an excuse to have the matter raised in higher quarters in Rome. The result seems to have been that Felix was removed from office, since in the following year, he was re-placed as procurator by Porcius Festus, a man apparently noted for his pro-Jewish sentiments (cp. Acts 24^{27}; 25^9).

How far rich Jews in Palestine and elsewhere in the Diaspora were persuaded to co-operate in Zealot activities through their own sincere religious aspirations, and how far through fear of the assassin's knife, we cannot know. Doubtless we should assume that a combination of patriotism and apprehension of sudden death, or, at least, social ostracism, won over many otherwise reasonable men. Jewish businessmen, after all, had far more to lose materially than they could ever hope to gain from subversive activities against the Roman guardians of peace. Again, we should not be deluded from the disparagement levelled by Josephus at the Zealots as "robbers" or "brigands" that they were ignorant peasants attracted to the fight by promises of rich pickings from the spoliation of the Jewish aristocracy and shopkeepers. The Zealot leaders at least were highly intelligent as well as fanatically dedicated men. Josephus, no mean scholar, began the war of AD 66 as a general in the northern region, under overall Zealot command. When he changed sides to serve the Romans as their spokesman, he left behind loyal Jews whose subsequent defiance of Roman might, while tragically vain from any rational viewpoint, was nevertheless directed throughout with cold efficiency and a high order of strategic appreciation. The terrible fallacy of the whole of their thinking, of course, was the religious belief that their forces would be augmented at the last moment by heavenly hosts, and that the Holy City would never be permitted by God to fall into barbarian hands.

The Jews of Caesarea may have succeeded in removing Felix from the procuratorship by their trouble-making, but it won them no friends in Rome. Nero, emperor since Claudius's death by poisoning in AD 54, was persuaded to annul the grant of equal civic rights to the Caesarean Jews, and thus added fuel to the smouldering fires of racial antagonism in that city. When next they were fanned into flame, six years later, the outbreak could not be extinguished before Jerusalem itself lay in ruins.

Festus died in office, and was succeeded by Lucceius Albinus in AD 62. Little is said of this procurator, except that during his two years of office he made as much money as he could by opening the gaol doors to any prisoner whose relatives could raise sufficient ransom. This may well have been so, but the story possibly owes something to another characteristically audacious aspect of Zealot activity. In order to secure the release of those of their number who had been captured and thrown into prison, the Sicarii would slip into the city by night and carry off an important hostage, whom they would then offer to exchange for a number of their own men. In this way they made a daring raid by night during one of the festivals and made off with the High Priest's son, who held an official position in the Temple guard. In exchange for his safe return, the Sicarii demanded ten of their own men, at the time held in custody by Albinus. Ananus, the High Priest, prevailed upon the procurator to release his prisoners, doubtless by offering a suitable bribe, and the exchange was effected. From the authorities' point of view, this transaction proved expensive, since the Zealots thenceforth knew that they could always bring about the release of political prisoners by kidnapping men of rank and wealth whose safety was of concern to the High Priest.

It is to Albinus's successor in office, Gessius Florus, that history has pointed the finger of accusation for setting the spark to the dry tinder of revolt. Thus Tacitus writes: "the endurance of the Jews lasted until Gessius Florus was procurator" (*Histories* v 10), and Josephus has: "it was Florus who constrained us to take up war with the Romans" (*Ant* XX xi 1 § 257). Our chronicler even suggests that Florus incited the Jews to revolt so as to cover up his own misdeeds, fearful that they might bring his maladministration to the notice of the emperor and secure his dismissal, as they had done in respect of his predecessors (*War* II xiv 3 § 282f.). In fact, of course, however inept Florus's handling of the Jewish problem, the situation was already out of any one man's control. Nevertheless, the procurator was probably right in believing that the Jews would seize upon some incident to claim a hearing of the imperial court of a complaint against him. It was again the troubled situation in Caesarea that offered the Jewish leaders their opportunity.

Nero's decree had annulled the privilege accorded Caesarean Jews of equal civic rights with the Greek inhabitants, and the atmosphere in the city had continued to be tense with racial hatred. In May of AD 66, an incident occurred which sent the Jews running off to lay a formal complaint with Florus against their fellow-citizens. The Jewish community had a synagogue situated in the heart of the city, and surrounded by land belonging to a Syrian. Despite all their attempts to buy the adjoining land, the owner had refused to sell, since he intended to develop the site for industrial purposes. He now put the work in hand, building workshops on his property and leaving only a small and inconvenient passage-way for the Jews to reach their place of worship. Young Jewish hot-heads tried to interrupt building operations by beating up the workmen, and the Greeks complained to Florus. The violence was stopped, but the Jews thereupon approached Florus with a substantial bribe of eight talents to induce him to frighten the Syrian landowner into abandoning his plans. Florus took the money and then promptly cleared off to let the protagonists fight the matter out between themselves. Insults, and then stones, began to fly, the cavalry were told to intervene, and the Jews withdrew to a nearby Jewish district to consider the next move. A deputation was sent to Florus at Samaria, to remind him of the eight-talent bribe and his obligations to fulfil his pledge. The procurator replied by arresting the Jewish notables and having them put in irons. This seems to have been a signal to the Jerusalem Zealots for a direct confrontation with the Roman troops. Their opportunity arose when, about this time, Florus sent to the Temple treasuries for seventeen talents, presumably an overdue tax payment. His envoys were met with abuse and demands for the procurator's dismissal. Florus then sent a cohort of military to enforce his demand, and to call for the surrender of those who had jeered at his messengers. When the culprits were not forthcoming, being unidentifiable, or because no one dared point the accusing finger for fear of reprisals from the ever-present Assassins, Florus let loose his men on an orgy of rapine and slaughter in the upper market of the city.

On the following day, two more cohorts from Caesarea entered the city and were met with a subdued but later overtly hostile demonstration. The soldiers responded with more force and made an attempt to hack their way through the crowded streets of the north quarter to the Antonia fortress and the Temple. The movement was blocked, however, by sheer weight of numbers, and as the mass of interlocked soldiers and civilians surged back and forth in the lanes and passageways, a more disciplined and clearly well-prepared force of rebels in the Temple area cut down the bridge connecting the Antonia fortress with the sanctuary. Thus, even if the Romans gained the former, they would still be separated from the Temple, the insurgents' main defence position. The first decisive step in the battle of the Holy City had been taken, and the Jewish war of liberation had begun.

21   Part of the vaulted roof of underground cisterns of the Antonia fortress now situated under
the convent of the Sisters of Zion, Jerusalem.

22(a)   A coin of the Second Jewish Revolt, marked with the
letters "*Sh-m-'*", an abbreviation of *Shim'on*, "Simon", its leader.

22(b)   A papyrus letter from the leader of the Second Revolt, beginning
"From Simon Ben Kosibah . . ."

23   A rocky gorge in the Wilderness of Judah, site of caves used by rebels of the Second
Jewish Revolt.

24 Part of the central arch of a triple gateway erected as the eastern entrance into Hadrian's
Aelia Capitolina. It stands over the ruins of Antonia, destroyed during the Roman attack of
AD 70. The northern arch has been incorporated into the altar of the chapel of the Sisters
of Zion convent, on the right of the picture.

CHAPTER XIX

The fall of Jerusalem

Florus reported the open revolt to the Roman governor in Syria, Cestius Gallus. An officer was immediately despatched to take stock of the situation and told to contact Agrippa II returning from Alexandria. They met at Jamnia and were joined by a deputation of Jews from Jerusalem lodging a formal complaint against the procurator, Florus. The king was now in a difficult position. It was one thing speaking up on the Jews' behalf in the presence of the emperor in Rome, and helping them manipulate procuratorial appointments to their advantage; it was another being required to play the role of protector of Jewish affairs actually in the midst of a rebellious Judaea. Agrippa's first duty was to his Roman patrons, who relied upon him to bridge the gap between gentile rule and subject Jewry. On the other hand, Judaea was not within his kingdom, for which at this moment he must have been extremely thankful. The country was the direct responsibility of the procurator and Syrian legate, who were answerable to Rome for maintenance of law and order in the province.

The best that Agrippa could do in the circumstances was to go along with the governor's representative and make a long and impassioned address to the Jerusalem citizens for reason. They gathered on a platform of polished flag-stones, called the Xystus, just outside the western wall of the Temple enclosure and below the Hasmonean palace on the western hill (Fig. 8). At the end of the oration the king and his sister Berenice were in tears, but if the aggressive passions of part of his audience had been washed away in the flood of their emotions, others, less sympathetically affected by the king's rhetoric, were hurling stones at him and demanding his expulsion from the city. The revolutionary leader, one Eleazar, son of the High Priest Ananias, and a captain of the Temple guard, took over control of the sanctuary and ordered an immediate cessation of the daily sacrifice for the emperor and Roman people. Since the days of Augustus, a bull and two lambs had been offered on the Jewish altar on the emperor's behalf, and at

Roman expense. To stop the ritual was tantamount to a declaration of war.

Agrippa, disappointed at the results of his pacificatory efforts, went home sulking, but was soon followed by a deputation of leading Jews. Now thoroughly alarmed at the course of events, they came asking that he should send military forces to save Jerusalem from the rebels. A similar request was sent to Florus. The procurator delayed acknowledging the failure of his policies by resorting to full-scale armed intervention, but Agrippa, still smarting from the insults he had received from the populace, sent troops from his own northern domain to support the anti-war party.

The Zealots had managed to gain control of the Temple mount, and a party had taken over the mighty fortress of Masada from its Roman garrison. In Jerusalem, Agrippa's troops were able, with the assistance of the anti-Zealot party, to secure the upper city for a time, although they could not dislodge the insurgents from their dominating position in the sanctuary. At length, the king's men were driven out even from the suburbs and forced to take refuge in Herod's palace-fortress on the west of the city, on a site now occupied by the so-called David's Citadel (Fig. 8). They were joined there by those citizens who had sought military assistance against the rebels from Agrippa and Florus. They were now very frightened men, and included in their number the High Priest Ananias and his brother. In Zealot eyes, their call for outside assistance to break the revolt was a crime against Judaism and their god. It was no less heinous than the action taken by the Jewish opponents of Alexander Jannaeus, a century and a half earlier, when they called for help from the Greek Demetrius III Eukairos against their own Hasmonean ruler.

The rebels were now free to pillage and burn the Hasmonean palace on the western hill and to enter the Records Office to destroy incriminating documents stored there. Their numbers augmented by reinforcements from Masada, the Zealots then laid siege to the Herodian palace-fortress, and in due course managed to undermine part of its outer defences and break in. Their main quarry, the pacifists, were ruthlessly ferreted out from their hiding places and murdered. The High Priest and his brother were found hiding in a ditch in the palace grounds and put to the sword. The king's troops and natives of the country were allowed to leave unmolested, but those Romans who had been left to garrison the citadel were sealed off in its three great towers, to face a

siege without food or water. It was now high summer, August/
September of AD 66, and the besieged men were soon in desperate
plight. Through their leader, a certain Metilius, they offered to surrender
on a pledge of safe conduct. The Zealots agreed, solemn oaths were taken
on either side, and the men filed out into the open courtyard. At the
command of their officer, they laid aside their shields and weapons, and
the Zealots waited until they had done so. Then they rushed in and
slaughtered every man. Only Metilius was allowed to live, and he
agreed to be circumcised and become a good Jew.

One interesting feature of these operations against the Roman
garrison and its supporters, is that they were in the main conducted by
another son of the famous Judas, hero of the opposition to the Quirinius
census of AD 6. His name was Menahem, and having collected arms and
men from Masada, he came to Jerusalem and seems to have set himself
up as the rightful leader of the insurgents, doubtless on the strength of
his father's pre-eminence in the Zealot movement. He led the attack
on the Herodian citadel, but before its denouement, was himself set
upon and killed by a rival faction of the rebels under Eleazar. Menahem
had gone up to the Temple in robes of state, to offer sacrifice, rather as if
he had assumed the role of king and High Priest in the manner of the
old Hasmonean rulers. Perhaps he even laid claim to messianic office,
as "the one who should come" in the fullness of time. In any case,
there was a rival group of insurgents who would have none of this and,
despite his bodyguard, he was driven from the sanctuary into hiding in
the area of ancient Ophel, south of the Temple. There the mob hounded
him out, tortured and killed him. A few of Menahem's party managed
to escape into the desert and found their way back to Masada. Among
them was Eleazar, son of Jair, part of whose speech as commander of
the last of the defenders of that fortress we have already quoted (see
above, p. 206).

One would very much like to know more about the rival factions
within the Zealot movement. Certainly this incident is not the only
evidence of splits within the leadership. As the end drew near and outlying provinces were being overrun by the Romans, the Zealot commanders were forced to retire with their staffs upon Jerusalem. Each of
equal rank in the field, once in headquarters they eyed each other with
suspicion, lest one should seize some advantage in power and prestige
against his fellows. This might seem to us a surprising display of petty
jealousy in such a moment of grave consequence, when the whole

future of Jewry hung in the balance. But we have to understand that personal rank within this eschatological movement was not merely a matter of bars or pips on the shoulder. One's place in the order of precedence was determined by God's favour. Leaders were chosen by lot, as in the old days high priestly office had been allocated, and the fall of the dice was determined by the will of the Almighty. Thus, when the Zealots gained control of the cultus they elected a new High Priest by this manner, and brought forth scathing remarks from Josephus for having let the lot fall upon an imbecile "who scarcely knew what the high priesthood meant" (*War* IV iii 8 §155). Their answer would doubtless have been that at least this was better than making the sacred office a pawn in the power game, to be bought and sold at the whim and profit of aliens.

Whatever rank was held by the Elect in the present world order would obtain in God's Kingdom. To lead the Sons of Light in the immediate apocalyptic battle would be to assume the mantle of king-messiah, the strong right arm of the new world government in the millennium of theocracy immediately to follow. Thus in the Dead Sea Scrolls we have the same concern with rank. The Elect are gathered before their Messiah in the ordering of the Messianic Banquet, as set out in one of the documents:

"(This is the order of the session) of men of repute, (who are called) to meet for the Council of the Community. When (God) begets the Messiah with them, there shall come (the Priest), the head of all the congregation of Israel, and all the priests, (elders of the children of) Aaron, (invited) to the Meeting as men of repute. And they shall sit (before him, each) according to his rank, corresponding to his (station) in the camps and marches. And all the heads of the (elders of the Congregation) shall sit before them, each man according to his rank. And (when) they are gathered at the communion (table, or to drink) the new wine, and the communion table is laid out, and the new wine (mixed) for drinking, (let no man stretch forth) his hand on the first of the bread or the (wine) before the Priest; for (he will) bless the first of the bread and wine, (and will stretch forth) his hand on the bread first.

"And afterwards, the Messiah will (stretch forth) his hands upon the bread, (and then) all the Congregation of the Community (will give blessings), each according to his rank. . . ."

One gathers that this is the pattern for the Messianic Banquet to be held in the new Kingdom, after the great purge of the present war. The chief characters here are the Priest, the first of the two great leaders in the New Age, the direct intermediary with God, the Messiah, the Davidic "Son of God" who was to be the chief executive power of the kingdom, and the Chosen People who were to rule the world. All have their assigned ranks, with the priestly Messiah, "The Priest", as he is simply called in the Scrolls, at the head.

This careful ordering of the congregation before the Messiah or Christ is reflected in the curious incident recorded in Luke's Gospel, when Jesus at his Messianic Banquet, or "Last Supper", promises his disciples that they should "sit on the thrones judging the twelve tribes of Israel". His followers take to arguing among themselves at this most solemn moment "which of them was to be accounted the greatest" (22^{30}; ^{24}). As we may now understand, this was not just a matter of personal pride; it had a direct bearing upon their respective ranking in the coming Kingdom.

If we knew more about the internal administration of the Zealot movement, and particularly of its manner of designating and allocating ranks in the field, we should perhaps be in a better position to understand the background of the struggles for leadership recorded unsympathetically by Josephus. In this connection, it is possible that we can seek first-hand information on the discipline and religious bases of Zealotism in the Dead Sea Scrolls with more confidence than we have customarily allowed ourselves. Some scholars have from the beginning identified the documents as "Zealot" in origin, against the trend of opinion that designated them as "Essene". In fact, the rigid division that historians have tended to erect between the two parties of Judaism was probably never justified: both stem from a common source. Their differences are rather in degrees of emphasis than in radically divergent religio-political outlooks.

But as far as identifying historical events and personalities, the Scrolls have severe limitations. As with any such esoteric movement, proper names, where they are at all found in the records, are used as pseudonyms, intentionally cloaking the identities of actual persons. Their lives, or those of their families and successors, were too often at risk from antagonistic orthodoxy or military authorities to allow the use of real names of people and places. The Dead Sea Scrolls speak of the sect's leader as "the Teacher of Righteousness", as, no less cryptically, the New Testament gives the hero of its story the name of Moses' successor and Israel's first guide into the Promised Land, Joshua/Jesus.

The Scrolls refer to divisions within the movement, speaking of past betrayals and historically unidentifiable renegades from the true path. This is no more than what we should expect of any such exclusive and highly emotive religious body as Essenism/Zealotism. But we should need to know far more of its secret and most distinctive doctrines than seems at present possible if we are fully to understand the nature and extent of its rival factions. Later historians of twentieth-century extreme Protestantism may find it hardly less difficult to understand the schisms, often most bitterly sustained, within such fringe sects as the Plymouth Brethren.

Menahem's ill-fated bid for Zealot leadership was only one of several struggles for power during the final phases of the war. In the autumn of AD 67, the Roman general Vespasian, who had by now been placed in charge of the campaign to end the revolt, had succeeded in clearing the whole of the Galilee area of rebels. The Zealot base at Gischala (modern el-Jish: Fig. 7) in Upper Galilee was in Roman hands, and its com-mander, John of Gischala, had been forced to flee south with his surviving men to Jerusalem. Once in the city, John began a struggle for power with Eleazar, already recognised as the local commander of Zealot forces. It ended for the time being with Eleazar managing to maintain control of the strategically paramount fortified Temple area, whilst John held sway in the rest of the city.

By the spring of AD 68, Vespasian had suppressed the revolt through-out Judaea, and was encamped in Jericho, mopping up local pockets of resistance and preparing to move up to Jerusalem for the final assault. Zealot groups roamed where they could, terrorizing villages whose inhabitants refused them food and shelter. The local group commander in the Judaean region was a certain Simon Bar-Giora, of equivalent status and function to that of John of Gischala. When Simon also came to join the headquarters staff in Jerusalem, there developed a feud between all three leaders. At one stage in the struggle for control, Eleazar held the inner courts of the Temple area, John the outer courts with their buildings, while Simon ruled the remainder of the city. Vespasian could take his time about securing his own position, since the signs were that the rebels would destroy themselves by their quarrel-ling. As it happened, Vespasian was soon otherwise engaged with imperial affairs back home. The emperor Nero died on the 9th June AD 68, his successor Galba, called from Spain to the throne, was killed in the following January, and Otho, who followed next, committed suicide three months later, following his defeat by the generals of Vitellius. Rather than see the despised Vitellius succeed to the imperial purple, Vespasian's troops proclaimed their general emperor, echoed soon by embassies and peoples throughout the empire. Vespasian was thus fully occupied in securing his position, and detailed his son Titus to continue with suppressing the Jewish revolt. The year AD 69 had passed without further action in this respect, but in the spring of the following year, Titus moved his legions up from Jericho to invest Jerusalem.

Even then, the feud for leadership continued in the city. While the Romans were at the walls, John of Gischala managed to infiltrate some of his armed men into the Temple courts during Passover celebrations (March–April). In the ensuing battle he was able to wrest control of the sanctuary from Eleazar, and the two factions thenceforth coalesced, to face Simon within and Titus without the city walls (*War* V iii 1 § 98ff.). It was not until the Roman siege engines were actually battering down the outermost rampart, that all three parties reluctantly joined to face the common foe: "The rival factions shouted across to each other that they were doing all they could to assist the enemy, when they ought, even if God denied them lasting concord, for the present at least to postpone their mutual strife and unite against the Romans . . ." (*War* V vi 4 § 278).

After a three months' siege, the Romans broke into the Antonia fortress and from thence into the Temple area. The holy place was burnt to the ground and John of Gischala and Simon Bar-Giora were rounded up from their hiding-places within the city. John was condemned to perpetual imprisonment, Simon to be sent to Rome for the triumph and then executed. The subjection of the entire city was finally accomplished on the 26th September AD 70 (*War* VI x 1 § 435).

The revolt continued in the outlying fortresses of Herodium, near Bethlehem (Pl. 14), Machaerus on the eastern side of the Dead Sea, and, most tenaciously, in Masada. The first two were taken by the Romans comparatively easily, but Herod's great palace-fortress on the western shore of the Dead Sea held out for three years, under the command of Eleazar, son of Jair (see above, p. 235). For the Romans it was a hollow victory. When, on the 2nd May AD 73, they finally broke through the walls, they found only the charred remains of the palace and its stores of food, and, scattered among the ruins, the corpses of the citadel's last defenders, men, women, and children. At Eleazar's urging, they had taken their own lives in a gruesome suicide pact, rather than offer their living bodies to the hated gentiles:

"For a while they caressed and embraced their wives and took their children in their arms, clinging in tears to those parting kisses, at that same instant, as though served by hands other than their own, they accomplished their purpose, having thought of the ills they would endure under the enemy's hands to console them for their constraint in killing them. And in the end not one was found a truant in so daring a deed: all carried through their task with their dearest ones. . . . Unable, indeed, any longer to endure their anguish at what they had done, and feeling that they wronged the slain by surviving them if it were but a moment, they quickly piled together all the stores and set them on fire; then, having chosen by lot ten of their number to despatch the rest, they laid themselves down each beside his prostrate wife and children, and, flinging their arms around them, offered their throats in readiness for the executants of the melancholy office. . . . Finally, then, the nine bared their throats, and the last solitary survivor, after surveying the prostrate multitude . . . set the palace ablaze, and, collecting his strength, drove his sword clean through his body and fell beside his family" (*War* VII ix 1 § 391ff.).

There were five survivors of this holocaust. An old woman, one other, "a relative of Eleazar's", and five children had remained hidden in an underground water conduit while the mass slaughter was taking place above their heads. When they heard the shouts of the Romans entering the breached walls, they emerged and told their grisly story.

Recent excavations have brought to light the remains of Herod's fortress surmounting the Masada rock. In the ruins were found relics of the last stand made by its defenders, among them eleven potsherds inscribed each with a single name. It has been suggested that these could well have been the tokens by which the ten Zealot commanders decided who was to be the last survivor of the suicide pact charged with killing his fellows and firing the palace:

"These, having unswervingly slaughtered all, ordained the same rule of the lot for one another, that he on whom it fell should slay first the nine and then himself last of all" (§ 396).

One of the pieces of pottery had on it the name "Ben Jair", that is, the Zealot leader Eleazar, "son of Jair". It might be considered ungracious to speculate on the identity, or even true sex of the "old woman", described as "a relative of Eleazar's", and as being "superior in prudence and training (*phronēsei kai paideia*) to most women", who hid her female companion and accompanying five children underground during or after the mass slaughter of their fellow-Zealots above. Perhaps, too, we should not enquire too closely how that prudent person could so "lucidly report both the speech (of Eleazar) and how the deed was done (§ 404), if she were in hiding the whole time. Nevertheless, one cannot help wondering if Josephus did not come by his remarkably complete knowledge of these last dramatic days and hours of Masada's resistance through the first-hand report of Eleazar himself. Does Josephus know more about the "relative of Eleazar" and her "prudence" than he cares to divulge? Certainly, if Eleazar had felt no guilt in escaping the suicide pact disguised as an old woman, and was thus enabled to usher perhaps his wife and family from this tomb of Zealot hopes, he would have had some sympathy from Josephus, who had done much the same thing earlier on in the war. At the time, our chronicler was a commander of the insurgent forces in the Galilee area. With a few of his men he had taken refuge in a cave but was discovered and surrounded by Roman forces. Their fate seemed sealed, and Josephus suggested to his comrades that, to avoid the ignominy of falling alive into enemy hands, they should draw lots in a suicide pact:

"Let him who draws the first lot fall by the hand of him who comes next; fortune will thus take her course through the whole number, and we shall be spared from taking our lives with our own hands. For it would be unjust that, when the rest were gone, any should repent and escape" (*War* III viii 7 § 388).

Which is just what happened. Josephus, the organiser of the lot-drawing, found himself left with one remaining comrade, all the others lying dead around them in the cave. Without apparently very much pleading on his part, our historian's companion was persuaded to abandon the suicide pact at that stage, and give themselves up. Josephus thus survived that encounter and, indeed, the whole war, to the lasting benefit of future historians.

If our surmise that Eleazar, too, survived the war, he would not have sought far for reasons to justify his betrayal of the suicide pact. He had been, after all, second-in-command to Menahem, self-acclaimed king, perhaps Messiah, a son of that great Judas who brought the Zealot revolt into the open. The mantle of Jewish resistance to the gentile yoke had fallen upon him, Eleazar ben Jair, and with Jerusalem in ruins and the murderers of his master themselves dead or prisoners in Roman hands, who remained but he to continue the struggle?

For the underground movement did, indeed, continue. The doctrine of Jerusalem's invincibility had now to be readjusted, but those Jews who had managed to escape in time and joined the Diaspora, brought with them the fire of revolt. The cells of the mystic cult from which Zealotism was born were still to be found throughout the empire, and, despite all the efforts of the Roman and "orthodox" Jewish authorities to destroy them under their "messianist" or "Christian" designation, for some time yet they afforded a channel of clandestine communication and hope.

CHAPTER XX

Son of the Star

Josephus closes his account of the war with a note of some of its rever-
berations in the Diaspora. A party of the Sicarii managed to escape
the Roman net in Judaea and made their way to Alexandria. Apparently
they found there sufficient support for their cause to raise an insurrection,
despite the opposition of a larger body of Jews who wanted peace. The
Romans were, however, alerted and the Sicarii and their supporters
rounded up. The Roman governor reported the matter to Vespasian
who decreed that the Jewish temple at Leontopolis, at the southern end
of the Delta (Fig. 4), should be closed. He was clearly concerned that
this sanctuary should not, like the Jerusalem Temple, be made the
rallying-point for another stage in the revolt.

In Cyrene, a certain Jonathan, a weaver by trade, claimed messianic
authority and led some Jews into the desert to await signs and wonders
that would herald the Kingdom. They went unarmed, but their mission
being made known to the Roman governor Catullus, he immediately
sent an armed force of cavalry and infantry after them, and cut them
down. The few survivors he brought back for judgment. The incident
sounds fairly trivial, but Catullus was sufficiently convinced of its
dangerous potentiality as a signal for a general uprising in Africa, that he
took Jonathan in chains to Rome and arraigned him before the emperor.
Furthermore, Catullus seems to have had some evidence for believing
that behind the poor deluded weaver there was a considerable body of
support among rich Jews in Alexandria and Rome. He even named our
historian Josephus among the plotters. These charges failed for want of
evidence, and, needless to say, Josephus pours scorn on the whole idea.
But it hardly seems likely that Catullus would have brought such
grave accusations of sedition against influential Jews in Rome itself
if he had not been convinced that there was more to the affair than
one man's religious fanaticism.

For the time being, peace reigned, but the seeds of revolt had been
well sown in the fertile soil of Egypt and Africa. It needed only a

temporary relaxation of Roman watchfulness for them to blossom into a general Jewish insurrection. Towards the end of Trajan's reign, in AD 115, Roman troops were withdrawn in large numbers from Africa to take part in another campaign against the Parthians in Mesopotamia. No sooner had they gone than, on a general signal transmitted throughout the Eastern Mediterranean, the Jews asserted their independence of Roman rule.

Our main source for these events is the Roman historian Dio Cassius, writing in the second-third century. He tells us that in Cyrene, the Jews turned on their gentile neighbours and massacred large numbers of them. The survivors fled to Alexandria and raised the alarm. The old feud between Jew and Greek was at once resuscitated and the Jewish quarter became again the scene of fearful carnage. Elsewhere in Egypt, the Jews took the initiative and ran amuck, laying waste gentile villages and slaughtering their inhabitants. They had elected for themselves a king called Lykyas (Dio Cassius lxviii 32), and seemed intent on founding a Jewish kingdom in Africa, perhaps as a step towards making a triumphal return in Moses' footsteps from Egypt to the Promised Land. The insurrection was only crushed after Trajan had sent his ablest general, Quintus Marcus Turbo, to Africa, with a considerable naval and military force. Even then, the revolt was not entirely suppressed until after Hadrian had come to the imperial throne in AD 117.

The call to revolt had been made also in Cyprus. There, too, we are told, the Jews turned upon their Greek fellow-citizens and massacred thousands. Such was the hatred aroused among the islanders for the Jews, as a result of this deliberate attempt at genocide, that long after the revolt was put down, no one of that race was allowed to set foot in Cyprus. It was even said that should a Jew be driven there by adverse winds at sea, he would be instantly killed.

In Mesopotamia, the Jewish uprising behind Roman lines was presumably intended to hold down more soldiers who might otherwise be sent to quell the general insurrection throughout the Diaspora. Trajan's cavalry general, Lusius Quietus, treated the Jewish insurgents with barbaric ruthlessness. It may well be that his subsequent appointment as procurator of Judaea indicates that there, too, an uprising had taken place, or was expected to develop. But whatever happened on that occasion in Palestine, seventeen years later Roman forces were required to deal with a Judaean revolt in some ways no less extensive than the war of AD 66.

Unfortunately this important uprising lacks a chronicler of the first-hand knowledge of Josephus. We are dependent for the sparse documentation that we possess upon Dio Cassius (lxix 12–14) and the Church historian Eusebius (third–fourth century: *Ecclesiastical History* iv 6, 8) together with some late Jewish traditions and, most recently, documents found in caves in the Judaean desert. There is much uncertainty about the immediate cause of the revolt of AD 132. The emperor Hadrian had made a journey to the Orient in the years AD 130–131, and, in accordance with his declared aim of revitalizing Hellenism, the cultural basis of the Roman empire, he had given instructions for the rebuilding of cities and the establishment of monuments. Among his plans was the reconstruction of the ruined city of Jerusalem as a Hellenistic centre with a shrine to Zeus/Jupiter. It seems not improbable that this work was begun immediately after the emperor's return from the east, and that this paganization of the Holy City was the spark that set Judaea aflame. But if so, it was hardly more than an immediate call to arms long prepared, and, since the disturbances of AD 115, ready to hand. Dio Cassius makes it plain that Jewish support throughout the Diaspora was behind the present revolt, and seditious actions elsewhere at this time, partly underground and partly in the open, showed once more a closely integrated strategy.

The insurgents seem to have taken over Jerusalem at the outset of the rebellion, since they issued coins variously inscribed "for the liberation of Israel", and "for the liberation of Jerusalem". A new era was recognized as beginning with the declaration of this independence from alien rule, and coins marked "year 1" and "year 2" have survived. Of the former, some are also inscribed "the priest Eleazar", which indicates that the cultus in the city had been revived and that a start had probably been made with reconstructing the Temple. The other personality referred to on the coins and elsewhere is Simon, the self-styled "prince of Israel" (Pl. 22). His full name is variously given in our sources. According to Christian writers recording the events, he was known as Simon Bar-Kocheba, "Son of the Star", and we learn from Rabbinic literature that the famous contemporary scribe Rabbi Akiba so named him, as fulfilling the prophecy of Balaam: "a star shall come forth out of Jacob, and a sceptre shall rise out of Israel" (Num 24^{17}). In the Dead Sea Scrolls literature, that verse is similarly applied to the coming messianic figure, "the Interpreter of the Law", in this case, the priestly Teacher who was thought to arise at the End of Days in company with the Davidic "Prince". Simon's enemies, who rejected his claim to messianic office, called him rather, "Son of the Lie", Bar-Koziba. From caves in the Judaean wilderness, used as refuges by partisans in this revolt, have come letters written on parchment, papyrus and wooden slats, in Hebrew, Aramaic and Greek, which bear Simon's name and patronymic (Pl. 22). From these it appears that his real name was Bar-Kosibah (spelt out in Greek, *Chōsiba*), and so the honorific and depreciatory nicknames, "Son of the Star" and "Son of the Lie" were merely plays upon his actual name.

These letters and other archaeological remains which have recently come to light in the deserts on the west of the Dead Sea, vividly demonstrate the kind of warfare that Simon and his friends waged against the Romans for three years. How long they held Jerusalem we do not know, but it is certain that when the rebels were driven from the city, they found their administrative and military bases in other fortresses and in villages in southern Judaea. They did not again allow themselves to be besieged within Jerusalem's walls, but rather took the battle into more open places. They hid in caves in the wadies and gorges that cleave the limestone hills of the Judaean wilderness. From these hideouts, many of which have now been discovered, the guerrilla fighters could ambush the Roman troops and then rush back again into safety. Such is the rough nature of that country, transport of supplies by pack mule and men's backs could be undertaken almost under the nose of the enemy. In one Aramaic letter Simon informs the recipients that he has sent "two donkeys, that you will send with them two men . . . in order that they shall pack and send to you in camp branches and citrons. From your place, do you send others who will bring you myrtles and willows. . . ." The items involved were for use at the Festival of Booths, or Sukkoth, probably of autumn, AD 134.

It is clear also from the tenor of the documents that Simon and his men were exercising that same kind of terrorist control over people in the villages as his namesake, Simon Bar-Giora had done in the first revolt, in his capacity of commander of the Zealot forces in the Judaean region. Thus wheat is ordered to be confiscated; the men of Tekoa, near Bethlehem (Fig. 2), were to be punished because they were repairing their houses, and refusing to fight, and were to be forcibly mobilized, and so on. Some idea of the upheaval that the partisans were causing in the settled villages can be seen in the pathetic remains left in caves behind the Dead Sea coastal oasis of En-gedi (Figs. 2, 7). People had been obliged to flee from their homes and take refuge in these caves, and had taken with them their most precious possessions, cut-glass dishes, wooden bowls, keys, cosmetic utensils, and above all, family archives, including marriage deeds, covenants of gifts and sales, and the like (Pl. 17ᵃ⁻ᵉ). From the reference in one of Simon's letters to the custody of a boat at En-gedi and to a consignment of stores, we may gather that the influence of the "brothers", as they call themselves, extended also to other coasts of the Sea, and particularly to the villages on the east side, whose grain fields were required to feed the insurgent forces in the Judaea region.

When the revolt of AD 132 began, Tineius Rufus was the Roman governor of Judaea, but he was unable to suppress the uprising. Even when the governor of the adjoining Syrian province was ordered to help, the guerrilla tactics of the rebels made a decisive victory difficult to secure, since Simon's men avoided pitched battles. In the end Hadrian had to bring one of his most experienced generals, Julius Severus, back from Britain to lead the campaign. Despite the large levies of troops and auxiliaries put at his command, the only way Severus could bring the rebels to heel was by surrounding their hideouts and starving them to death or surrender. Again, remains of Roman camps around caves used by Simon's men and their families testify today to the nature and effectiveness of these tactics. The final stand by Simon and his remaining supporters took place at Beth-ter, a hill fortress near the modern village of *Bittir*, six miles south-west of Jerusalem (Fig. 2). Severus had to lay siege to the rebel stronghold, and remains of the Roman encircling wall may still be seen on the site. Simon was killed in the fighting, and thus ended the second agonising attempt to assert Jewish independence of Roman rule in Palestine.

Judaea had been devastated. Dio Cassius describes the province after the war as "almost a wilderness". Tens, or even hundreds of thousands of Jews had died by the sword, disease or famine. Jewish prisoners caused a glut on the world's slave markets. The unsaleable were sent to the circuses to give amusement to the foreign audiences as the victims were torn apart by gladiatorial weapons or the fangs of wild beasts. Losses on the Roman side were also considerable, and Hadrian's rescript to the Senate informing them of the end of the war omitted the usual formula that the emperor and his army were well (Dio Cassius lxix 14). The kind of warfare the Jewish freedom-fighters had forced upon the Roman legions brought its inevitable toll in mutual hatred and long-lived bitterness. For some three agonising years the soldiers had faced sudden ambush in the deep gorges of the desert (Pl. 16). Every crag and hollow, every cave in the cliffs, concealed a ruthless and desperate enemy who gave and expected no quarter. During the day the sun beat down, making every wady bed a furnace, and during the nights the air was bitterly cold. In every town and village, the inhabitants were cowed into sullen hostility, or had gone entirely, leaving piles of ashes to mock the hunger of the Roman foraging parties. Small wonder that the very name of "Jew" was thereafter an anathema to the Romans. It was banished even from the name of the province, to be known thenceforth as the land of the Philistines, or "Palestine".

More than ever, the Promised Land became a Roman possession. The Holy City, in accordance with Hadrian's earlier intention, was rebuilt as a Roman colony, but now with the added status of a token of victory (Pl. 24). Its name, Aelia Capitolina, was given to honour the emperor, and an equestrian statue proclaimed the city's imperial patronage. On the site of the Jewish sanctuary was erected a temple to Jupiter Capitolinus, and elsewhere in the city another shrine honoured the goddess of love. In later times, its sanctity was marked by its commemoration as the place where Jesus was temporarily laid to rest.

From this "New Jerusalem" all Jews were excluded, on pain of death. Yahweh had departed, and Jews had now to accustom themselves to living among the gentiles they had learnt to despise and, at times, to try and exterminate. They could only repair to their synagogues and pray to their god that he would "return to Jerusalem, Thy city, in mercy and dwell therein, as Thou hast spoken; rebuild it soon in our days as an everlasting building, and speedily set up therein the throne of David. . . ." ("Eighteen Benedictions", *Shemoneh Esreh*, xiv).

But the gospel of the "New Israel" was not dead. Even outside Judaism, another "Chosen Race, a royal priesthood, a holy nation" was already abroad, proclaiming the coming Kingdom of God in the world. Throughout the empire, small cells of believers, claiming kinship with the old Israel, were planning new forms of world conquest. But theirs was not the way of political revolution and the sword. Their leaders adjured them to "be subject for the Lord's sake to every human institution, whether it be to the emperor as supreme, or to governors as sent by him to punish those who do wrong and praise those who do right. . . . Honour all men. Love the brotherhood. Fear God. Honour the emperor" (I Peter 2$^{9, 13-17}$). These "messianists", or "Christians", preached a gospel of love and peace, and infiltrated the corridors of power with sweet words of God's redeeming love, revealed to mankind through a Jewish Messiah who healed gentile children and praised Roman centurions. In two centuries, their priests were powers behind the emperor's throne, and in due course, their papal armies ruled the world.

Chronological Chart

Egypt	The Jews	Babylon	Media	Assyria
	Hezekiah 715–687/6 Manasseh 687/6–642 Amon 642–640 Josiah 640–609 *Jeremiah* *Zephaniah* *Nahum*	Nabopolassar 626–605	Cyaxares 625–585	Fall of Nineveh 612
	Jehoahaz 609 Jehoiakim 609–598 *Habakkuk*	Nebuchadnezzar 605/4–562		
Defeat at Carchemish by Nebuchadnezzar 605 Neco II 609–593 Psammeticus II 593–588 Apries (Hophra) 588–569	Jehoiachin 598/597 Zedekiah 597–587 *Ezekiel* FALL OF JERUSALEM 587 EXILE		Astyages 585–550	
Invaded by Nebuchadnezzar 568		Nabonidus 556–539	Cyrus overthrows Astyages 550 and reigns over the Persian (Achaemenian) Empire 550–530	
	Cyrus' edict 538 *II Isaiah*	Cyrus takes Babylon 539		
Conquered by Cambyses 525	Zerubbabel Temple rebuilt 520–515		Cambyses 530–522 Darius I Hystaspes	

Malachi

Artaxerxes I 465–424
Longimanus
(Peace of Callias 449)

Nehemiah governor 445
Ezra 428?

Xerxes II 423
Darius II Nothus 423–404
Artaxerxes II Mnemon
404–358
Artaxerxes III Ochus
358–338
Arses 338–336
Darius III Codomannus
336–331

Bagoas governor

Egypt revolts 401
XXVIII–XXX Dynasties
Reconquered by Persia 342

(Philip of II Macedon 359)

(Alexander the Great 336–323) (Issus 333)

Occupied by Alexander 332

Seleucus I 312/11–280

The Jews under the Ptolemies

Ptolemy I Lagi 323–285

Antiochus I 280–261
Antiochus II 261–246
Seleucus II 246–226
Seleucus III 226–223
Antiochus III (the Great)
223–187

Ptolemy II Philadelphus
285–246
Ptolemy III Euergetes
246–221
Ptolemy IV Philopator
221–203
Ptolemy V Epiphanes
203–181
Ptolemy VI Philometor
181–146

(Magnesia 190)

Palestine part of Seleucid
Empire 198

Seleucus IV 187–175
Antiochus IV Epiphanes
175–163

Profanation of the Temple
Dec. 167
Judas Maccabeus 166–60
Rededication of the
Temple Dec 164

Egypt	The Jews	Babylon	Media	Assyria
			Antiochus V 163–162	
			Demetrius I 162–150	
			Alexander Balas 150–145	
	Jonathan 160–143/2		Demetrius II Nicator	
			145–139/8	
			Antiochus VI Epiphanes	
			145–142/1	
	Simon 142–134		Antiochus VII Sidetes	
			139/8–128	
	John Hyrcanus 134–104		Demetrius II Nicator	
Ptolemy VII 145–116			128–126/5	
			Antiochus VIII Grypos	
			125–96	
			Antiochus IX Kyzikenos	
			115–95	
	Aristobulus I 104–103		Thereafter claimants:	
	Alexander Jannaeus 103–76		Seleucus V 126/5	
	Alexandra 76–67		(assassinated); Seleucus VI	
	Aristobulus II 66–63		Epiphanes Nicator;	
	Pompey established control over Palestine 63		Antiochus X Eusebes	
			Philopator; Antiochus XI	
			Epiphanes Philadelphos;	
			Philip I, Demetrius III	
			Euxairos; Antiochus XII	
			Dionysus Epiphanes;	
			Antiochus III 73–64	
			Syria made a Roman	
			province by Pompey 64	
Ptolemy VIII Lathyrus 116				
Driven from Egypt by mother				
Cleopatra III 108/7				
Ptolemy IX and Cleopatra III 108/7–88				
Ptolemy VIII Lathyrus restored 88–80				
Ptolemy X 80				
Ptolemy XI 80–51				
Ptolemy XII and Cleopatra VII 51–48				
Ptolemy XIII and Cleopatra VII 47–44				
Ptolemy XIV and Cleopatra VII 44–30				
Egypt a Roman province 30				

Rome	Syria-Palestine			Nabataea
	Jews	Legates	Procurators	
Wars against Mithridates VI of Pontus 121/0–63	Hyrcanus II ethnarch and High Priest under Roman control 63	M. Aemilius Scaurus 62 Marcius Philippus 61–60 Lentulus Marcellinus 59–58		Aretas III 87–62 Obedas II 62–47
First Triumvirate: Pompey Caesar, Crassus, 60 Caesar's Gallic wars 58–51	Antipater 55–43	A. Gabinius 57–55 M. Licinius Crassus 54–53 C. Cassius Longinus 53–51		
War between Caesar and Pompey 49–46 Pompey defeated at Pharsalus 48	Antipater procurator of Judaea 47 Herod governor of Galilee 47	Vejento 50–49 Q. Metellus Scipio 49–48 Sextus Caesar 47–46		
Julius Caesar assassinated 44 Second Triumvirate: Antony, Octavian, Lepidus, 43 Brutus and Cassius defeated at Philippi 42	Herod and Phasael tetrarchs 41 Invasion of Parthians, death of Phasael, Herod appointed King of Judaea 40	C. Cassius Longinus 44–42		

	Syria-Palestine			
Rome	Jews	Legates	Procurators	Nabataea
	Parthians invade Syria 38			Malchus 47–30
	Herod marries Mariamne, fall of Jerusalem 37			
	Aristobulus High Priest murdered 35			
	Cleopatra visits Judaea 34			
	War with Nabateans 32			
Battle of Actium 2 Sept 31	Earthquake in Judaea 31			
Octavian (Augustus) sole ruler 31–AD 14	Hyrcanus II executed 30			Obedas III 30–9
	Mariamne and Alexandra executed 29			
	Famine 25			
	Rebuilding of Temple begun 18			
	Dedication of Temple 10			Aretas IV 9–AD 40
	Alexander and Aristobulus executed 7/6	P. Quintilius Varus 6–4		
	Antipater executed. Death of Herod 4			
	Archelaus tetrarch of Judaea, Samaria, Idumaea 4 BC–AD 6			
	Herod Antipas tetrarch of Galilee and Peraea 4 BC–AD 39			
	Philip tetrarch of Gaulonitis, etc. 4 BC–AD 34			
	Census AD 6	P. Sulpicius Quirinius AD 6		

Emperors	Palestine	Governors of Syria	Procurators
Claudius 41–54	former tetrarchies of Philip and Lysanias 37, of Herod Antipas 39, and rest of Palestine 41	L. Vitellius 35–39 P. Petronius 39–42 C. Vibius Marsus 42–44 C. Cassius Longinus 45–50	Cuspius Fadus 44–46 Tiberius Alexander 46–48 Cumanus 48–52
	Herod Agrippa dies 44 Palestine under procurators 44–66 Herod Agrippa II king of Chalcis 50, and later of Philip's former tetrarchy and cities of Galilee and Peraea	C. Ummidius Quadratus 50–60	Antonius Felix 52–60 Porcius Festus 60–62 Luccerius Albinus 62–64 Gessius Florus 64–66
Nero 54–68		Cn. Domitius Corbulo 60–63	
Rome burned 64	Riots against Jews in Caesarea, May 66 JEWISH REVOLT	C. Cestius Gallus 63–66 C. Licinius Mucianus 67–69	
Rival contenders Galba, Otho, Vitellius, Vespasian 68–69 Vespasian 69–79	Vespasian in Jericho 68 Jerusalem and Temple destroyed 70 Judaea again under procurators. Romans take Masada May 73		

Rome	Syria-Palestine			Nabataea
	Jews	Legates	Procurators	
Titus 79–81				
Domitian 81–96				
Nerva 96–98				
Trajan 98–117				Nabataea a Roman province 106
Campaign against Parthians in Mesopotamia 115	Revolt of Jews in Africa 115			
Hadrian 117–138	Jewish revolt crushed 117			
Hadrian's tour of Orient 130–131				
	Jewish Revolt under Bar Kokhebah 132–135		Tineius Rufus 132	
	Jerusalem rebuilt as Aelia Capitolina; Jews banished from city 135		Julius Severus 135	

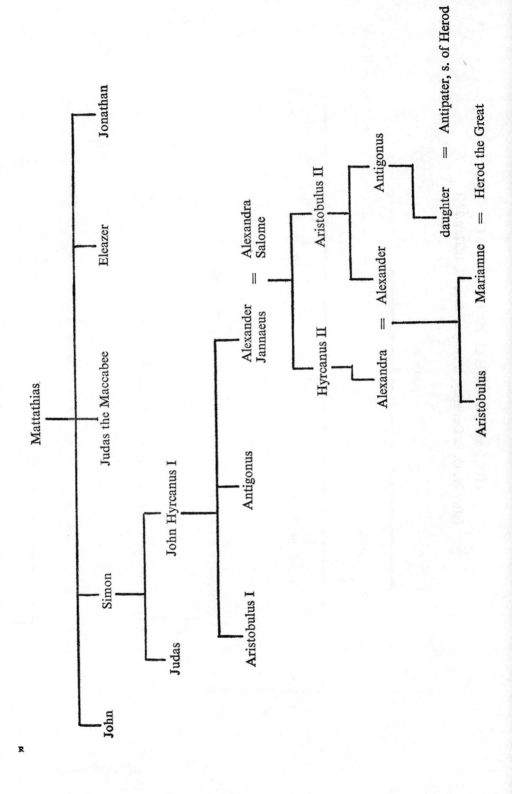

THE FAMILY OF HEROD THE GREAT

(after W. O. E. Oesterley, *History of Israel* ii, 1932, p.374)

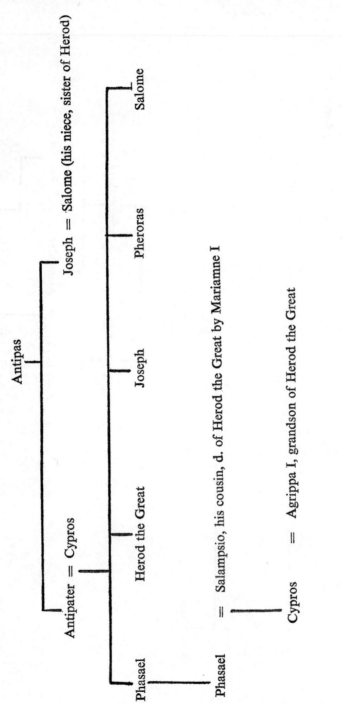
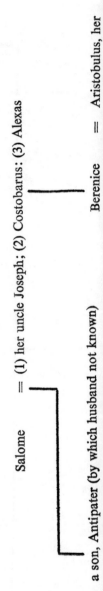

Herod the Great

by

Doris	Mariamne I	Mariamne II	Malthake	Cleopatra	Pallas	Phaedra	Elpis
Antipater	Alexander Aristobulus Salampsio Cypros	Herod	Archelaus Antipas Olympias	Herod Philip	Phasael	Roxana	Salome

Marriages: Antipater = d. of Antigonus, the Hasmonean
Alexander = Glaphyra, d. of Archelaus, king of Cappadocia
Aristobulus = Berenice, d. of Salome, sister of Herod the Great, by Costobarus
Herod = Herodias, his niece, d. of Aristobulus (see below)
Archelaus = Glaphyra, widow of his half-brother Alexander
Antipas = Herodias

of daughters: Salampsio = Phasael, her cousin
Cypros = Antipater, her first cousin, son of Salome, Herod's sister
Olympias = Joseph, her cousin, son of Joseph, Herod's brother

The main line of descent was through Aristobulus, Herod's second son by
Mariamne I:

Aristobulus (= Berenice)

Herod of Chalcis   Agrippa I   Herodias
(= Berenice, his niece)   (= Cypros, grand-niece   (= (1) Herod (2) Antipas)
                             of Herod the Great)

Berenice   Mariamne   Drusilla
(= (1) Herod of Chalcis   (= (1) Azizus
    (2) Polemon of Cilicia)   (2) Felix)

Agrippa II   Agrippa

SUGGESTED FURTHER READING

(listed chronologically, the more recent preceding)
General works on the relevant history and religion:

G. Fohrer, *Geschichte der israelitischen Religion*, Berlin, 1969

Bo Reicke, *The New Testament Era*, London, 1969

M. Simon and A. Benoit, *Le Judaisme et le Christianisme Antique*, Paris, 1968

D. S. Russell, *The Jews from Alexander to Herod*, London, 1967

F. V. Filson, *A New Testament History*, London, 1965

W. Förster, *Palestinian Judaism in New Testament Times*, Edinburgh, 1964

F. F. Bruce, *Israel and the Nations*, London, 1963

E. L. Ehrlich, *A Concise History of Israel from the Earliest Times to the Destruction of the Temple in AD 70*, London, 1962

F. C. Grant, *Ancient Judaism and the New Testament*, Edinburgh, 1960

N. K. Gottwald, *A Light to the Nations*, New York, 1959

B. W. Anderson, *The Living World of the Old Testament*, London, 1958

G. Ricciotti, *The History of Israel*, 2 vols., Milwaukee, 1955

R. H. Pfeiffer, *History of New Testament Times and an Introduction to the Apocrypha*, New York, 1949

C. Guignebert, *The Jewish World in the time of Jesus*, London, 1939

W. Bousset, *Die Religion des Judentums im späthellenistischen Zeitalter* (ed. H. Gressmann), Tübingen, 1926

L. E. Browne, *Early Judaism*, Cambridge, 1920

More detailed treatments within the same areas:

S. Zeitlin, *The Rise and Fall of the Judaean State*, 2 vols., Philadelphia, 1952

J. Bright, *A History of Israel*, London, 1960

V. Tcherikover, *Hellenistic Civilization and the Jews*, Philadelphia, 1959

M. Noth, *The History of Israel*, London, 1958

S. W. Baron, *A Social and Religious History of the Jews*, vol. i, Philadelphia, 1962

F.-M. Abel, *Histoire de la Palestine*, 2 vols., Paris, 1952

W. O. E. Oesterley, H. Loewe, and E. I. J. Rosenthal, *Judaism and Christianity*, 3 vols., London, 1937–38

J. Bonsirven, *Le judaïsme palestinien*, 2 vols., Paris, 1934–35

S. A. Cook, F. E. Adcock, and M. P. Charlesworth (edd.), *Cambridge Ancient History*, vol. X, Cambridge, 1934

M. J. Lagrange, *Le judaïsme avant Jésus-Christ*, Paris, 1931

G. F. Moore, *Judaism in the First Centuries of the Christian Era*, 3 vols., Cambridge, Mass., 1927–30

G. Kittel, *Urchristentum, Spätjudentum, Hellenismus*, Stuttgart, 1926

K. Lake and F. J. F. Jackson (edd.), *Beginnings of Christianity*, 3 vols., London, 1920–26

C. F. Kent, *History of the Jewish People*, London, 1919

J. S. Riggs, *A History of the Jewish People*, London, 1919

E. Schürer, *A History of the Jewish People in the Time of Jesus Christ*, 5 vols., Edinburgh, 1892–1901.

Ancient texts in translation:

J. B. Pritchard (ed.), *Ancient Near Eastern Texts Relating to the Old Testament*, (third ed.), Oxford, 1969
  The Ancient Near East. Supplementary Texts and Pictures Relating to the Old Testament, Princeton, 1961

D. Winton Thomas (ed.), *Documents from Old Testament Times*, London, 1958

G. R. Driver, *Aramaic Documents of the Fifth Century* BC, Oxford, 1957

A. Cowley (ed.), *Aramaic Papyri of the Fifth Century* BC, Oxford, 1923

The Works of Flavius Josephus in various editions, but especially with the Greek text in the Loeb Classical Library.

R. H. Charles (ed.), *The Apocrypha and Pseudepigrapha of the Old Testament*, 2 vols., Oxford, 1913

With particular reference to the various chapters of this book:

CHAPTER I

M. Noth, *The Laws in the Pentateuch and Other Essays*, Edinburgh, 1966

N. K. Gottwald, *All the Kingdoms of the Earth*, New York, 1964

J. Marshall Holt, *The Patriarchs of Israel*, Nashville, 1964

A. Kuschke (ed.), *Verbannung und Heimkehr* (Festschrift für W. Rudolph), Tübingen, 1961

R. de Vaux, *Die Hebräischen Patriarchen und die Modernen Entdeckungen*, Düsseldorf, 1961

A. Altmann, *Tolerance and the Jewish Tradition*, London, 1958

C. F. Whitley, *The Exilic Age*, London, 1957

E. Janssen, *Juda in der Exilzeit*, Göttingen, 1956

H. H. Rowley, "The Book of Ezekiel in Modern Study" in *Bulletin of the John Rylands Library*, 36 (1953) pp. 146–90

For the fertility origins of Yahwism and the Sacred Mushroom Cult of the Near East:
John M. Allegro, *The Sacred Mushroom and the Cross*, London and New York, 1970

CHAPTER II

P. R. Ackroyd, *Exile and Restoration*, London, 1968

J. M. Myers, *The World of the Restoration*, Englewood Cliffs, 1968

Y. Aharoni, *The Land of the Bible*, London, 1967

A. T. Olmstead, *History of Palestine and Syria to the Macedonian Conquest*, Michigan, 1965

K. Galling, *Studien zur Geschichte Israels im Persischen Zeitalter*, Tübingen, 1964

G. E. Wright, *Biblical Archaeology* (rev. ed.), London, 1962

D. Winton Thomas, "The Sixth Century BC: a Creative Epoch in the History of Israel" in *Journal of Semitic Studies* 6 (1961), pp. 33–46

C. H. Gordon, *The World of the Old Testament*, London, 1960

H. H. Rowley, *Darius the Mede and the Four World Empires in the Book of Daniel*, Cardiff, 1959

A. T. Olmstead, *History of the Persian Empire*, Chicago, 1948

G. G. Cameron, *History of Early Iran*, Chicago, 1936

A. C. Welch, *Post-exilic Judaism*, Edinburgh, 1935

W. F. Lofthouse, *Israel after the Exile*, Oxford, 1928

C. C. Torrey, *The Second Isaiah*, New York, 1928

CHAPTER III

L. H. Brockington, *Ezra, Nehemiah and Esther*, London, 1969

J. Gray, *A History of Jerusalem*, London, 1969

B. Porten, *Archives from Elephantine*, California, 1968

D. Winton Thomas (ed.), *Archaeology and Old Testament Study*, Oxford, 1967

J. M. Myers, *Ezra, Nehemiah*, New York, 1965

W. F. Albright, *The Biblical Period from Abraham to Ezra*, New York, 1963

I. Epstein, *Judaism* (Pelican A440), London, 1959

A. Alt, *Kleine Schriften zur Geschichte des Volkes Israel*, vol. ii, München, 1953

H. H. Rowley, *The Servant of the Lord and Other Essays on the Old Testament*, 1952

J. Simons, *Jerusalem in the Old Testament*, Leiden, 1952

W. Hinz, *Iran; Politik und Kultur von Kyros bis Rezâ Schah*, Leipzig, 1938

H. W. Robinson (ed.), *Record and Revelation*, Oxford, 1938

A. Lods, *The Prophets and the Rise of Judaism*, London, 1937

W. O. E. Oesterley, *A History of Israel*, vol. ii, Oxford, 1932

A. S. Peake, *The People and the Book*, Oxford, 1925

L. W. Batten, *Ezra and Nehemiah*, Edinburgh, 1913

CHAPTER IV

M. Hengel, *Judentum und Hellenismus*, Tübingen, 1969

W. F. Albright, *From Stone Age to Christianity*, Baltimore, 1957

W. O. E. Oesterley, *The Jews and Judaism During the Greek Period*, London, 1941

M. I. Rostovtsev, *The Social and Economic History of the Hellenistic World*, 3 vols., Oxford, 1941

G. H. Box, *Judaism: in the Greek Period*, Oxford, 1932

E. R. Bevan, *Jerusalem under the High Priests*, London, 1924

R. H. Charles, *Religious Development Between the Old and New Testaments*, London, 1914

CHAPTERS V–VI

R. Hanhart, *Drei Studien zum Judentum*, München, 1967

R. de Vaux, *Ancient Israel: Its Life and Institutions*, London, 1961

J. C. Dancy, *A Commentary on I Maccabees*, Oxford, 1954

K.-D. Schunck, *Die Quellen des I und II Makkabäerbuches*, Halle/Saale, 1954

S. Tedesche and S. Zeitlin, *The Second Book of Maccabees*, New York, 1949

F.-M. Abel, *Les Livres des Maccabées*, Paris, 1949

E. Bickermann, *The Maccabees: An Account of their History from the Beginnings to the Fall of the House of the Hasmoneans*, New York, 1947

E. Bickermann, *Der Got der Makkabäer*, Berlin, 1937

E. R. Bevan, *The House of Seleucus*, 2 vols., London, 1902

CHAPTERS VII–VIII

John M. Allegro, *The Dead Sea Scrolls* (Pelican A376: rev. ed.), London, 1967

M. Black, *The Scrolls and Christian Origins*, London, 1961

H. Sérouya, *Les Esséniens*, Paris, 1959

G. H. C. MacGregor and A. C. Purdy, *Jew and Greek*, Edinburgh, 1959

J. T. Milik, *Ten Years of Discovery in the Wilderness of Judaea*, London, 1959

D. Howlett, *The Essenes and Christianity*, New York, 1957

L. Finkelstein, *The Pharisees*, 2 vols., Philadelphia, 1946

R. T. Herford, *The Pharisees*, London, 1924

CHAPTERS IX–X

John M. Allegro, *The Treasure of the Copper Scroll* (rev. ed.), New York, 1964

J. Gray, *Archaeology and the Old Testament World*, London, 1962

J. T. Milik, *Discoveries in the Judaean Desert of Jordan: III*, Oxford, 1962

S. Lieberman, *Hellenism in Jewish Palestine*, New York, 1950

N. H. Snaith, *The Jews from Cyrus to Herod*, Wallington, 1949

M. Radin, *The Jews among the Greeks and Romans*, Philadelphia, 1915

CHAPTERS XI–XV

A. Schalit, *Köning Herodes*, Berlin, 1969

S. Sandmel, *Herod: Profile of a Tyrant*, Philadelphia, 1967

E. M. Smallwood, "High Priests and Politics in Roman Palestine", in *Journal of Theological Studies* 13 (1962) pp. 14–34

S. Perowne, *The Life and Times of Herod the Great*, London, 1956

H. Willrich, *Das Haus des Herodes zwischen Jerusalem und Rom*, Heidelberg, 1929

CHAPTER XVI

S. G. F. Brandon, *Jesus and the Zealots*, Manchester, 1967

M. Simon, *Jewish Sects at the Time of Jesus*, Philadelphia, 1967

M. Hengel, *Die Zeloten*, Leiden, 1961

S. E. Johnson, *Jesus and His Own Times*, London, 1958

W. R. Farmer, *Maccabees, Zealots, and Josephus*, New York, 1956

J. Klausner, *Jesus of Nazareth*, New York, 1926

CHAPTER XVII

F. F. Bruce, *New Testament History*, London, 1969
A. Momiagliano, *Claudius: the Emperor and His Achievement*, Cambridge, 1961
F.-O. Busch, *The Five Herods*, London, 1958
S. Perowne, *The Later Herods*, London, 1958
A. H. M. Jones, *The Herods of Judaea*, Oxford, 1938

CHAPTER XVIII

J. Jeremias, *Jerusalem in the Time of Jesus*, London, 1969
H. St. John Thackeray, *Josephus, the Man and the Historian*, New York, 1967
G. A. Williamson, *The World of Josephus*, London, 1964
F. J. Foakes Jackson, *Josephus and the Jews*, London, 1930
A. Schlatter, *Geschichte Israels von Alexander dem Grossen bis Hadrian*, Stuttgart, 1925

CHAPTER XIX

Y. Yadin, *Masada, Herod's Fortress and the Zealot's Last Stand*, London, 1966
G. R. Driver, *The Judaean Scrolls*, Oxford, 1965
H.-F. Weiss, *Der Pharisäismus im Lichte der Überlieferung des Neuen Testaments*, Berlin, 1965
P. Benoit, J. T. Milik, and R. de Vaux, *Discoveries in the Judaean Desert of Jordan: II*, Oxford, 1961
C. Roth, *The Historical Background of the Dead Sea Scrolls*, Oxford, 1958
S. G. F. Brandon, *The Fall of Jerusalem and the Christian Church*, London, 1957
H. J. Schoeps, *Urgemeinde, Judenchristentum, Gnosis*, Tübingen, 1956

CHAPTER XX

M. A. Beek, *A Short History of Israel, from Abraham to Bar Cochba*, London, 1963
Y. Yadin, *The Finds from the Bar Kokhba Period in the Cave of Letters*, Jerusalem, 1963
A. Fuks, "Aspects of the Jewish Revolt in AD 115–117", in *the Journal of Roman Studies* 51 (1961), pp. 98–104
Y. Yadin, "Expedition to the Judaean Desert, 1960", in *Israel Exploration Journal*, vol. 11 nos. 1–2 (1961) pp. 2–72, pl. 1–24; vol. 12 nos. 3–4 (1962) pp. 227–57, pl. 43–48
H. J. Leon, *The Jews of Ancient Rome*, Philadelphia, 1960

Index

Map references follow page references and are given with figure number and page
in italics.

Biblical Index